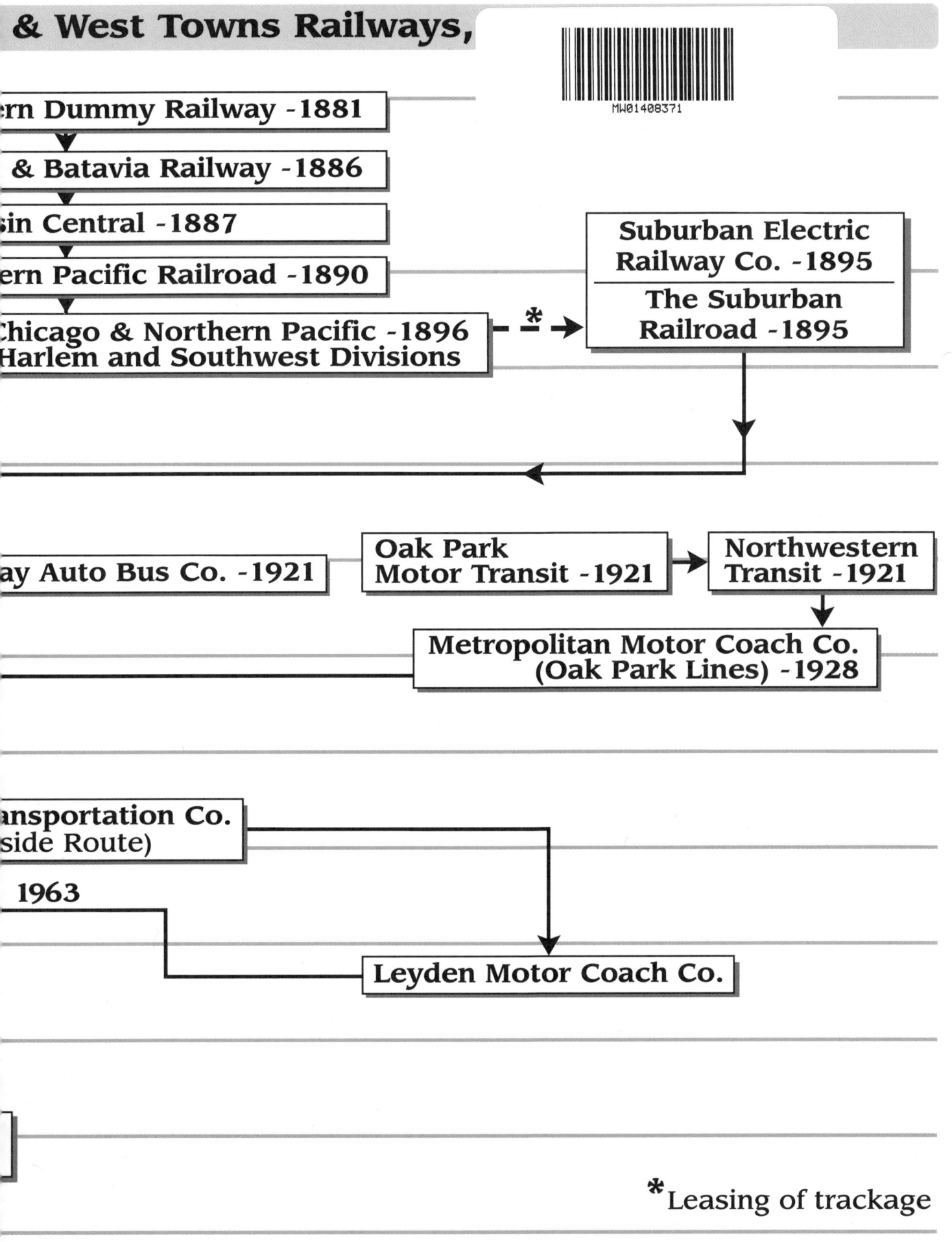

The Chicago & West Towns Railways

By James J. Buckley

Edited by Richard W. Aaron

Bulletin 138 of the Central Electric Railfans' Association

The Chicago & West Towns Railways
Transit Service in Chicago's Near West Suburbs

By James J. Buckley

Edited by Richard W. Aaron

Bulletin 138 of the Central Electric Railfans' Association

© 2006 by the Central Electric Railfans' Association
An Illinois Not-for-Profit Corporation
Post Office Box 503, Chicago, Illinois 60690, U.S.A.

CERA DIRECTORS 2004

J. Terrell Colson	Frederick D. Lonnes
Graham Garfield	Bruce G. Moffat
Daniel D. Joseph	Dennis McClendon
Walter R. Keevil	Ludwig Scheuerle
Jeffrey L. Wien	

All rights reserved. No part of this book may be commercially reproduced or utilized in any form, except for brief quotations, nor by any means electronic or mechanical, including photocopying and recording, nor by any informational storage retrieval system, without permission in writing from the Central Electric Railfans' Association.

The Chicago & West Towns Railways was designed by Jack Sowchin. Production was coordinated by Bruce Moffat.

CERA Bulletins are technical, educational references prepared as historic projects by members of the Central Electric Railfans' Association, working without salary due to their interest in the subject. This bulletin is consistent with this stated purpose of the corporation: To foster the study of the history, equipment and operation of electric railways.

ISBN-13: 978-0-915348-38-1
ISBN-10: 0-915348-38-1

Library of Congress
Control number: 2006921796

Preceding page: *Chicago & West Towns car 163 was westbound in River Forest on Lake Street near Park Avenue. The photographer's vantage point was the Soo Line Railroad overpass. Circa 1946.*
Donald N. Idarius photo/George E. Kanary Collection

Preface

Chicago has always been America's transportation capital. In the current age of jet airplanes, Chicago's airports have always been traffic leaders in the nation. Chicago also has been America's railroad capital. It has been the place where the east coast and west coast railroads interchanged more passengers and freight than anywhere else. *Trains* magazine was a little more exuberant when it claimed, in its July 2003 issue, "If you are a railroad, this city is the most important place on Earth!"

Chicago has also been America's transit capital. During the late 1800s, when cable railways were in vogue, Chicago, not San Francisco, operated the world's largest cable car system. As technologies advanced, costs changed, and population grew, Chicago's street railways evolved into the world's largest system. Chicago is the home to an innovative rapid transit system which has always been the second largest in the nation. Urban transportation has also been provided by a world famous network of world-class interurban electric railways. The vast commuter services operated by the main-line railroads continue to provide urban transit. If you wanted to study American transit and could only visit one city, Chicago is that place.

In this city of rail opulence, what then is the significance of the Chicago & West Towns Railways? Based on data provided in *First & Fastest* magazine, in 1935, it operated a grand total of five streetcar routes, owned 70 passenger cars, and in 1931 operated 35 miles of line. In contrast, the Chicago Surface Lines in 1935 operated 97 distinct routes, owned a fleet of 3,742 passenger cars, and operated 529 miles of line. In 1935, Chicago's rapid transit system had a fleet of 1,781 motor and trailer passenger cars and operated 81 miles of line. Chicago's electric interurban railways and the main line railroads, as well, provided some local service on hundreds of miles of track with large fleets of equipment. The West Towns was a few grains of sand on the beach of Chicago transit.

This carrier, however, earned an emotional appeal far greater than its size. Imbedded in the West Towns' system was the most beautiful electric railway in the Chicago area: The La Grange line. This line ran through the woods. It crossed rivers and highways on its own bridges. It ran on reserved medians. It crossed and ran alongside main line railroads. It featured the largest segment of streetcar open track or private right-of-way operation in the Illinois portion of the Chicago metropolitan area. It was part streetcar line, part suburban railway and part interurban. It operated a fleet of traditional "old" cars and had a management that was unusually friendly to railfans. It was a microcosm of the totality, beauty, and glamour of non-main line electric railway operation.

The West Towns, unfortunately, had more than its share of economic and political problems. The company was an unwanted child. It's service territory was gerrymandered such that it could never earn much of a profit. Two of the five West Towns operating streetcar lines, Lake Street and Madison Street, were extensions of the Chicago routes of the same name. To make service more inconvenient and expensive for patrons, passengers on these streets wishing to continue their journey past the Chicago city limit were required to change carriers and to pay an additional fare. To complicate matters, in its early years, the West Towns was regulated by each of the small municipalities in which it operated. Since elected officials' interests were always served by low fares, fare increases were always an area of great contention. The municipal governments were also known to act independently of each other thereby causing another series of problems. The political nightmare in which the West Towns operated always tested management and plagued profitability.

The Chicago & West Towns did a satisfactory job of providing reliable transportation and a commendable job in producing service innovations. Recognizing the need for complementary crosstown service and westward expansion, the West Towns was a early adapter of buses. The first of which were purchased in 1932 to initiate service on an extension of the Madison Street car line. Several competing bus operations, such as the complementary lines of Marigold and the adjacent lines of Leyden, were purchased. After 1948, when the final streetcars were retired, the West Towns became the second largest motor bus operator in the state of Illinois.

The demise of the West Towns as a independent entity was the result of deteriorating economics. In the 1980s, the West Towns operated for five years with state funding until it was purchased in 1988 with public money. At the time of this writing, the West Towns routes are operated by Pace, an arm of the Illinois Regional Transportation Authority. Many former West Towns routes have been lengthened and integrated into a commuter bus system serving adjacent municipalities. Public ownership also permitted the establishment of uniform transfer privileges between all transit carriers in the metropolitan region, making travel much more equitable.

Contents

Preface 3
Table of Contents 4
Acknowledgments 6
James J. Buckley 7

SECTION 1

The Predecessor Companies 8

Chapter 1: The Beginnings 9
The Cicero & Proviso Street Railway Company 9
    Electrification 9
    The Chicago Avenue Line 13
    Carhouses 15
The Ogden Street Railway 16
Chicago Consolidated Traction Company 20
Chicago & Northern Pacific Railroad 23

Chapter 2: The Suburban to La Grange 29
The Cicero & Proviso Street Railway Company 29
    Suburban Railroad 33
    Extensions 35
Chicago Riverside & La Grange Railroad Company 40
    Suburban's Receivership 40
    Tough Times 41

Chapter 3: County Traction Company 43
    Ripping Up the Rails 46
Chicago & Southwestern Railway Company 51
    County Traction Buys the Suburban 55
    Labor Issues of 1913 59

SECTION 2

The Chicago & West Towns Railway 60

Chapter 4: The Early Years 61
    Fare Issues 62
    Franchise Extensions 63
    Chicago Strike 64
    Five-Cent Fare Suits 64
    Street Improvement Projects 65
    World War I Fare Increases 66
    1919 Strike and Higher Fares 68
    More Fare Changes 68
    West Suburban Transportation Company 69
    Bus Extensions 69

Chapter 5: The Growing 1920s 73
    Derailments in Berwtn 73
    Harlem Avenue 75
    New Cars 76
    St.Charles Road 76
    Lake Street Extension 79
    Other Changes Affecting Streetcar Service 80

Chapter 6: Buses to Hines Hospital 83

Chapter 7: Crosstown Bus Service in Oak Park 87
    Oak Park Motor Transit 87
    Northwestern Transit Company 88

Chapter 8: The Depressing 1930s 91
    Brookfield Zoo 91

      Elevated Transfers 92
      Oak Park Carbarn Fire 93
      Abandonment of the Chicago Avenue Line 94
      Roosevelt Road Problems 100
      Abandonment of the Berwyn-Lyons Streetcar Route 101
      LaGrange Line Improvements 103
      Additional Bus Service 105
  Chapter 9: Competition from Bluebird **107**
  Chapter 10: The End of Streetcar Service **109**
      The End of an Era 116
      Financial Woes 116
      Transition to Buses 117
      Freight Service 117

SECTION 3

Streetcar Lines of the Chicago & West Towns **120**
  Chapter 11: Berwyn-Lyons 121
  Chapter 12: Chicago Avenue 131
  Chapter 13: Lake Street 143
  Chapter 14: Madison Street 155
  Chapter 15: La Grange 167

SECTION 4

Cars, Buses and Buildings **186**
  Chapter 16: Cars and Buses **187**
      Cicero & Proviso Street Railway Company 187
      Known Roster Information 187
      Ogden Street Railway Company 188
      County Traction 188
      Cars Leased from Chicago Railways 188
      Equipment Roster 190
      Cars of the Suburban Railroad 191
      Chicago & West Towns Railway Company 195
      All-Time Equipment Roster 216
      Roster of Buses 220
  Chapter 17: Facilities **223**
      Car Houses and Garages 223
      Power Plants 226

SECTION 5

After the Streetcars Quit **228**
  Chapter 18: The Road to Pace **229**
      Facilities 233
      Equipment 231
      Corporate Form 233
  Chapter 19: Epilogue **237**

SECTION 6

Appendices **240**
  Bibliography 241
  Appendix 1: Chicago & West Towns Key Financial and Operating Statistics 242
  Appendix 2: Suburban Railroad Co. Key Financial and Operating Statistics 244
  Index 246

Acknowledgments

This book is mainly possible because of a group of four men. As all four liked to photograph trains, they would arrange, when convenient, to go together. Then, they would swap the resulting negatives and prints. One operated his own dark room and would develop and print film for the others. All four published. Two were masters at the short magazine article while the other two were more comfortable with larger projects. One was a great model builder and the other three helped him construct an award winning layout in the basement of his home. The men, Jim Buckley (1918-1994), Joe Diaz (1924-2002), Bob Gibson (1924-1999), and Don Idarius (1921-2004) were friends for over fifty years.

For this project, the roles of Jim Buckley and Bob Gibson were critical. The basis of this bulletin is *Chicago & West Towns Railways* published in 1952 as Electric Railway Historical Society bulletin #3. This 60 page soft-covered book was authored by Bob Gibson. The publication staff included Jim Buckley. Jim, in a role that earned him recognition of being the leading researcher of and source for statistics for Chicagoland electric railways, continued to research the West Towns. About a decade later, he had prepared an enlarged history of the railway. Even though this was never published, Jim continued his research to learn more about the West Towns. This bulletin represents over 40 years of research and writing by Jim and Bob.

Joe Diaz made a number of significant contributions to the Chicagoland railfan community. For some years, he ran a model traction meet in downtown Chicago. During the 1970s, Joe published *The Street Railway Review*. Nineteen issues were published over a five year period. Later, Joe wrote a regular column and feature articles for *First & Fastest*, the current journal of Chicagoland electric railways. When Joe learned of CERA's interest in publishing a bulletin about the Chicago & West Towns, he opened his voluminous files to us. Because some time earlier, Joe had hoped to publish a West Towns book of his own, he had car drawings and line art produced. These are included in this bulletin. He provided us with a large number of photos from his collection which also appear in these pages.

In his later years, Don Idarius was a principal contributor of feature articles to *First & Fastest*. In his capacity as the senior West Towns expert, he proofread this manuscript and provided many valuable insights and suggestions. He was a major photographer of the Chicago & West Towns and many of his photographs have been selected for inclusion in this bulletin. Don also was a key contributor to CERA by providing an annual program at the monthly membership meetings of his trademark movies. He was a willing and eager teacher and when you had the privilege of being invited to his home, was a wonderful host.

The enlarged manuscript prepared by Jim Buckley in the mid-1960s laid fallow for almost three decades. In 1991 he gave the manuscript to Roy Benedict in hopes that Roy would be able to find a publisher. Some time later, in 1997, Bill Shapotkin and Roy talked about the unpublished manuscript. Ray DeGroote saw the Buckley manuscript early on and supported its publication. By 1998, the board of Central Electric Railfans' Association approved publishing an expanded bulletin based on Jim Buckley's work.

As someone who never rode the blue and white trolleys of the Chicago & West Towns, the joy in producing this bulletin came from working with people who had a special interest in seeing this book published. These include:

Ms. Lori Thielen of the Berwyn Historical Society, Ms. Marilyn Faber of the La Grange Area Historical Society, Ms. Ellen Lempera, Head of Reference at the Cicero Public Library, and Mr. Frank Lipo and Ms. Diane Hansen of the Historical Society of Oak Park and River Forest. Three other men opened their files of photographs and memorabilia to us for this project: John F. Humiston (1913-2003), Bob Hansen, and George Kanary. Bruce Moffat, not only acted as CERA's publication program manager, but also provided a wealth of material from his extensive personal collection. Special thanks go to Roy Benedict, Bruce Moffat, and Bob Hansen for answering an unending list of questions about this or that which came up during the editing. LeRoy Blommaert provided photo postcards from his collection and provided access to the collections of Carl Klaus and Joe May. John Humiston's brother, Cutler, contacted children of former Chicago & West Towns employees to find historical items. Art Peterson cataloged the West Towns assets of the Krambles-Peterson Archive which allowed us to select those items that we found of interest. Walter Keevil produced stunning prints from seventy year old black and white negatives. Mac Sebree, Tom Jones, Rich Phillipi, and Steve Goldmann provided access to the collection of the Motor Bus Society. Neal Samors and Michael Williams provided valuable editorial and proofreading services. Major proofreading credit also goes to Glenn Andersen, Roy Benedict, Bob Breeze, Ray DeGroote, Bob Hansen, Don Idarius, George Kanary, Bruce Moffat and Bill Shapotkin. Other thanks go to many photographers who contributed a photo or two to this project. Their names are listed adjacent to their photos.

In these projects, a major contributor always thanks his spouse for her help and support. Mine deserves more credit than usual. Jan has spent her career as an editor of periodicals in the food service industry. She not only is an accomplished "word smith," and lent much pro-bono time to this manuscript, but also had the most unpleasant task of teaching me the more obscure facets of Word Perfect.

Richard W. Aaron
Chicago, Illinois
March 2005

James J. Buckley

James J. Buckley (1918-1994) was one of the deans of the Chicago train buff community. He is probably best known for his work with the Electric Railway Historical Society. This organization published 49 bulletins and acquired a collection of Chicago area transit vehicles including Chicago & West Towns streetcar 141, two trolley buses, and eight other Chicago streetcars. Jim authored two books for ERHS, *The Evanston Railway Company* and *The Hammond, Whiting & East Chicago Railway*, and provided inputs to most of the others.

Jim was also a major participant at CERA. He served for many years on the publication staff and, for a few years, was a director of the association. With his unsurpassed expertise in rosters and technical data, he provided material support for over 20 CERA bulletins. In the list of credits for each bulletin, his contributions earned such titles as Publications Co-Director and Roster Editor. He was the author of CERA B-84, *Gary Railways*; CERA B-93, *Chicago & Interurban Traction Company;* and wrote a major article in B-88 about the Philadelphia Suburban Transportation Company. Jim also contributed programs to the monthly CERA membership meetings.

Jim was particularly creative in developing and researching data sources that others overlooked. He was an expert in using bankruptcy and abandonment court records, builder's order files, and newspaper articles to check and cross check electric railway roster data. He also became an expert in interviewing employees and former employees of transportation companies to get their insights on the property for which they worked. As he traveled, he would visit libraries in the cities he visited to research the street railway and interurban operations that once existed there. Jim's records survived him and his work is still quoted in currently produced books and periodicals as the authoritative source for specific items of electric railway history.

As many railfans prefer, Jim traveled extensively to seek out information to add to the knowledge base of transportation systems. He enjoyed visiting Central and South America and became exceedingly knowledgeable about the railway networks in Mexico and Central America. At the time of his death in June 1994, Jim was doing what he loved, researching electric railway operations. This time in Bremen, Germany.

SECTION 1
The Predecessor Companies

1 The Beginnings

The Cicero & Proviso Street Railway Company

Left: *Suburban Railroad car 107 was seven years old when photographed at the Hillgrove and Brainard Avenue terminal of the railroad. In this photo, looking southwest, the Chicago, Burlington & Quincy Railroad's Stone Avenue station platforms are visible. The car's motorman and La Grange pioneer, George Dieke, was standing in the car's vestibule. The conductor is unknown.*
La Grange Area Historical Society Collection

Cicero was named by Augustus Porter, an early settler who came to the region by way of the Erie Canal, for his hometown of Cicero, New York. Developed by early farmers and land speculators, Cicero was a railroad suburb. The Galena & Chicago Union Railroad began operating through the northern portion of the area in 1849, around the same time as the Chicago, Alton & St. Louis Railroad was finished in the southern portion. By 1860, there were only about 10 families living in the area following creation of the township of Cicero in 1857. Cicero grew very slowly before the Civil War, but began to draw new residents when, in 1863, the Chicago, Burlington & Quincy Railroad began operating trains in the area. With that growth in population, Cicero became an incorporated town by a special state charter.

The first attempt to provide street railway service in this area was by horse car. On June 19, 1886, the Town of Cicero granted the People's Horse Car Company the right to build a railway on Lake Street between the town's eastern border at Pulaski Road and Austin Avenue, a distance of 2-1/2 miles. The ordinance called for the route to be in operation by December 31, 1886. Unable to meet this deadline, the Town granted the company an extension until June 30, 1887 to complete the project. The ordinance granting the extension required the People's Horse Car Company to reimburse the Town of Cicero for the cost of improving Lake Street. The company was unable to raise the funds necessary to build the line and the franchise expired.

On February 15, 1889, the Cicero & Proviso Street Railway Company was incorporated by E. A. Cummings and D. J. Kennedy. Initial capitalization was $250,000, but was increased to $1 million about a year and a half later. Like many railways, the line was conceived to enhance real estate values in the area through which it would operate. The company soon secured a franchise from the Town of Cicero to build an electric railway. Prior to the opening of the railway, the Chicago & North Western Railway was the key public carrier of passengers into downtown Chicago, but with the absence of competition, fares were high and service was inadequate.

Construction of the railway started in Spring 1890. The route began on Chicago's western fringe at Madison Street and Pulaski Road, which was a 1/2 block west of the West Chicago Street Railroad cable car line, and continued west on Madison to Harlem Avenue where it turned north to Lake Street. From the intersection of Lake Street and Harlem Avenue the line continued east on Lake Street to Cicero Avenue and then south to Madison Street for the return trip to Pulaski. The entire line was double tracked, thus providing service in both directions.

Horse car service began on Madison Street, between Pulaski and Austin Avenue, on the afternoon of October 24, 1890. The horse cars were judged to be so unique that schools were closed early so that the children could take a ride. On November 29, 1890, horse cars were placed in service on the Lake Street portion of the line. Horse cars ran hourly from Pulaski and Madison Street to Laramie Avenue and Lake Streets via Madison Street, Cicero Avenue, and Lake Street. In January 1891, service on Madison Street was extended to Harlem Avenue.

Electrification

A move toward electrification began with the construction of a power generating plant at Lake Street and Harvey Avenue in Oak Park in April 1890. Other infrastructure improvements included a new car barn on Madison Street, about 80-feet west of Pulaski, and a waiting room at the corner of Madison Street and Cicero Avenue. Over the years, the Oak Park site would become the headquarters and primary car barn of the lines.

Four streetcars that had been ordered from Pullman to open the line arrived at the Austin Avenue team track of the Chicago & North Western Railway on January 29,1891. For some reason, the crews of the Cicero & Proviso had some difficulty

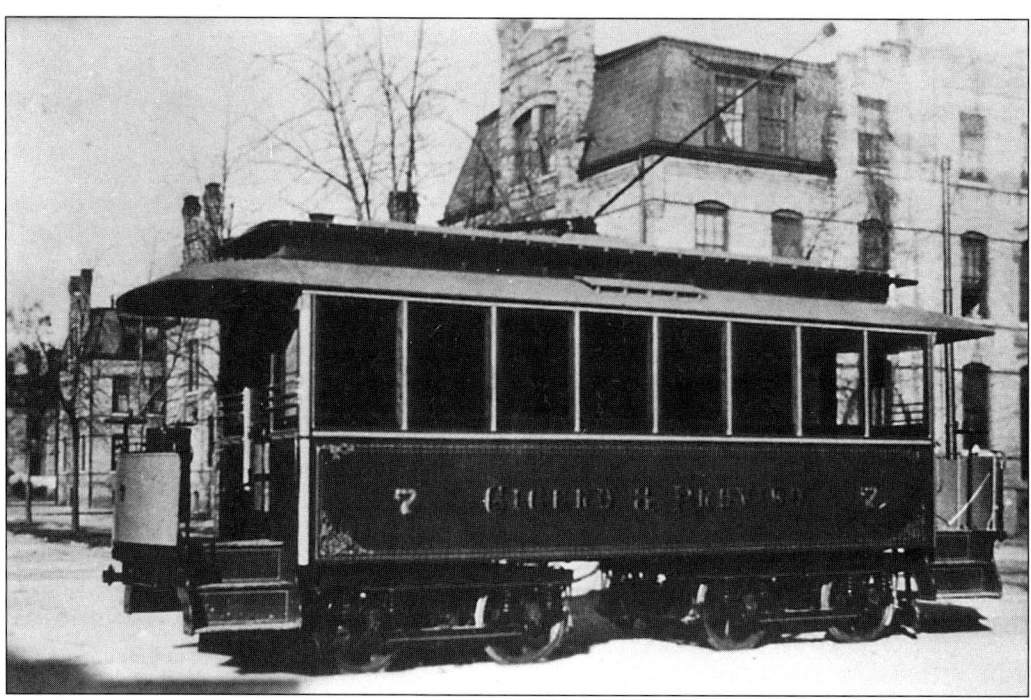

Cicero & Proviso Street Railway car 7 posed for the customary official photograph before being shipped from the builder's plant. It was one of 12 identical cars supplied by the Pullman Palace Car Company in 1891.

Chicago Public Library, Special Collections and Preservation Division

unloading them. The unloading finally was completed by late the next afternoon. The four cars were positioned on the street railway's tracks near the team track where they remained awaiting the completion of the power plant and the training of crews.

The ceremonial opening of the line was held on February 26, 1891, at the company's Oak Park power plant, although the first electric car ran during test service on February 12, 1891. It was reported that those who saw the trolleys operate were pleased, and hopes were high that the streetcar line would improve the quality of life in Chicago's western suburbs. The entire railway was ready to operate on opening day, and business was strong during the first week of operation. All four cars were more than ample to handle the passengers, and the little cars ran close to capacity the first Sunday of operation carrying loads of 70 to 80 persons per car.

Early operations could be difficult because the streets were not surfaced as we know them today, as the only pavement on the streets was the area between the car tracks. Residents took advantage of the pavement by using it as a street or sidewalk. On wet days, the tracks were even more preferred because the horses would tend to get stuck in the mud of the unpaved street. It is claimed that more than one motorman, if delayed unduly by a wagon, simply plowed his streetcar into it at full speed. This action destroyed the wagon and all of its contents, but cleared the right-of-way.

Eight additional streetcars were delivered to the Cicero & Proviso on Saturday, April 4, 1891. These cars were ordered as part of the original order for 12 vehicles, but the new cars were powered with higher horsepower motors. (The 15-horsepower motors, supplied on the first batch, had proved inadequate.) When the new cars were placed into service, the original four cars were returned to Pullman for installation of larger motors.

Several extensions to the initial system were built over the next few years. A one and a half mile extension was built on Madison Street from Harlem Avenue to the Des Plaines River. This extension was opened on August 8, 1891 and was built to serve the Concordia Cemetery. On Saturday, September 19, 1891, a branch was opened on Des Plaines Avenue between Madison Street and Twelfth Street. The branch served the Forest Home and Waldheim cemeteries.

In the early years, ridership was high because of the "novelty" value of a streetcar trip and the lack of competition. By its first summer, the railway needed to expand its infrastructure to handle the ever-growing passenger traffic. The power house was enlarged and additional rolling stock, consisting of ten open trailers, was delivered in June 1891. On warm summer Sundays, the road carried loads of 12,000 to 14,000 passengers.

During 1892, the railway again expanded in response to a 35% increase in business. Twenty-four of the popular open cars and 6 single-truck closed motor cars

The Cicero & Proviso used a simple form for a transfer. The date of issue was printed on the transfer and the conductor punched the document for time of day and direction of travel. The original transfer was printed on yellow paper stock with black ink.
Richard R. Andrews Collection

A joint Cicero & Proviso and Lake Street Elevated Railroad ticket enabled the bearer to complete five continuous one-way journeys using both companies. The ticket was punched for each ride segment. The form was printed with black ink on a salmon colored paper stock.
Historical Society of Oak Park and River Forest Collection

For corporate purposes, the Cicero & Proviso issued a buff colored ticket for complementary rides.
Historical Society of Oak Park and River Forest Collection

were added and a new brick car house was built to replace the old wooden shed. In addition, construction was started on a larger powerhouse adjacent to the new car house.

Further expansion was planned for a line to continue on Madison Street into Maywood. The three men who were principal promoters of the Maywood extension also controlled substantial real estate holdings in the area — E. A. Cummings, President of the Cicero & Proviso, Frank Bollard and James Darlow. Before the expansion could happen, a major trestle over the Des Plaines River and the lowlands west of the river would have to be built. Due to a slower economy in 1893, obtaining the funding for the extension was much slower than improvements for other parts of the railway. Service was opened to the eastern edge of the trestle during the Summer of 1893, and the formal opening of an extension to Maywood was held on November 11, 1893.

On Tuesday, January 15, 1894, a streetcar was placed in service via Madison Street and 19th Avenue to the Chicago & North Western Railway station at Melrose Park. This shuttle car became known as the "Madison Street Transfer." This extension was opened without fanfare or ceremony.

By 1894, the Village of Maywood was seeing major growth, including the opening of a Norton Brothers factory, employing 1,000 workers, the construction of the 120 acre Harlem Race Track at Twelfth Street near Harlem Avenue, and the opening of a picnic ground and pavilion on Madison Street at 19th Avenue. Furthermore, new housing was being built in subdivisions in the area, as well as a new model town being built on a 200 acre tract. These developments greatly expanded the market for passenger traffic for the Cicero & Proviso.

The growth of Maywood also prompted the railway to continue its Lake Street line westward. This plan, however, was slowed by the Village of River Forest, which wanted the railway to pay for paving between the rails, something that it customarily had done elsewhere. The issue was finally resolved and construction began on Monday morning, September 23, 1895. Ninety-pound rail was laid on oak ties set below the level of the street. Planking was then laid over the ties and cedar blocks were set on the planks. This construction method was described as being especially well-adapted for high speed operation and smooth running. Financing of this construction was possible by the issuance of a $2,500,000 bond issue

Chapter 1: The Beginnings

In this map drawn to represent the Cicero & Proviso in 1898, the cartographer used the oldest commonly known names of streets. The name of West 48th Street was changed to 48th Avenue in 1895 to reduce confusion with the numbered streets on the south side of Chicago. The name of 48th Avenue was changed to Cicero Avenue in 1913. Many other west side street names, using this numbering system, such was West 44th Street, were also changed to numbered avenues in 1895. West 44th Street became 44th Avenue which later was renamed Kostner Avenue. The name of Robinson Avenue was later changed to West 52nd Street and then to 52nd Avenue. It was renamed Laramie Avenue in 1913.

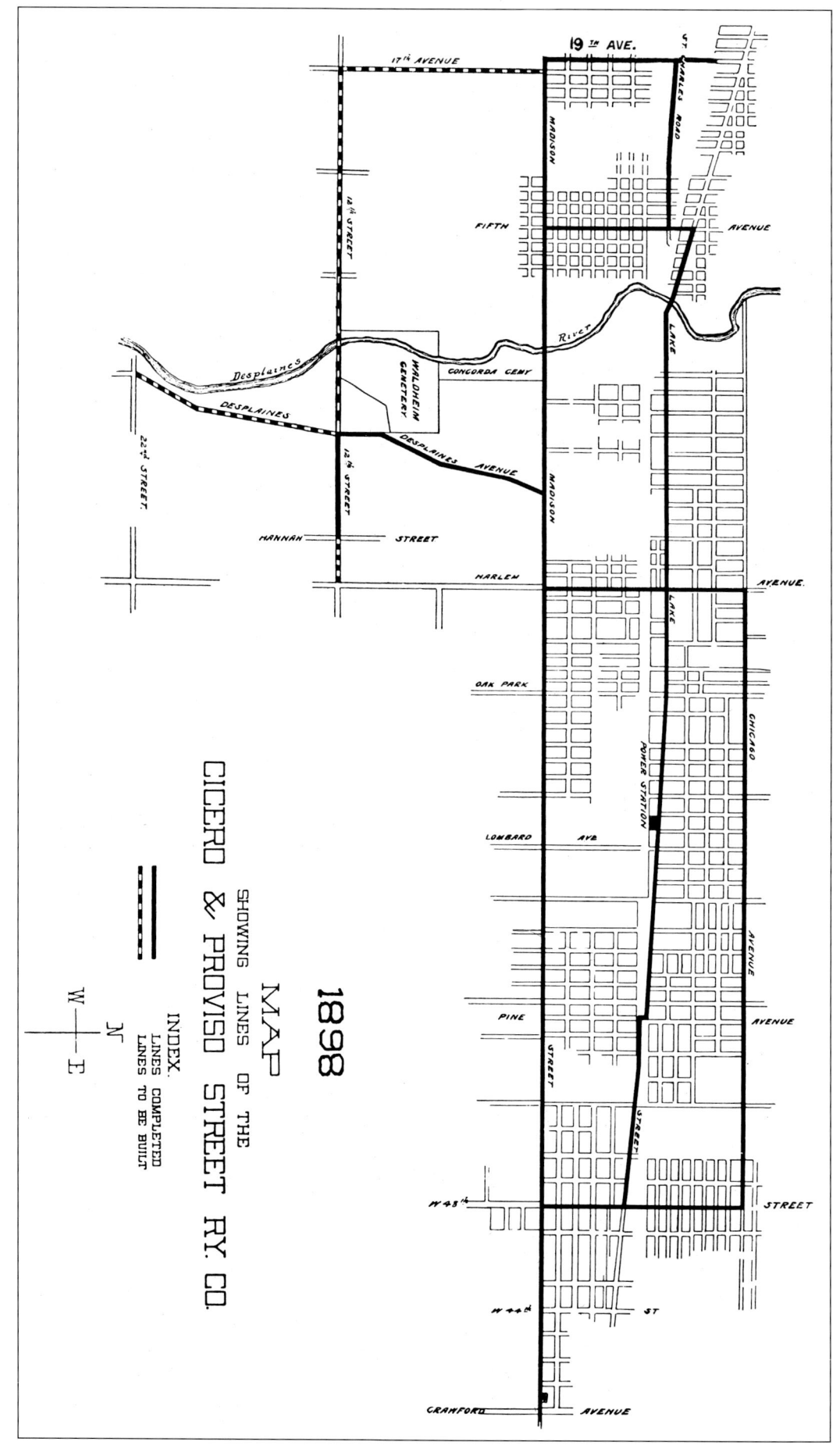

The Chicago & West Towns Railways

Early spring rains appear to have flooded the tracks of the Lake Street carline west of the Des Plaines River. The crew and passengers of the eastbound single-truck streetcar wait departure time by sitting on the bridge railing wondering if the waters had reached their full height. Circa 1900.

LeRoy F. Blommaert Collection

which included refinancing $871,000 of existing debt.

Construction moved ahead rapidly, permitting service to open to the Des Plaines River on Sunday, December 1, 1895. Work on the trestle was delayed because a telephone pole line needed to be relocated and, as would be expected, the telephone company did not want to pay for the work. With a contractual deadline of December 27, 1895 in place to secure a subsidy from the Village of Maywood, the trestle was finished and the line extension to Fifth Avenue was opened with no time to spare on December 27, 1895.

The Cicero & Proviso added another extension to the Madison Street line when track was installed on St. Charles Road between 19th Avenue in Melrose Park and Fifth Avenue in Maywood on December 13, 1895. As a result, the "Madison Street Transfer" car was no longer needed. On December 27, 1895, the railway chose to route the Madison Street cars on this new trackage. In the morning the cars were routed via 19th Avenue while in the afternoon, cars were routed via Fifth Avenue. There was some grumbling from the riding public that this arrangement was inconvenient for passengers wishing to travel in the direction opposite to that of the streetcar flow. The company installed turnouts which permitted operation around the loop in both directions. However, the railway preferred to operate all cars via Fifth Avenue, St. Charles Road, and 19th Avenue.

The Chicago Avenue Line

Construction of a Chicago Avenue line was taking place concurrently with that of the Madison Street and Lake Street routes. The Cicero & Proviso had obtained a franchise from Cicero for operation of a streetcar line from the town limits at Laramie Avenue, west to Harlem Avenue and then south to Lake Street. However, the company wanted to operate the line from Cicero Avenue and Chicago Avenue because the West Chicago Street Railroad Company's Chicago Avenue streetcar line terminated there. The City of Chicago would not grant the Cicero & Proviso a franchise for this one-half mile line segment without compensation. The Chicago City Council, at the behest of 28th Ward Alderman Sayle, finally approved a franchise ordinance. The Cicero & Proviso would not have to pay the city anything for the first five years of operation of the streetcar line. In the second five-year period, the company would be required to pay the city 1/4 of 1% of the route's gross receipts. Finally, in the final five-year period of the franchise, the Cicero & Proviso would pay 1/2 of 1% of gross receipts. The granting of this franchise permitted construction to begin in September 1894.

On Saturday, January 19, 1895 the Chicago Avenue line was formally opened. Beginning at the Chicago & North Western Railway's crossing at Cicero Avenue the line traveled north to Chicago Avenue and west on Chicago to a terminal at

Chapter 1: The Beginnings

Harlem Avenue. The Chicago & North Western crossing took additional time to complete because the railroad was in no hurry to help a competitor.

Further extensions took place in 1895 when the Cicero crossing of the Chicago & North Western was completed in March and rail was laid on Harlem Avenue, from Chicago Avenue south to Lake Street in July. This track project was completed in two weeks by an 80-person crew employed by the contractor, J. B. Toughy & Company. At the same time this project was being executed, a second track was being positioned on Harlem Avenue between Lake Street and Madison Street. When placed into service, Chicago Avenue cars were through-routed with the "Forest Home Shuttle" via Harlem Avenue, Madison Street, Des Plaines Avenue, and Twelfth Street to a terminal at the Harlem Race Track. This series of extensions helped relieve the overcrowding on the Lake Street line during the rush hours because patrons living north of Lake Street now had an alternative way to travel.

Business in 1895 was much better than in the previous year. Record-level crowds used the line on Memorial Day weekend, and additional open cars were acquired to handle the customers. On the Madison Street line that weekend, streetcars pulled from one to three trailers, and even standing room on these vehicles was at a premium.

During 1896, the company instituted several small operating changes. After much public discussion and consternation, destination signs were installed on the cars during May 1896. Also in May 1896, the Lake Street line was extended to a new terminal in Maywood on Fifth Avenue at the Chicago & North Western Railway's tracks. The railway had hoped to cross the North Western's tracks to connect to Madison Street, but this never materialized. A sewer construction project on Madison Street near Cicero Avenue necessitated a temporary route change on the east end of the line. In the original routing, Lake Street cars would turn south on Cicero to reach Madison Street. In the temporary routing, these cars would continue on Lake Street to Pulaski Road to turn south. Finally, the Cicero & Proviso leased two party cars, the "Arcturus" and "Sunbeam," from the West Chicago Street Railroad to see if a party car business could be established. The experiment was unsuccessful.

One of the more interesting structures along the Cicero & Proviso line was the Madison Street Loop House. It was built to serve as the terminal and waiting station for the Madison Street cable route of the West Chicago Street Railroad Company. The one story brick structure was located on Madison Street near Springfield Avenue. Before it was constructed, passengers wishing to transfer to and from the cable cars had to walk the half-block between Pulaski and Springfield. In January 1896, a renovation was completed which changed the track arrangement. The building now contained a large loop for the cable cars which utilized the outermost doors of the structure. Within the large loop was a smaller loop which was provided for the use of the Madison Street, Cicero Avenue, and Lake Street trolleys of the Cicero & Proviso. The terminal building also contained a restaurant, waiting room, and several stores. After the Cicero & Proviso stopped using this facility in 1911, it remained in streetcar use by the West Chicago Street Railroad Company successors until the Chicago Transit Authority abandoned streetcar service on the Madison Street route in the early 1950s. At that time, the property was sold for redevelopment.

During this same time period, significant changes in the ownership and control of the railway were taking place. In 1894, the Cicero & Proviso Street Railway Company was purchased by Charles T. Yerkes. The Cicero & Proviso was formally leased to the Yerkes-controlled West Chicago Street Railroad, on May 12, 1896. Operations of the Cicero & Proviso by the West Chicago continued until early 1899 when many of the Chicago area street rail companies began to be consolidated. The first step in this change was the formation of the Chicago Consolidated Traction Company on January 28, 1899. On December 1, 1899, the next step was implemented and the Consolidated assumed control of the Cicero & Proviso as well as six other street railway companies that operated on the north and west sides of the City of Chicago. Chicago Consolidated Traction and Chicago Union Traction Company had entered into a 50-year agreement covering the joint use of streetcars and trackage. As a result, all of these streetcar operations were run by Chicago Union Traction and the outlying lines were operated by Chicago Consolidated Traction.

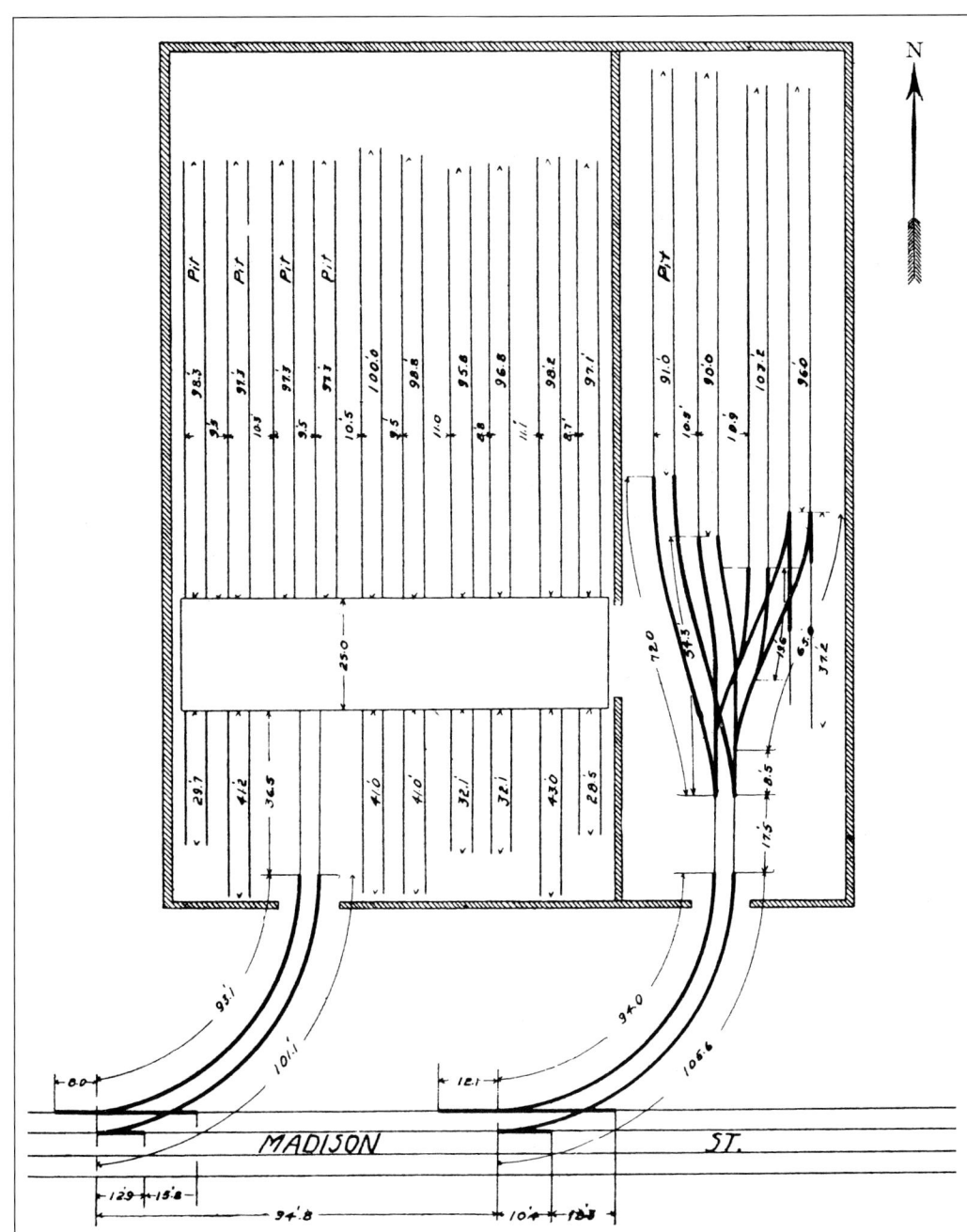

A 1910 valuation report contains a drawing of the trackwork in the Madison Street carbarn as it existed after the 1894 addition was completed. The building was 150 feet wide by 175 feet deep. The original (east) bay had 4 tracks while the new (west) bay had 10 tracks, accessed by a transfer table.
Bruce G. Moffat Collection

Carhouses

The major depot for the Cicero & Proviso Street Railway was on Madison Street near Pulaski Road. The two-story structure was built in 1890 on the north side of Madison Street about 100 feet west of Pulaski. The 50-foot wide building contained two small offices on each side of a single lead track. The lead track led inside the building to four storage tracks, each about 100 feet long. In 1894, this facility was enlarged to include a single story addition containing ten tracks. A transfer table was used in the addition to position cars.

This depot was used by both the Cicero & Proviso Railway and the Ogden Street Railway. All of the Cicero & Proviso runs came from this depot. In addition, the facility served the Berwyn-Lyons and Cicero Avenue routes of the Ogden Street Railway. The cars for the Berwyn-Lyons route were transferred to the West Chicago Street Railroad's Lawndale Avenue depot on July 4, 1897.

A one and two-story carhouse was built in 1892 on Lake Street at Cuyler Avenue in Oak Park. The upper story of the building housed the company's offices and storage, while the lower story was used as a machine shop. This depot was used only for storage at this time and not as an operating depot.

Chapter 1: The Beginnings

A car has passed Prescott Avenue in Lyons and continues westward on Ogden Avenue to its terminal at Lawndale Avenue. The street, including the area between the tracks, was unpaved. Circa 1900.

Roy G. Benedict Collection

The Ogden Street Railway

The Ogden Street Railway was incorporated on October 1, 1891, about a year and a half after the incorporation of the Cicero & Proviso. The ownership of the Ogden Street Railway was the same as that of the Cicero & Proviso. The purpose of the corporation was to build and operate an electric railway linking the Des Plaines River valley to the manufacturing district in the southwestern portion of the suburbs of metropolitan Chicago. The railway did not own any rolling stock and all cars were leased from either the Cicero & Proviso or the West Chicago Street Railroad.

In 1893, the Cicero Town Board passed an ordinance granting the Ogden Street Railway the right to construct a single track line on the west side of Cicero Avenue from Madison Street to Twelfth Street. This trackage was built a year later.

In December 1894, the Cicero Town Board granted the Company five very valuable franchises for street railways lines:
1. On Cicero Avenue from Madison Street to Ogden Avenue.
2. On Twelfth Street from Pulaski to Harlem Avenue.
3. On Ogden Avenue from Cicero Avenue to the town line at Harlem Avenue.
4. On Laramie Avenue from 25th Street to 35th Street.
5. For a route on many streets known as the Berwyn-Lyons line.

The line on Laramie Avenue between 25th Street and 35th Street was to be placed in service when a new viaduct over the Chicago, Burlington & Quincy Railroad was completed. The Berwyn-Lyons route franchise began at Cicero Avenue and 25th Street and ran via 25th Street, Central Avenue, 26th Street, Ridgeland Avenue, Stanley Avenue, and Harlem Avenue to a terminal in Lyons at Harlem and Ogden Avenues.

On June 25, 1895, streetcar service was initiated on Cicero Avenue between Madison Street and Harrison Street and a few weeks later, in July, the line was extended south to Twelfth Street. Initial excitement in the line boosted first-week traffic greatly, and exceeded the company's expectations. The line was constructed hurriedly and was built only as a single-track railway with a few passing sidings, however, by October 1895, the double-tracking was completed.

The formal opening celebration for the Berwyn-Lyons line was on Saturday, May 28, 1896. Three trains, each consisting of a motor car and two trailers, were required to carry the invited guests from the western terminal of the Madison Street car line at Springfield Avenue and Madison Street for a ride over the line. The Berwyn Improvement Club organized a local celebration to commemorate the line's opening, including a brass band and tenor quartets. One person even wrote a poem for the occasion.

The 6-1/2 mile line known as the Berwyn-Lyons route was double-tracked, with cars running every ten minutes. Cars carried a destination sign reading, "Hawthorne, Morton Park, Clyde, Lavergne and Berwyn." When the line opened, its western terminal was at 31st Street and Harlem Avenue in Berwyn. The owners had hoped to operate a streetcar line north on Harlem Avenue to Twelfth Street, but the necessary frontage consents north of 31st Street could not be obtained. Since the railway could not build

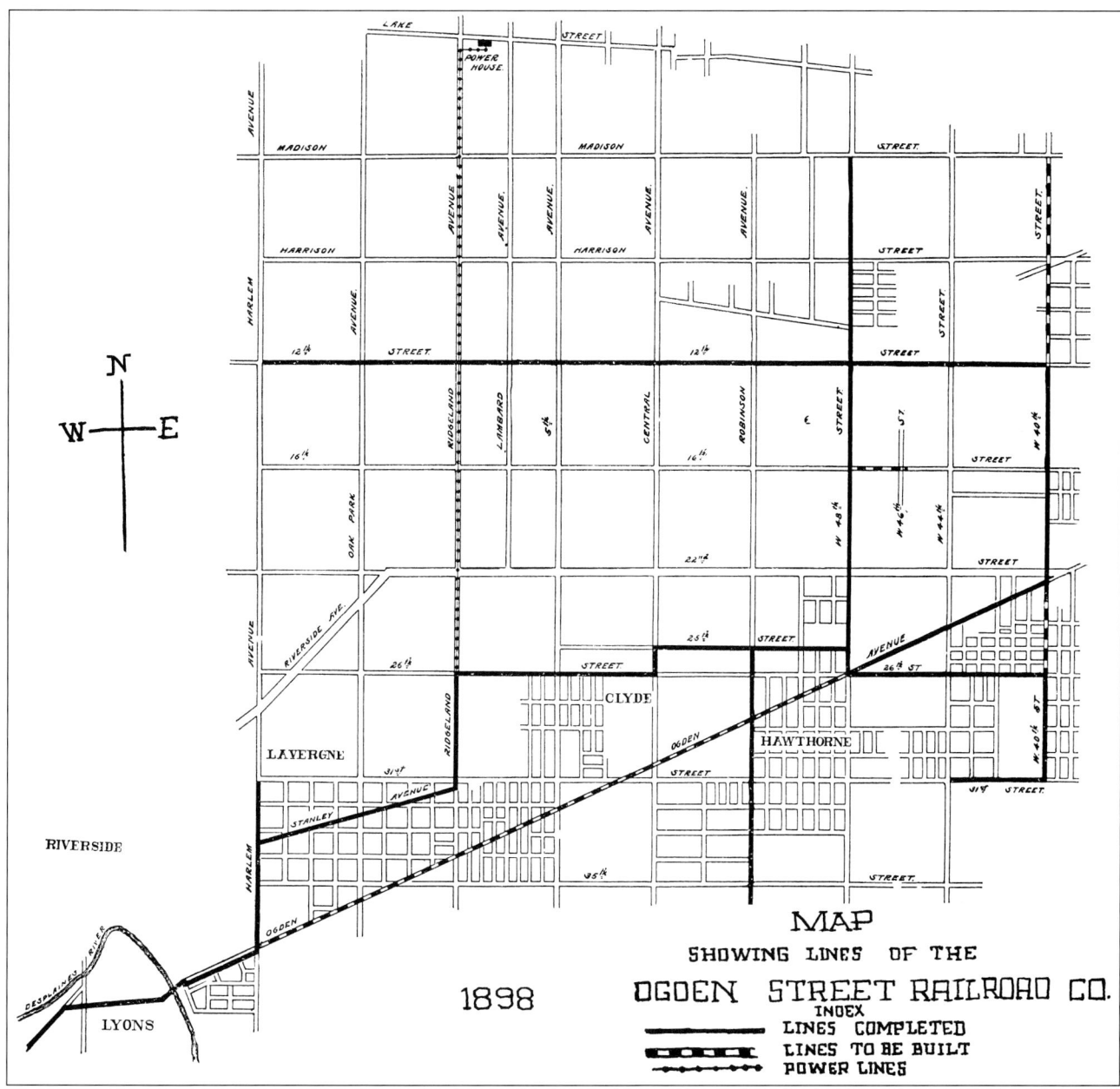

When the cartographer prepared this map, he misnamed the railway. The correct name is the Ogden Street Railway Company. In addition, the oldest known street names were used. Today, Fifth Avenue is known as Austin Avenue, Robinson Avenue is named Laramie Avenue, West 48th Street is named Cicero Avenue, West 46th Street is called Kenton Avenue, West 44th Street is known as Kostner Avenue and West 40th Street is called Pulaski Road.

north of 31st Street on Harlem, it elected to build tracks to the south. Almost immediately, a double track railroad was constructed south of the Chicago, Burlington & Quincy Railroad's tracks on Harlem Avenue. On Sunday, June 1, 1896, the contractors of the Ogden Street Railway were trying to install a crossing of the railroad's tracks without permission. The "Q's" management felt that safety was an overriding issue in allowing the street railway to cross its tracks and did its best to stop construction. Two switch engines were run back and forth across Harlem Avenue to prevent the crews from completing the crossing. Later, debris consisting of some old box cars and scrap was dumped into the street blocking the crossing for the Ogden Street Railway Company, as well as all other street traffic on Ogden Avenue.

In December 1896, the parties agreed to a single-track crossing, and with that the streetcar line was extended to Ogden Avenue. Even though this new crossing was protected with signals, a major accident took place on Wednesday, January 13, 1897, less than a month after the line extension opened. During a blizzard, a snow sweeper got stalled on the crossing and was hit by a westbound train, throw-

Chapter 1: The Beginnings

ing it into the path of an eastbound train. Fortunately, the sweeper's crew saw the trains coming and were able to escape in time. This accident resulted in the "Q's" management directing the company to operate a shuttle car south of the crossing. Passengers wanting to ride on the southmost segment of the line had to walk across the tracks to change streetcars, an arrangement that continued for several years.

Extension of the line west into Lyons proved difficult. The company was unable to obtain a franchise to operate west on Ogden Avenue from Harlem Avenue to Lyons. Instead, the company was forced to purchase its own right-of-way on the south side of Ogden Avenue and also build a trestle across the Des Plaines River. In Spring 1897, the route was extended to the east side of the river and in August 1897 the trestle was completed, beginning service into Lyons.

At this time, Lyons was "wet" while the municipalities to the east were "dry." So on warm summer evenings, thirsty patrons filled the cars to capacity traveling to the town's bars and taverns. And on the weekends, it became a popular spot for picnics. Business was very good on this line, and the railway frequently operated two trailers behind a motor car to handle the load.

There were several other service changes during 1897. On July 2, 1897, a second east-end terminal for the Berwyn-Lyons route was placed in service. The new terminal was at Ogden Avenue and Pulaski and cars were routed via Ogden Avenue, Cicero Avenue, and 25th Street to join the original line. In October 1897, the Twelfth Street route was placed into service operating west from Pulaski to Harlem Avenue. In November 1897, track was laid on Laramie Avenue from 25th Street south to the Hawthorne Race Track at 36th Street. Service on this new Laramie Avenue trackage was provided as an extension of the Cicero Avenue line. Cars terminated at Lake Street and Cicero Avenue where transfers could be made with the Lake Street "L." The route utilized Cicero Avenue and 25th Street to reach the new Laramie Avenue trackage. Trackage rights were obtained from the Cicero & Proviso on Cicero Avenue between Lake Street and Madison Street.

The last extension built by the Ogden Street Railway turned out to be a fiasco. The management of the railway had wanted to develop a Harlem Avenue streetcar route. To this end, the company contracted to have track laid on Harlem Avenue south from Ogden Avenue to 39th Street and north from 31st Street to the point where the Illinois Central Railroad crossed Harlem Avenue near 26th Street. Connections could have been made with the cars of the Suburban Railroad at 26th Street and Harlem Avenue. However, the management of the Ogden Street Railway and Illinois Central Railroad could not come to an agreement over this crossing. By February 1900, the government of the Town of Cicero dictated that the Ogden Street Railway have these unused tracks removed because they interfered with team traffic. There is no proof that the company complied with Cicero's request.

ROLLING TO BERWYN   Tune, Marching Thru' Georgia

I. Oh, listen to the humming of the trolley on the wire,
    See the crowds awaiting for the coming of the flyer,
    See the cars a-coming, flashing out electric fire
    As they go rolling to Berwyn.

Chorus:
    Hurrah, Hurrah, we hail th' electric fire;
    Hurrah, Hurrah, we swell the chorus higher;
    Thus we sing the advent of the trolley and the wire
    As it goes rolling to Berwyn.

II. Oh, how the people waited for the coming of the car,
    How the prophets prophesied its coming from afar,
    How the dread injunction often did its progress bar,
    As it came c-r-a-w-l-i-n-g to Berwyn.
Chorus:

III. Don't you see the flashing of the bright electric spark,
    Don't you hear the hubbub; children scream and canines bark;
    That's the car a-coming through the wilds of Morton Park
    As it goes flying to Berwyn.
Chorus:

IV. Still, it's coming nearer; everybody takes a ride;
    Glad to get to Berwyn; see them come from every side;
    No one but the Board of Education left in Clyde,
    As we go rolling to Berwyn.
Chorus:

V. No more the monthly ticket sale will fill our souls with woe;
    No more the punctured tires make our indignation glow;
    But on the new electric railway to the city we will go,
    As it goes rolling thro' Berwyn.
Chorus:
                                                  "The Berwyn Poet"

Decades before Frank Sinatra sang about My Kind of Town, *the Berwyn Male Quartet entertained audiences with their rendition of* Rolling to Berwyn, *the unofficial theme song of the Ogden Street Railway Company.*
Berwyn Historical Society Collection

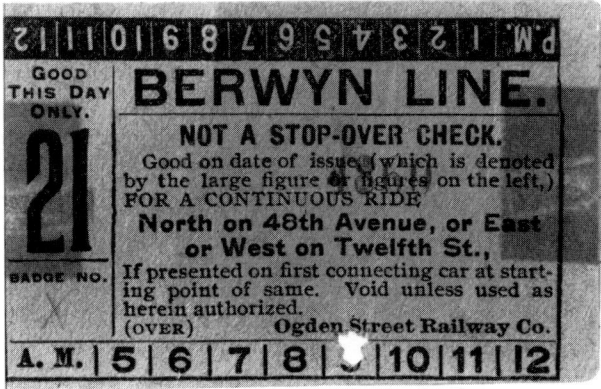

Due to the common management, the Ogden Street Railway company used the same style of transfer as did the Cicero & Proviso. This form was printed with black ink on salmon colored paper stock.
Richard R. Andrews Collection

These three Barclay photographs illustrate the financial plight of the Cicero & Proviso and its successor companies. The railway was built as a stand-alone corporation by real estate promoters who needed transportation to sell their land. Twelve years after the first streetcar line opened, insufficient real estate development had taken place to generate traffic levels necessary for the street railway company to pay its bills and earn a profit. A ride down Madison Street and Roosevelt Road in 1903 was a ride through a prairie. The land was eventually developed. During the entire twentieth century, except for some brief periods of time, population densities in the territory served by the Cicero & Proviso were generally inadequate to profitably support the service.

All three photos: Philander W. Barclay/ Historical Society of Oak Park and River Forest Collection

By the early 1900s, photographers began to record street scenes. In this view, circa 1903, an east bound Madison Street car stopped at Ridgeland Avenue to pick up two passengers. Car 255 was leased from Chicago Consolidated Traction, the new parent of the Cicero & Proviso. The photograph shows considerable undeveloped land adjacent to the north side of the unpaved Madison Street.

In the warm months, open streetcars were used. Passengers enjoyed the gentle breezes the car generated as it moved down the track. Car 5821 was equipped with canvas side curtains to protect passengers from sudden rainstorms. It required a staff of two: A motorman to operate the vehicle and a conductor to collect fares. Since the car had no center aisle, fares were collected from the outside running boards. Car 5821, leased from Chicago Consolidated Traction, was proceeding westward on Roosevelt Road at Ridgeland Avenue, circa 1903.

The Photographer

Philander W. Barclay (1878-1940) was a bicycle repairman by trade, but an historical photographer by preference. He rode a bicycle throughout early Oak Park to obtain his images. By the time of his death, he had produced over 1,000 photos. These photographs are now part of the collection of the Historical Society of Oak Park and River Forest. A century later Barclay's photos are the best that were taken of early train operations in Oak Park.

An open car operated through block after block of undeveloped real estate in Oak Park. The photograph shows Madison Street looking west at Oak Park Avenue in 1903.

Chapter 1: The Beginnings

A single-truck car waited on Fifth Avenue at Lake Street in Maywood. The Chicago & North Western Railway's tracks are in the background.
Joe May Collection

Chicago Consolidated Traction Company

On February 27, 1899, the first major consolidation of street railway companies in the Chicago area was completed when eight north and west side street railway companies, including both the Cicero & Proviso Street Railway and the Ogden Street Railway, were merged into the Chicago Consolidated Traction Company. Seven of these companies were already controlled by Cicero & Proviso owner Charles T. Yerkes. The final step of the merger took place on March 1, 1899 when deeds were filed in the recorder's office conveying all property and franchises of the eight street railway companies to the Chicago Consolidated Traction. As with many railroad mergers, the promoters of the consolidation hoped that the combined operations would eliminate duplicate activities and therefore make the operation more profitable.

To effect the consolidation, Yerkes forces obtained passage of legislation known as the Allen Law in the Illinois Senate and House of Representatives. This law permitted the consolidation of street car companies and also extended by 50 years the expiration period of the franchises for street railway operation that were granted by the municipalities. It was reported that Yerkes paid $500,000 to both state houses to obtain passage of the Allen Law.

In early 1902, the power house on Lake Street at Cuyler was partially destroyed by fire. The loss estimate was $125,000. The power station was soon rebuilt and returned to service.

On October 25, 1902, the Illinois Supreme Court ruled that the Chicago Union Traction and Chicago Consolidated Traction were one and the same company. This ruling meant, among other things, that the two companies had to allow free transfers between their lines.

By 1908, the economic reality of the transit industry had run another cycle. The Chicago Union Traction was sold at a foreclosure sale on January 25, 1908. The purchasing company was named the Chicago Railways Company. Physical reorganization

Postmarked in 1907, this postcard shows a Lake Street single-truck car. It is waiting for its next scheduled run at Fifth Avenue and the Chicago & North Western Railway tracks in Maywood.
C. R. Childs photo/Bruce G. Moffat Collection

was forced on the transit lines about a year and a half later. On October 10, 1910, the Chicago City Council passed an ordinance requiring that all former Chicago Consolidated Traction property within the city limits be acquired by Chicago Railways. The ordinance was accepted by Chicago Railways on December 6, 1910. This resulted in all of the lines, buildings, and cars of the Chicago Consolidated Traction being sold to Chicago Railways on December 27, 1910 for about $4 million. On the very same day, the lines outside the City of Chicago were purchased by the newly created County Traction Company.

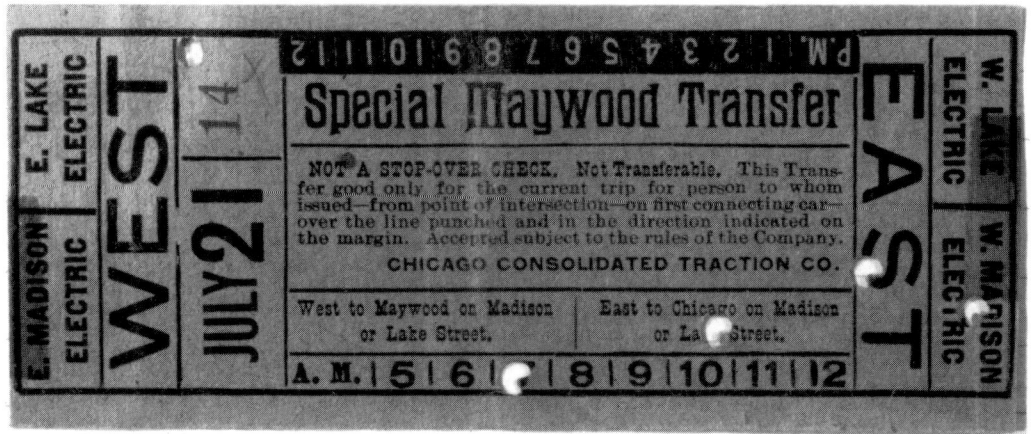

Black ink on light purple paper stock was used to print a special Maywood transfer. The form allowed the bearer to pay one fare to ride between Maywood and Chicago. Circa 1903.
Richard R. Andrews Collection

Chapter 1: The Beginnings

In the early 1900s, a Chicago Consolidated Traction streetcar departed the Lawndale Avenue terminal in Lyons and operated eastbound on Ogden Avenue.
Roy G. Benedict Collection

For some long forgotten reason, a contingent of Chicago Consolidated Traction's motormen, conductors, and shop employees were positioned on a single truck open car to pose for a photograph. The scene is at the Cicero & Proviso's car barn on Madison Street, a little west of Pulaski. Circa 1900.
Carl P. Klaus Collection

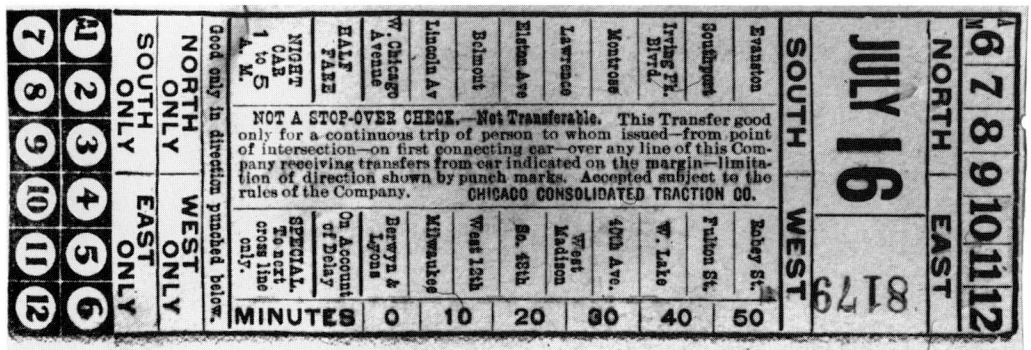

With the creation of Chicago Consolidated Traction, transfer forms became more complicated. The form lists the former Cicero & Proviso and Ogden Street Railway lines plus those on the north side of Chicago. The transfer was printed with black ink on yellow paper stock. Circa 1910.
Richard R. Andrews Collection

Chicago & Northern Pacific Railroad

The major railroads in the Chicago area had competition from many large and small transportation investors. These entrepreneurs hoped to gain a piece of the freight and passenger markets, as well as create an interest in their real estate developments. One of these short-lived companies was the Chicago & Northern Pacific, a subsidiary of the Northern Pacific Railroad. This railroad was positioned between the present day Union Pacific Railroad (formerly the Galena Division or west line of the Chicago & North Western) and the Burlington Northern Santa Fe Railroad (formerly the Chicago, Burlington & Quincy Railroad).

The beginnings of the Chicago & Northern Pacific can be traced to the formation of the relatively obscure Chicago & Western Dummy Railway Company. On August 21, 1881, an entrepreneur and resident of the Town of Austin, Charles R. Vandercook, secured an ordinance from Cicero to build a "dummy" railway line. This line would begin near the western terminal of the West Chicago Street Railroad's Madison Street car line, and travel a route north via Pulaski, west via West End Avenue (in Chicago) and Randolph Street (outside Chicago) to a Western terminal at Wisconsin Avenue in Oak Park. Regular service on the Chicago & Western Dummy Railway began on November 27, 1881.

The term "dummy" is not used in railway terminology very often today. It refers to a small, low-speed steam locomotive that was developed for street railway operation. The "dummy" locomotive was built to look like a passenger coach, with the boiler and propulsion equipment masked from public view. About a decade later, electrical propulsion proved to be economically and operationally superior and these locomotives were withdrawn from street railway service.

The railroad was beset by many difficulties during the 1880s. Due to a big winter snowstorm, the railroad was closed from January 1, 1883 to the end of February. In Spring, the line was sold to a Chicago banker, John Buehler. Under new ownership, the line was extended in June 1883 via Randolph Street, Park Avenue, and Des Plaines Avenue to Harrison Street, adjacent to Waldheim Cemetery. In October 1883, a train derailed resulting in serious injuries to one passenger. At a time when fares were 5 to 15¢ per ride, the passenger received a court award for the staggering sum of $4,500 for his injuries. In January 1885, another snowstorm closed the railroad for six weeks. Soon thereafter, the railroad was forced into receivership and the property was sold. The new owner, the Chicago, Harlem & Batavia Railway Company, was incorporated on January 1, 1886. It reported in a filing that

An early photograph of the line shows a one-car West Chicago & Western Dummy Railway train at Randolph Street and Harlem Avenue in 1881. The locomotive was named "Waldheim" in recognition of the cemetery on the line with the same name. The coach was mislettered "West Chicago Dummy Railway Co."

Chicago Public Library, Special Collections and Preservation Division

Chapter 1: The Beginnings

In the late 1880s, Chicago, Harlem & Batavia engine #3, the Austin, *and coach #4 waited between trips at the company's station, slightly north of Madison Street at Pulaski Road. The standard gauge locomotive and coach were more substantial than the narrow gauge equipment they replaced.*
Historical Society of Oak Park and River Forest Collection

Engine #2, the Oak Park, *stopped at the modest Oak Park station in the late 1880s. The one car train operating on a single track railroad was more than adequate to meet service demands.*
Historical Society of Oak Park and River Forest Collection

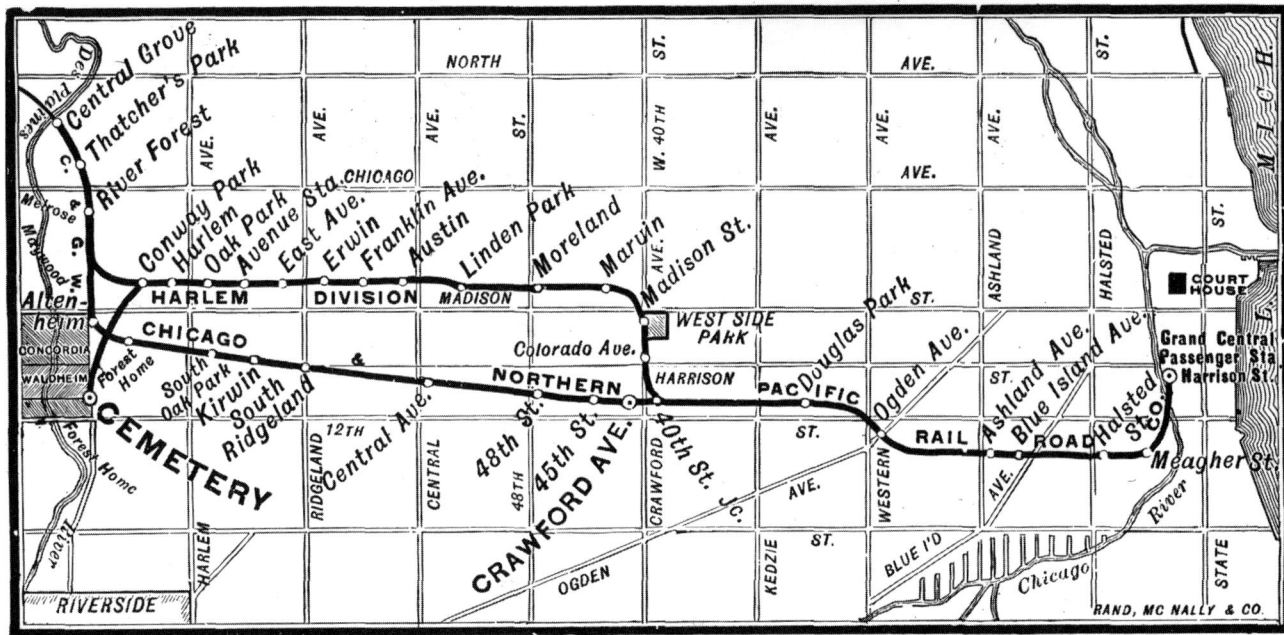

Reproduced from an 1896 timetable, this map shows the trackage of the Chicago & Northern Pacific. To the north of the main line is the Harlem Division, the former Chicago, Harlem & Batavia Railway.

it had purchased the property for $100,000 cash and then issued $50,000 in bonds for the purchase of new rolling stock, locomotives, and other improvements. Ironically, there never seemed to be any effort to extend the railway to Batavia, a town on the Fox River about 25 miles west of Harlem Avenue. However, an attempt to extend the railway west to Maywood failed when the local government refused to pay the cost of a bridge over the Des Plaines River.

To no one's surprise, even with the plant improvements, the Chicago, Harlem & Batavia suffered from insufficient traffic. The major business generator for the railway was its connection with the Madison Street horse car line. However, connections between the two carriers were not coordinated, and both carriers were at fault. The Oak Park *Vindicator* complained that passengers were forced to wait while the railway's locomotives took on water, while the horse car, just two blocks away, would be departing on its trip east into Chicago. It was not any better for a westbound passenger either. The horse car company elected to change horses one block away from the railway's station. Passengers would watch the C H & B's train pulling away, realizing that they might have to wait as long as 40 minutes for the next one. These poor connections did little to help stimulate patronage.

The Chicago, Harlem & Batavia ex-

The June 17, 1882 timetable lists 17 trains in each direction. The form was printed on dark blue paper with black ink. The headways were irregular, being as great as 71 minutes or as little as 34 minutes. An unusual feature of the timetable was the publishing of arrivals and departures at Waldheim, a station that was not only "not yet completed" but also not even started.

Krambles-Peterson Archive

Chapter 1: The Beginnings

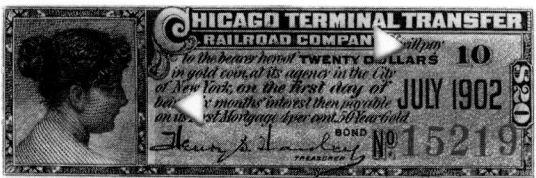

To help finance its purchases, The Chicago Terminal Transfer issued 50-year 4% first mortgage bonds in denominations of $1,000. The security had interest coupons attached which the bond's owner would detach and present to the company's agent for payment.
Krambles-Peterson Archive

isted as an operating railroad for less than two years. It was leased to the Wisconsin Central Railroad on November 15, 1887. Five days later, it purchased the Chicago, Harlem & Batavia outright. The former dummy line would now be known as the Harlem Division of the Wisconsin Central. Under the new ownership, the line was renovated and improved. The first change was to extend the line south on Pulaski to connect with the Wisconsin Central's main line. The following spring, the route was closed for several weeks to permit grading and installation of a second track and to eliminate two sharp curves. The line was also extended on the west end to connect with the Wisconsin Central, allowing Harlem Division trains to reach River Forest and Thatcher Park. Through service into Chicago started on August 24, 1888.

The formal ownership position changed again as the Northern Pacific Railroad entered the picture. The motivation for the Northern Pacific's interest in the Wisconsin Central was a way to bring its trains into Chicago at the new Grand Central Station. Establishing a subsidiary to hold the Chicago properties, the Chicago & Northern Pacific Railroad was organized. On March 11, 1890, ownership of the Harlem Division was transferred to this new company.

In July of 1890, the owners of Chicago & Northern Pacific created a new company called the Chicago & Southwestern Railroad to provide construction supplies for a new railway locomotive manufacturing plant being built by the Grant Locomotive Works. Plans called for the railroad to provide both freight and passenger service to the works. The Southwestern was routed to tie into the Chicago & Northern Pacific main line at Kilbourn Avenue and run southward to 16th Street, west to Harlem Avenue, and north to rejoin the Chicago & Northern Pacific's main line. The railroad would serve what was to be, at the time it was designed, the largest manufacturing plant in the midwest. The ownership of the Northern Pacific even purchased a large tract of land west of Central Avenue to create employee housing. Unfortunately, the Grant Locomotive Works closed in 1893 due to losses incurred during a strike and a decrease in demand for railway locomotives prompted by the "Panic of 1893." These events meant that passenger traffic on the Chicago & Southwestern was anemic at best.

The deteriorating economic environment affected the Chicago & Northern Pacific almost immediately. Earnings fell off due to competition from the extensions of the elevated lines and from the new streetcar lines being opened. However, problems at the parent road, the Northern Pacific, brought the entire operation tumbling down. The Northern Pacific failed to meet its financial obligations, and both the Northern Pacific and the Chicago & Northern Pacific entered bankruptcy in 1893.

Ownership changed again in both 1896 and 1897. In May 1896, another transportation operator agreed to lease both the Harlem and Southwestern Divisions as a way to rapidly enter the market for street railway services. This company, named the Suburban Railroad, wanted to compete against the Cicero & Proviso and the West Chicago Street Railroad. Both of these firms were now controlled by Charles T. Yerkes. The Suburban Railroad began operating the passenger services on the Harlem and Chicago & Southwestern Divisions on November 15, 1896. Two days later, the Chicago & Northern Pacific's receivers approved its sale to the Suburban.

The Chicago & Northern Pacific remained in receivership until the Chicago Terminal Transfer Railroad was organized to acquire it in June 1897. With a July 1, 1897 takeover, main line suburban service to Thatcher Park was terminated as well as the Suburban's right to use Grand Central Station. In an attempt to provide its former customers with some sort of transportation, the Suburban initiated service on Harrison Street. The Chicago Terminal Transfer fell back into receivership and was purchased by the Baltimore & Ohio Railroad Company in January 1910. Its wholly owned subsidiary, the Baltimore & Ohio Chicago Terminal Railroad, began operating the property on April 1, 1910.

Chicago *Terminal Transfer Railroad Company operated several key routes in the Chicago area. The western-most belt, as shown in the map above, was the longest The north-south route, roughly parallelingWestern Avenue, tied the railway into Grand Central Passenger Station. The western lines included the former Chicago & Northern Pacific.*

Chapter 1: The Beginnings

The Grant Locomotive works was to be built on the one-square-mile site bounded by Cicero Avenue on the east, Roosevelt Road on the north, Central Avenue on the west, Cermak Road on the south. Bruce G. Moffat Collection

2 The Suburban to La Grange

Suburban Electric Railway Company

The Suburban Electric Railway Company was chartered May 17, 1895 under the General Railroad Act of the State of Illinois for the purpose of building an electric railway from the City of Chicago to cities, towns and villages in the counties of Cook, Lake, DuPage and Kane in the State of Illinois. These lines would connect with the western terminals of both the Lake Street and Metropolitan elevated lines. The company was incorporated with $1,250,000 capital represented by $100 par value common stock and a bond issue for a like amount was to be issued. Officers of the company were Charles H. Crossette, president; David B. Lyman, treasurer; and Homer K. Galpin, secretary. The main line was to follow the Chicago, Burlington & Quincy Railroad to La Grange and eventually to Aurora. After this line was completed an extension to Elgin was to be built. (Obviously, these plans were made before the Aurora, Elgin & Chicago Railway came into existence and initiated service between Chicago and Aurora in 1902.)

The idea of building this railway originated with developer George P. Townsend and railroad promoter Charles S. Leeds. Other participants included Henry Cooper, a manager of Marshall Field's partner Levi Leiter's LaGrange real estate interests, and David B. Lyman, a LaGrange lawyer and president of the Chicago Title & Trust Company. Associated with these men was J. Schneider, president of the National Bank of Illinois. When Townsend formed a partnership with Charles Leeds to build the line, they agreed that each would share whatever profit was made on the project

Leeds traveled to New York City to raise funds to build the railway. He interested Irwin C. Stump, manager of the estate of the late Senator George Hurst in the project. Before investing, the plans for building the electric railway were thoroughly examined by both Stump and Hurst's widow. After study, they agreed to purchase $110,000 face value of bonds of the railway for $100,000.

In Chicago, David B. Lyman was a very successful real estate promoter. His statements on behalf of the company carried great weight in helping the company

Suburban Railroad's car 504 was operating westbound on Randolph Street, just east of Harlem Avenue. The photograph was taken in 1903 during the years of joint operation on this track segment with the Lake Street "L." In the background, an "L" train was standing at the Wisconsin Avenue station. Oak Park police officer William Lembke observed the approaching trolley.
Philander W. Barclay photo/ Historical Society of Oak Park and River Forest Collection

Chapter 2: The Suburban to La Grange

A neatly striped 507 was ready to depart Cermak Road and Pulaski Road for La Grange circa 1910. Fred Borchert photo

secure the necessary franchises. On July 27, 1895, the Cicero Town Board passed an ordinance granting the company the right to build a double track car line along the following streets:

Thoroughfare	Double Track Car Line Segment
Harrison Street	Cicero Avenue to Harlem Avenue
Laramie Avenue	Madison Street to 25th Street
22nd Street	Cicero Avenue to Harlem Avenue
Riverside Drive	22nd Street to the west limits of the township
Cicero Avenue	22nd Street to 39th Street

Thoroughfare	Single Track Car Line Segment
Laramie Avenue	Chicago & North Western Railway tracks to Madison Street

This franchise was granted for 50 years by the Cicero Town Board. As part of the agreement, the company agreed to pave between the rails with cedar blocks, pay $1,000 per mile for the use of streets occupied, and pay an annual license fee of $20 for each car the company operated. The license fee was to be collected after the road was in operation for 10 years. One mile was to be in service by July 1, 1896 and the whole system by July 1, 1897. The board also approved the Suburban's plan to purchase the Harlem Division of the Chicago & Northern Pacific Railroad.

The population of the towns lying west of Cicero Avenue appeared to have the potential to generate significant levels of traffic. The company proposed to run special funeral trains to the three large on-line cemeteries: Concordia, Waldheim and Forest Home. The territory along the Des Plaines River was very popular for picnics and the long suburban route would also attract trolley parties. The company hoped all these sources of ridership would produce a profitable investment.

Seventeen miles of double track railway were to be built. Starting at the Cicero Avenue station of the Garfield Park branch of the Metropolitan Elevated, the main line would follow Harrison Street, Harlem Avenue, entering Riverside on 26th Street (crossing the Illinois Central Railroad at grade at the Parkway suburban station), Des Plaines Avenue, through the woods on private right-of-way (about 34th Street) and into Brookfield, crossing both the Des Plaines River and Salt Creek (on deck-type girder bridges), Monroe Avenue, Broadway Street, Lincoln Avenue (crossing the Indiana Harbor Belt Railway at grade), private right-of-way paralleling the Indiana Harbor Belt, and Hillgrove Avenue to a terminal at Brainard Avenue in La Grange. A branch line was planned on Laramie Avenue between Harrison & 25th Streets and a connecting line on 22nd Street between Cicero Avenue & Harlem Avenue. In addition, 13 miles of track that were the Harlem Division of the Chicago & Northern Pacific Railroad Company were to be leased.

A construction contract for the railway was awarded to the Suburban Construction Company of New Jersey, a new company created and controlled by Leeds. The company was incorporated with capital stock of $100,000. The four principals owning it, including Leeds, each held $24,200 of the stock while the remaining $3,200

ACCIDENT ON CHICAGO SUBURBAN.

On the morning of September 14, at 6:45 o'clock there was a collision between two cars on the Chicago Suburban Railroad at a point about 400 ft. north of the switch on 16th street leading into the yards and directly east of the Harlem race track. There was a very heavy fog which obscured the view and made the accident possible. According to the usual morning schedule the south-bound car was to be at the switch, on the side track, leaving a clear road for the north-bound car to pass over the three-quarters of a mile of single track.

The south-bound car had, however, been detained up the line by a derailed car, and was not on the side track. Standing near the switch and on the side track was a car that was being examined by a motor inspector. As the north-bound car approached the meeting point the motorman glanced at the side track and saw this car which he supposed to be the one he was to meet, and turned on the current to get over the stretch of single track as rapidly as possible.

Almost as soon as the switch was passed the south-bound car was seen approaching at full speed to make up for lost time. Both motormen shut off the current and applied the air brakes; the rails, however, were wet from the mist and caused the wheels to slide.

Almost before the motormen had realized their danger the cars met, breaking in the front ends, as shown in the illustration. Nearly all the passengers on the cars were bruised by being thrown against the seats or cut by broken glass, 21 being so injured, some quite seriously but none fatally. The two motormen were seriously hurt, and it is astonishing that neither was killed.

When the car bodies struck, the trucks were thrown forward, breaking or bending the center pins, brake rods, etc.; the trucks and motors were apparently little damaged. The total damage to the cars is estimated at $500. That the accident was not more serious is due to the effective action of the Christensen air-brakes with which the cars are equipped. The fog was so dense that one could not see more than 20 feet.

of the stock was held by three others.

This firm's contract called for it to construct the track, overhead lines and power house; furnish machinery and rolling stock; and to equip and operate the road for two years from date of completion. For building the road, Suburban Construction was to receive an amount of bonds not less that $600,000 nor more than $1,250,000, depending on the amount of work to be done. Construction began in 1895. Construction was subcontracted with C. E. Loss & Company for the first 5 miles of the line east from La Grange, but by the end of the year, only about 2-1/2 miles were built. On December 28, 1895, the name of the company was changed to the Suburban Railroad Company.

In April 1896, Leeds entered into a construction contract with the Naugle, Holcomb & Company in return for $260,000 in bonds of the railway. On November 28, 1896, the contract was extended and expanded to include constructing and equipping the railroad as projected, furnishing the leased lines with electricity, and operating the system for two years. The Harlem Division of the Chicago & Northern Pacific Railroad was leased to Leeds as of November 15, 1896. Naugle, Holcomb & Company would receive the remaining $1,139,000 in bonds and receipt of beneficial interest in 8,650 shares of capital stock of the road for performing the work. The capital stock was deposited with D. B. Lyman, trustee, under an arrangement whereby, in the final distribution, each of the four principals would receive $50,000 face value of stock. In addition, $50,000 (face value) of the stock was claimed by Irwin C. Stump as commission for helping to place the $110,000 bonds with the Hurst Estate.

In 1897, Suburban Railroad's cars 109 and 110 were involved in the railroad's first collision.

Chapter 2: The Suburban to La Grange

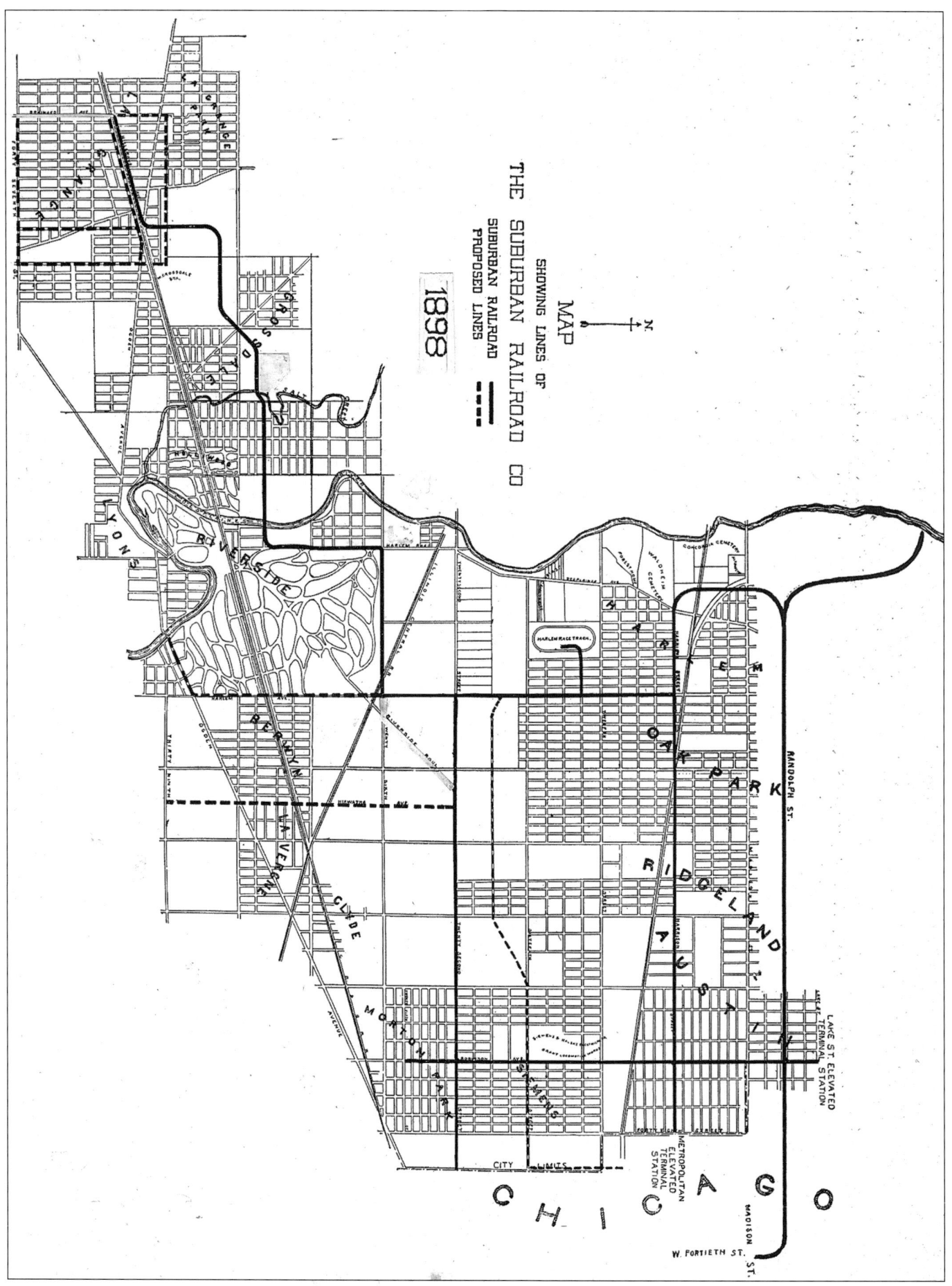

Suburban Railroad car 103 was traveling east on Harrison Street at Ridgeland Avenue in 1903. To call Harrison Street "a street" seems a bit overstated because, except for the streetcar tracks, it has yet to be paved. On this day, due to track maintenance, the south track was out of service and the streetcar was traveling eastbound on the normal westbound track.

Philander W. Barclay photo/ Historical Society of Oak Park and River Forest Collection

Suburban Railroad

Construction on the line was stopped when the trustees of the Hurst estate, annoyed with the local politics, had second thoughts about their investment in the road. Cicero did not want the railway built with T-rail track (girder rail was more expensive) and all the frontage consents had not yet been obtained. An injunction restraining the company from laying tracks on Harlem, Des Plaines and Ogden Avenues within the Village of Riverside was issued in November 1895. The judge ruled that the village could not grant any street car company franchises for longer than 20 years; that the ordinance was not accompanied by the necessary frontage consents; and that the Suburban Electric Railway Company would be exceeding its charter by operating as an ordinary common carrier railroad.

Construction resumed on December 27, 1896 when 70-pound T-rail track was laid on Harrison Street, east from Harlem Avenue. By June 1897, the line was finished from Harrison Street and Cicero Avenue to the car house at Harlem Avenue and 22nd Street. The track on Harlem Avenue, north of 19th Street actually belonged to the Chicago & Southwestern, another division of the Chicago & Northern Pacific. The Suburban Railroad leased this railroad to get the use of Harlem Avenue. The portion of this line between the main line of the Chicago & Northern Pacific and 19th Street was electrified and shared with steam trains. The first two cars were delivered in May 1897; the first trial trip was run on May 29, 1897. During the second week of June 1897, regular service began between the car house at 22nd Street and Harlem Avenue and the Metropolitan elevated station at Cicero Avenue and Harrison Street on a ten-minute headway.

During the 1897 construction season, the builders of the railroad experimented with a gasoline driven motor car. Earlier

Chapter 2: The Suburban to La Grange

Car 507 would depart from its Pulaski and Cermak Road terminal with a full load. Not only could passengers on the Pulaski and Cermak lines transfer to the Suburban here, but also so could riders on the Ogden Avenue line. Circa 1907.

James J. Buckley Collection

This transfer, printed on yellow paper with black ink, was used by the Suburban Railroad around 1900.

Richard R. Andrews Collection

work on the electrical overhead was accomplished with the aid of a tower car towed by a steam locomotive. Exhaust smoke from the locomotive frequently interfered with the men at work on the tower car, so the Patton Motor Car Company offered to supply one of their new vehicles to replace the steam locomotive. The Patton Motor Car was a two-axle car powered by an electrical generator with a gasoline engine attached to it. Both axles had a motor mounted on them. The motor cars were equipped with a battery bank (and recharging apparatus) to provide power in excess of that supplied by the gasoline engine when needed. The car was an operational success and was kept in use for the balance of the construction season.

In June 1897, George P. Townsend filed suit in the Superior Court of Cook County for a partnership accounting because Henry N. Cooper, a minority stockholder in the construction company, had filed a series of lawsuits seeking various injunctions against the railroad company. Interests representing Leeds had purchased almost all of the capital stock of the Suburban Construction Company. Then, at a meeting held in New Jersey, a vote was held to annul the Naugle, Holcomb & Company contract despite the fact that most of the work had been completed and the contractors were in possession of the railroad. The litigation branched out into at least four local suits and two more in New Jersey where the Suburban Construction Company was organized. The active litigation caused Naugle, Holcomb & Company to halt construction.

Charles T. Yerkes, always known for his shrewd financial manipulations, went into action by purchasing the holdings of Naugle, Holcomb & Company for $472,000 in cash. At the same time, he bought the interests of the Suburban Construction Company, which had gone into receivership. Immediately after both purchases, plans were made to make the railroad primarily feed Yerkes' Lake Street "L" by routing the cars over Laramie Avenue to Lake Street. Infrequent, inconvenient service was maintained to the Metropolitan's Garfield Park line for franchise purposes.

Some local residents thought that Kountze Brothers, a New York City investment banking firm, was really financing the Suburban Railroad as part of its work with financing the Metropolitan West Side Elevated. Therefore, it was taken for granted that the ties between the Metropolitan and the Suburban could not easily be broken. The change in car routing caught the Metropolitan's management totally by surprise.

Suburban Railroad 109 and two trailers posed on Cermak Road at Harlem Avenue. When this photograph was taken, Cermak Road had not been paved.
Electric Railway Historical Society Collection

Extensions

The Suburban Railroad wanted to make an agreement with the Metropolitan West Side Elevated to allow it to run its cars downtown over the elevated line. The Suburban offered to construct an incline between Cicero and 50th Avenues on the Garfield Park branch connecting the two lines, and even went so far as to secure an ordinance for this structure and options for the needed land. The elevated company, however, showed no interest in this connection.

Obtaining the necessary permission to route the car line through Berwyn proved difficult as well. The railroad wanted to use Riverside Drive, a diagonal street between 22nd Street and 26th Street. However, the township wanted to develop Riverside Drive as a 150-foot wide boulevard with a parkway in the middle of the thoroughfare. The township would not grant the railroad the use of this right-of-way and the Suburban was unable to get frontage consents to build on Riverside Drive.

Instead, the railroad had to reroute by using 22nd Street to Harlem Avenue and south on Harlem Avenue to 26th Street through land known as the Gage Farm, which was owned by the City of Chicago. The Cicero Town Board denied Yerkes' Ogden Street Railway's petition for right-of-way through the farm because it lacked the necessary frontage consents. However, another obstacle was an injunction secured by the Village of Riverside to prevent construction of the road from Harlem Avenue west to the Des Plaines River. The Suburban finally got the injunction dissolved in June 1897. The night that the court voided the injunction a large force of men completed the missing mile of track in less than 13 hours.

The formal opening of the La Grange line took place on July 3, 1897. Cars operated on a 15-minute headway between LaGrange and the Metropolitan Elevated Station at Harrison Street and Cicero Avenue. This route was profitable from the very beginning. Pre-operation estimates were for about 5,000 passengers a day, but during the first month it was hauling over 6,000 people daily. Gross receipts averaged about $750 a day while operating expenses were not even $400 a day. Company officials were very pleased, and expected that once the road was completed it would be carrying 25,000 people daily.

Obtaining the right to operate streetcars on Laramie Avenue between Madison and Lake Streets was another interesting situation. At this time, Laramie Avenue was the dividing line between the City of Chicago and the Town of Cicero. The Suburban Railroad only had a franchise for a single track on what had been the Cicero side of the street and was having a very difficult time trying to obtain a franchise from the City of Chicago to lay a second track on their side of the street. The Suburban attempted to set the poles anyway, but was forcibly stopped. Unable to come to terms with the city, the company finally laid the second track on the Cicero side of the street from Madison Street to Lake Street over the strong objections of nearby property owners.

Meanwhile, another debate was raging over how the car line was to cross Washington Boulevard which happened to occupy Laramie Avenue for a few hundred

Chapter 2: The Suburban to La Grange

Suburban Railroad car 105 has turned south on Cuyler Avenue from Randolph Street about 1903. The trackage in the foreground on Randolph Street was the Suburban's line to Wisconsin Avenue, formerly owned by the Chicago, Harlem & Batavia. The destination sign on the car told where the streetcar terminated, "Harrison Street to Harlem Avenue Only." It did not go to the Harlem Race Track.

Philander W. Barclay photo/ Historical Society
of Oak Park and River Forest Collection

feet. Ultimately, the Suburban agreed to buy the property at this corner and relocate Washington Boulevard to eliminate the jog at Laramie Avenue. The city reciprocated by granting a franchise for a track to be built in the city, allowing both tracks to be placed in the center of the street for the entire distance. The line was completed and put into service on September 19, 1897.

The most important work yet to be completed was the installation of track on 22nd Street, between the town limits at 46th Avenue and Harlem Avenue, a distance of a little over three miles. The Town of Cicero had obtained an injunction restraining the company from using the parkway in the center of the street for its tracks. Town officials were also rather confused about the company's intentions in leasing the Chicago & Southwestern and wondered why the company would run service on two lines so close together. What they did not know was that the Suburban planned to electrify the C&SW's Harlem Avenue trackage and run streetcars over it. After the injunction was dissolved, a large force of men was put to work on 22nd Street and the track was completed on Tuesday, September 28, 1897, with regular service beginning the following day. Every other La Grange car was rerouted from Lake Street via Laramie Avenue and 22nd Street on a 40-minute headway. These cars alternated with those via Harrison Street. Shortly afterward, a shuttle car was put in service on 22nd Street, between Kenton & Laramie Avenues.

The steam railroads were usually reluctant to allow the electric railway lines to cross their tracks. The Suburban was prevented from building several crossings on Laramie Avenue between Harrison Street and 25th Street by court injunction. On October 13, 1897, the courts ruled in favor of the Suburban in the matter of crossing tracks operated by the Chicago Great Western and Chicago Terminal

Transfer, successor to the Chicago & Northern Pacific, in the Town of Cicero. The Suburban was given permission to lay temporary "jump" crossings, but was required to have a flagman at these crossings during the time the cars were operating. These events took place about a year before the Chicago Great Western built a yard at this location.

When the Chicago Great Western constructed its main Chicago freight yard between Cicero and Central Avenues, the Suburban agreed to build a bridge to carry the car line over the yard and purchased a used bridge from the Chicago City Railway Company for this purpose. This bridge had a storied past, as it was originally erected in Chicago spanning 61st Street, a little west of State Street, as part of the street railway improvements made for the 1893 World's Fair. Later, when the steam railroads were elevated at this point, the rickety bridge nicknamed "robber's roost" was no longer needed and was placed in storage.

The Suburban was now operating eight routes totaling 57.5 miles of track. It owned 33.5 miles of track and the other

Suburban Railroad car 505 was proceeding northward from Park Place on Woodside Road, the continuation of Des Plaines Avenue in Riverside. The photograph, circa 1905, shows substantial development of single family homes. Residents using public rail transportation into Chicago could use either the Suburban or take a short walk to the Riverside station of the Chicago, Burlington & Quincy Railroad.
Fred Borchert photo

24.0 miles were leased from the Chicago Terminal Transfer. Forty-seven miles were electrically operated by 20 motor cars and 18 trailers, and the remaining 10 miles were served using one steam engine and four cars.

On May 1, 1899, the Cuyler Avenue branch of the Lake Street Elevated Railroad Company, an 0.8-mile long line between Randolph Street and Harrison Street, was leased to the Suburban for an annual rent of $2,000. This route was put in service on May 30, 1899 to coincide with the opening day of the Harlem Race Track. When the race track trains were not running, regular service on this branch was furnished by the Suburban. Later, the elevated company operated its own car. Cuyler service was interrupted several times until it was permanently terminated on July 3, 1905.

Chapter 2: The Suburban to La Grange

Around the corner and two blocks west, Suburban Railroad car 507 crossed the Des Plaines River. The pedestrian walks on both sides of the tracks were a convenient feature for area residents wishing to access Zoo Woods from Riverside. The north walkway was removed in subsequent bridge re-buildings. Circa 1905.

Fred Borchert photo

In the first week of October 1900, at the direction of Charles T. Yerkes, all La Grange cars were re-routed via Harrison Street and Cuyler Avenue connecting with the Lake Street "L" trains at Randolph Street. The reason for this change was money. Since Yerkes controlled both properties, he wanted to maximize revenue by not allowing convenient passenger transfer between the Suburban and the rival Metropolitan "L."

To meet the terms of the franchise on Harrison Street, east of Cuyler Avenue, the Suburban had to make at least six trips a day. However, only a few La Grange cars would make this trip, forcing people who wanted to take the Lake Street "L" to transfer at Cuyler Avenue to a shuttle car.

In January 1901, Charles T. Yerkes offered to sell the Suburban Railroad. On January 28th, he contacted Mr. W. W. Gurley, President of the Metropolitan West Side Elevated Railroad Company to present his proposition. In a follow-up letter to Gurley the next day, Yerkes gave an asking price of $1.1 million for his holdings in the property. The terms were $1 million in cash and $100,000 would remain in escrow until he could deliver $86,000 in bonds and 2,470 shares of stock held by others.

The Metropolitan studied Yerkes' proposal, and discovered that in the six months from January 1900 to June 1900, the Suburban earned $16,632.60 or about $91 per day, equaling about 1,800 daily fares. Of course, this was during the winter and spring seasons when the Suburban had no special attractions on the line, such as the summertime picnic business and horse racing at both the Harlem and Hawthorne race tracks. It was evident that the Suburban was just covering its operating expenses.

In addition, even though the line was well constructed, little attention had been given to maintenance. At this time, it was estimated that anywhere from $50,000 to $100,000 would be required to put the road in suitable condition for long-term operation. The Metropolitan's management thought that the Suburban would be a good feeder for the elevated line in time, but nevertheless recommended against

38

The Chicago & West Towns Railways

> Chas. T. Yerkes.
> ~~XXXXXXXXXXXXXXXXXXXX~~
> ROOM 619,
> ROYAL INS. BLDG.
> CABLE ADDRESS, YERKES, CHICAGO.
>
> Chicago, Jan. 29th, 1901.
>
> Mr. W. W. Gurley,
>   Chicago.
>
> Dear Sir:-
>
> In accordance with our conversation of yesterday, in relation to the Suburban Railroad, I wish to say, that there are in all 12,500 shares of the capital stock, of which I hold 10,025 shares. There are five Directors, each one of whom has one share of stock and I hold the certificates and power of attorney for same. The State Construction Co., which I control, has 2,470 shares, making a total capital of 12,500 shares.
>
> There have been issued $1,250,000 bonds, of which I hold $1,137,000; Naugle Holcomb & Co. hold $86,000 and there has been sold $27,000.
>
> I propose to sell all of my holdings, including the capital stock and all of the bonds, except the $27,000, for $1,100,000. The amount of cash to be received would be $1,000,000 and the $100,000 to remain in escrow until I was able to deliver the $86,000 bonds and the 2470 shares of stock.
>
> I would say that the company is free of floating debt, except what might be called the regular running expenses. I would also inform you that the Lake Street Elevated R. R. Co. has the right to run its cars over about one mile and a half of track of the Suburban Co., for which they pay an annual sum of $6,000.
>
> Very truly yours,
>
> Chas T. Yerkes

In early 1901, Charles T. Yerkes sent this letter to the Metropolitan "L" president W. W. Gurley confirming their earlier conversation and offering to sell his interest in the Suburban Railroad. Mr. Gurley must have been astonished to learn that his competitor wanted to sell him a valuable feeder for his "L" lines. After the Metropolitan studied the matter, Yerkes' proposal was quietly rejected.
Secretary, Chicago Transit Board

purchasing the road.

In the spring of 1901 Yerkes found a buyer, Blair & Company of New York City, and sold his interest in the Lake Street "L", plus other elevated lines (Northwestern and Union elevated railroads) for $5 million and left Chicago for London where he was active in extending the city's underground system until his death in 1905. The Suburban was not part of that transaction, remaining with Yerkes and his estate until 1913, when it was finally merged into the Chicago & West Towns Railway.

On May 1, 1901, the La Grange cars were rerouted back to their original terminal at Harrison Street and Cicero Avenue. Alternate cars were routed via Harrison Street and Harlem Avenue and via Harrison Street, Laramie Avenue, and 22nd Street. A shuttle car operated on 22nd Street between Kenton and Laramie Avenues. The Metropolitan's Garfield Park route gained about 2,000 fares per day.

Chapter 2: The Suburban to La Grange

The 106 and an unidentified trailer posed for the company photographer in 1897.   Western Electrician

Chicago, Riverside & La Grange Railroad Company

In 1903, the Suburban Railroad created a wholly-owned subsidiary to build a car line on 22nd Street between Pulaski Road and Kenton Avenue. This trackage would connect the Suburban with the Chicago system and would provide passengers the option of transferring to the Chicago car lines that ran on Pulaski, 22nd Street, and Ogden Avenue. The main reason for this extension was to serve the Western Electric Company's massive Hawthorne Works which was then under construction at the southeast corner of Cicero Avenue and 22nd Street.

The new company was chartered as the Chicago, Riverside & La Grange Railroad Company on March 7, 1903 under the laws of the State of Illinois. On March 23, 1903, an ordinance from the City of Chicago was secured authorizing construction of a double track electric railway on west 22nd Street between Pulaski and Kenton Avenues (the city limits). The line was to be operated by the Suburban as part of its system.

The six-block extension formally opened on Saturday, May 23, 1903. In addition to passenger traffic, package freight was now carried on the cars. This was the first time that package freight was allowed to be handled on streetcars in Chicago. Soon after the line opened, the Western Electric Company leased a car from the Suburban to carry workers without charge between the plant and the intersection of Pulaski and 22nd Street.

On January 9, 1911, an ordinance was passed by the Chicago City Council authorizing an operating agreement between the Southern Street Railway Company and the Chicago, Riverside & La Grange providing for the rehabilitation and joint operation of the line. Beginning on July 16, 1911, the Chicago City Railway (operating the Southern Street Railway) extended service on its 22nd Street line to Kenton Avenue. The Suburban continued to operate the La Grange cars to Pulaski.

On July 2, 1914, the Southern Street Railway Company purchased the tracks of the Chicago, Riverside & La Grange on which it had been operating under lease. The purchase price was $18,378.26. Beginning Monday, August 6, 1914, the Suburban ceased operating cars to Pulaski Road, terminating all runs at Kenton Avenue.

Suburban's Receivership

In 1902, the Chicago Title & Trust Company, trustee of the Suburban's first mortgage bonds, filed an application with the Circuit Court of Cook County for a receiver to take over the company. At the time, the company owed over $400,000 interest on its bonds. On July 30, 1902 Mr. Louis S. Owsley, the company's treasurer since July 1897, was appointed receiver. One of his first decisions was to terminate the Suburban's lease of the Chicago & Southwestern, except for the tracks on Harlem Avenue north of 19th

In this heavily retouched photo, a Suburban Railroad 500 series car pulled a single trailer through Brookfield. The trailer was converted from a motorized Cicero & Proviso car of the 13-24 series.
La Grange Area Historical Society Collection

Street, which were retained.

The reason for the company's failure was simple — there were not enough passengers in the near west suburbs to support all of the carriers vying for business. The Suburban not only had competition from the Lake Street and Metropolitan "L" lines, but also the Chicago & North Western, Chicago Great Western, Illinois Central, and Chicago, Burlington & Quincy railroads. In addition, the Chicago Consolidated Traction Company street cars competed with the Suburban for the cemetery, race track, and picnic business.

In October 1906, the Metropolitan West Side Elevated Railway Company announced plans to extend its Douglas Park branch to Cicero, primarily to serve the rapidly expanding Western Electric Company. The Suburban said when this was done, the La Grange cars would be rerouted down 22nd Street, connecting with the Douglas Park elevated trains instead of operating via Harrison Street to connect with the Garfield Park elevated trains. When the Douglas Park extension to Kenton Avenue finally opened on May 22, 1907, the new routing was placed in effect. The Harrison Street cars now terminated at Harlem Avenue and 22nd Street.

Of course, with any change in service people are inconvenienced, and passengers did complain about these new routings. The company knew that Kenton Avenue would not be the "L's" permanent terminal; in fact, it was extended westward in five stages: to Cicero Avenue on December 16, 1907; to Laramie Avenue on August 16, 1910; to Central Avenue on August 1, 1912: to Lombard Avenue on August 1 1915; and to Oak Park Avenue on March 16, 1924. A final extension to Harlem Avenue never materialized.

Tough Times

During the period from 1902 through 1912 the company was not earning much money and was unable to maintain its property suitably. By 1907, the tracks on Harrison Street were described as being a disgrace to the Village of Oak Park. The company was looking for a way to abandon the street trackage since the service was no longer profitable. The Village of Oak Park threatened to tear up the tracks on Harrison Street if the company did not act to repair them, but this was what the company wanted, and the village did not make good its threat.

As late as 1910 plans were made for a joint line on Harlem Avenue between Grand and Ogden Avenues, using both Chicago Consolidated Traction Company and Suburban Railroad Company tracks. There were several gaps between the tracks of the two companies, both of

Chapter 2: The Suburban to La Grange

The Suburban Railroad served the northeast corner of La Grange, terminating in Hillgrove Avenue at Brainard Avenue. This photo, taken around 1900, shows the Chicago, Burlington & Quincy Railroad's tracks in the foreground. Motorman Henry Quinlan and conductor William Schact posed in front of wooden Suburban car 112.
La Grange Area Historical Society Collection

which were in the hands of receivers. With neither company having any money, these plans never materialized.

In September 1909, the Village of La Grange passed an ordinance authorizing the paving of Hillgrove Avenue with brick. This street was considered the busiest in downtown La Grange, except for a block on La Grange Road and a block on Burlington Avenue. The condition of the unpaved street was so bad that heavy wagons could not use it. The village also required the Suburban to install costly girder (grooved) rail, but the company did not have the funds to comply, delaying the paving for over a year. In 1910, the street was finally paved, but with the old T-rail track still in place. It would have been expensive to replace the rail because there were two lumber yards on the north side of the street which had spur tracks off the Burlington that would have to be upgraded. The village complained about the Suburban not paying its share of these costs, but to no avail.

There were also complaints from west suburban passengers about overcrowding during the rush hours. Especially vocal were employees of the Western Electric Company, many of whom had moved their residences out to the western suburbs and rode the cars to work. The Suburban added trailers on some runs to provide more capacity, but the switching facilities at the end of the line at Brainard Avenue were inadequate to permit a motor car to run around its trailer(s).

The key step in ending the receivership of the Suburban was the holding of a judicial sale. On February 27, 1912 the sale was held pursuant to the order of probate Judge Cutting in the Cook County Circuit Court. The sale of the Suburban Railroad Company and its Chicago, Riverside & La Grange Railroad Company subsidiary was ordered on the application of the receiver, Louis S. Owsley, representing the estate of Charles T. Yerkes. The only bidder for the property was Emil G. Schmidt, president of the County Traction Company, who paid $300,000 for the property and merged it with County Traction.

3 County Traction Company

The County Traction Company was formed as a result of the process to end the bankruptcy of the Chicago Consolidated Traction, whose properties located within the limits of the City of Chicago were awarded to the Chicago Railways Company. In the negotiations leading up to this division, the management of the Chicago Railways Company felt that the outlying lines were more a liability than an asset and declined to take them over. Furthermore, the parties involved elected not to seek a special ordinance from the City of Chicago that would have been required for the Chicago Railways to absorb the outlying lines. Thus, those traction lines outside the City of Chicago came under the control of County Traction.

The County Traction Company was incorporated on November 21, 1910 by Alan C. McIllvaine, T. E. Rein, George Blanchard and John D. Wild. Initial stock capitalization was valued at $100,000, pending transfer of the rail properties. County Traction became a legal entity when, on December 27, 1910, Judge Peter Grosscup of the United States District Court in Chicago signed the necessary court orders to end the receivership of the Chicago Consolidated Traction. The judge approved the sale of the company and its subsidiaries to Andrew Cook, a vice president of the Harris Trust & Savings Bank of Chicago. He had been chairman of the reorganization committee and trustee for the bondholders of the Chicago Consoli-

The Country Traction emblem rarely appeared on rolling stock. Streetcars operating on the former Cicero & Proviso and Ogden Street Railway lines were leased and carried the name of the lessor. Suburban Railroad's name was not deleted from its cars when the ownership changed.

Circa 1905, a single-truck closed streetcar, bearing the markings of Chicago Consolidated Traction, crossed the Des Plaines River on an eastbound trip over the Berwyn-Lyons route and was approaching Harlem Avenue.

Roy G. Benedict Collection

Chapter 3: County Traction Company

The County Traction system in 1912

The 1912 map shows the trackage operated by County Traction. In addition to the west side routes, County also operated a car line in Evanston. The cartographer erred in his presentation by labeling the Suburban as a railway rather than as a railroad. Several streets are better known by their current names including 40th Avenue (now Pulaski Road), 46th Avenue (now Kenton Avenue), and 72nd Avenue (now Harlem Avenue).

44   *The Chicago & West Towns Railways*

About 1910, a "Buffalo Car" turned north off Stanley Avenue onto Ridgeland Avenue with the Lavergne station of the Chicago, Burlington & Quincy Railroad in the background. The car, leased from the Chicago Railways, earned its nickname because it was purchased second hand from the International Railway Company of Buffalo, New York. County Traction leased 15 of these cars and they were considered by some observers as "Chicago Railways' castoffs."
A. J. Schumann photo/LeRoy F. Blommaert Collection

dated Traction. Acting in this capacity, Mr. Cook subsequently sold Consolidated's assets to the Chicago Railways Company and the County Traction Company.

The property that was transferred to County Traction included 52.6 miles of track and the former Cicero & Proviso Street Railway Company's car house and the power plant on Lake Street in Oak Park. Curiously, no rolling stock was included in this sale. County Traction planned to run all its cars out of the Lake Street facility and trackage rights were obtained from the Chicago Railways on Lake Street (between Austin Boulevard and Cicero Avenue) and Cicero Avenue (between Lake Street and 22nd Street) to deadhead Cicero Avenue and Berwyn-Lyons cars back and forth to this depot. All of the equipment that had operated on these lines had already been acquired by the Chicago Railways Company, which simply leased them back. This division of property created some unusual situations. For example, on Irving Park Road, from Austin Avenue to Dunning, just west of Narragansett Avenue, the north track belonged to the County Traction Company while the south track was the property of Chicago Railways. In this case, service was provided by Chicago Railways. A similar situation occurred on 26th Street between Kenton Avenue and Cicero Avenue. Initially, service was not provided on this trackage by either company, but later the Chicago Railways and its successor, the Chicago Surface Lines, rerouted some service over this trackage.

On December 28, 1910, the day following the dissolution of the Suburban's receivership by Judge Peter Grosscup, many of the physical connections between the lines of County Traction and Chicago City Railways were severed by contractors hired by County Traction.

The new company got off to an inauspicious start when the new management took over at midnight on December 27, 1910. The company failed to inform passengers that the one seat ride across the city limits had been discontinued. Late-night riders were quite surprised when they were forced to change cars and pay a second fare at the city limits on the Oak Park and Cicero lines. Initially, service was not provided on the Chicago Avenue line at all. Single-truck cars were placed into operation on the Madison Street route. The most significant change coming out of the reorganization proceedings was the abolishment of the 5¢ fare. No longer would the two companies provide "through car" transportation between the near suburbs and the city for a nickel. Travel times were also increased because most passengers now had to wait for a connecting car at the city limits. All this caused widespread consternation among the citizenry the near western suburbs.

Chapter 3: County Traction Company

Ripping Up the Rails

As noted earlier, County Traction had hired contractors to sever track connections with the Chicago Railways. One group of men was instructed to remove about 25 feet of rail at Madison Street and Austin Boulevard. If the tracks were severed it would be impossible for either company to operate through cars if pressed to do so by local politicians. When these men arrived on the site at 9:30 a.m. on December 28, 1910, they were attacked by the crowd that had assembled. In turn, the workers defended themselves with their picks and shovels and the police had to use their billy clubs to break up the disturbance. The crews of the Chicago Railways Company also had their own run-in with the police. Work crews had been sent out primarily to install crossovers so that their cars could turn back at the city limits. In doing this, crews were also instructed to remove the connecting tracks on the Chicago side. These men were stopped by the police and were informed that they could only install switches.

What made matters even worse was the generally poor condition of the rolling stock. The streetcars that were leased from the Chicago Railways Company were old and not in the best of condition. The public not only resented these castoff trolleys that were forced upon them, but, in some cases, took direct action against the company by damaging and derailing equipment. On Madison Street in Oak Park and River Forest, kids threw snowballs at the streetcar crews without any interference from the police. On other streets, the kids rolled snowballs bigger than themselves and positioned them on the tracks so that, by the end of the day, there was no service on the lines of County Traction.

At this time, County Traction had no valid franchises to operate its routes. All existing franchises were invalidated by the division of property and the refusal of the Chicago Railways Company to allow anything but its own cars on its tracks. An immediate application for new franchises was made to the eight suburbs involved, and Alan C. McIllvaine, the attorney representing County Traction, claimed that if the franchises were not forthcoming, the lines would be scrapped, and the tracks and equipment sold as junk, thus depriving the suburbs streetcar commutation to the city. The officials of the Village of Forest Park decided to call McIllvaine's bluff. Streetcar operation in that suburb was stopped, and village police even arrested a crew for attempting to take a stranded car back to the car house. Forest Park village Board President Mohr and the Board of Trustees claimed that the reorganization of the transit companies was just downright theft, and its only object was to rob the people of another fare. The board felt that it might as well fight the battle out there, because if they turned to the courts for relief, the courts usually favored the investors of the traction companies. The board thought that the public spirit and good will would carry greater weight than all of the court proceedings.

The opinion of the board was that County Traction could not expect them to pass an ordinance granting them permission to operate in their village unless it included the same privileges that had been contained in franchises in the past. Simply stated, the village wanted through cars into Chicago at a 5¢ fare, and the village held a strong hand because it had good elevated train service into the city provided by the Lake Street and Garfield Park "L" lines. The Village of Oak Park was also in a strong negotiating position since the village was also served by the two "L" lines. The village enacted an ordinance to permit the Chicago & Oak Park Elevated to resume service on the now dormant

County Traction's transfer form for July 4, 1911 was printed on purple paper stock with black ink.

Richard R. Andrews Collection

Cuyler Avenue line south to Harrison Street. The company leased a streetcar and resumed service on this spur on January 10, 1911.

Not to be outdone, Cicero officials began to strengthen their bargaining position. Mr. L. E. Meyers located several horse cars and placed them in service on December 28, 1910 on 25th and 26th Streets running west to the town limits at Berwyn. No fares were collected. Then, representatives of the Cicero Town Board began negotiating for the transfer of their "municipally owned and operated" transportation system to the larger, adjoining transit operator Chicago Railways. Had this merger been completed, the town would have demanded that the nickel fare and through-routed car service be restored.

Town officials tried to justify their actions by claiming that the workers employed in the large manufacturing plants in Cicero, for the most part, lived in Chicago. They believed that the hauls in Cicero would be short and would enable the Chicago Railways to operate the lines at a profit. It was claimed that cash receipts at one of the elevated stations increased by $700 in 3 days after the horsecar service was established. Finally, town officials recognized that, although County Traction and Chicago Railways were separate companies, many people, because of the reorganization, held securities in both firms.

County Traction stated that the reason for such drastic action in the beginning was that if they had accepted transfers, even for a single day, the municipalities served could have gone to court to secure an injunction against them for discontinuing the transfers. Thus, the court could have held that by issuing and accepting these transfers, the County Traction and Chicago Railways would be admitting the legal and binding force of the old Chicago Union Traction contracts. These old contracts were considered by many to be the primary reason why the Chicago Union Traction and Chicago Consolidated Traction declared bankruptcy. The Chicago Railways had repudiated this obligation long ago and was upheld in various court rulings. Had such an injunction been granted, it would have taken years to resolve the issue in the courts.

However, the complicated legal explanation did not prevent the company from instituting a series of petty acts. Residents of Oak Park who had purchased tickets entitling them to transfer to the Lake Street elevated line, without extra charge,

With the Chicago & North Western Railway's tracks in the foreground, car 3814 waits on Fifth Avenue in Maywood, circa 1910.

Fred Borchert photo

Chapter 3: County Traction Company

Chicago Union Traction car 3831 was in service on Madison Street, circa 1911. The leased "Buffalo Cars" mainly were used on the Berwyn-Lyons and Madison Street routes.

Fred Borchert photo

found the tickets worthless as the streetcars no longer connected with the elevated trains. These tickets had been sold by Chicago Consolidated Traction up to the time that County Traction took over the lines, and now were only valid on the one and one-half mile Chicago Avenue line (from Austin Boulevard to Harlem Avenue).

Patrons on the Madison Street cars also were treated poorly. Those passengers wishing to ride into Maywood were not informed that the route now ended at Harlem Avenue. When they reached the new terminal they were asked to leave the car and walk north, through the slush and snow to Lake Street. When they boarded the Lake Street car, another fare was required. County Traction certainly knew how to alienate its customers.

With all these problems, the matters were again referred to the courts. After reviewing what had transpired, Judge Peter Grosscup said that he had been misled. He stated that he would have never entered the order for confirmation had he understood what consequences would ensue, and he then entered an order reopening the entire case, thereby giving the municipalities and companies until February 12, 1911 to work out a solution. In the meantime, he decreed that the Chicago Railways' pay-as-you-enter cars would be required to carry passengers to the city limits where transfers would be given to the County Traction lines. Furthermore, the Chicago Railways were ordered to accept County Traction transfers at the city limits good for one ride in the same general direction, and heated shelters were required at the transfer points. The companies accepted this plan under the judge's threat that he would set aside the sale and division of Chicago Consolidated Traction if they failed to abide by his ruling. The 5¢ fare to and from Chicago was restored on December 31, 1910, but service continued to be "sporadic."

The suburban municipalities continued to press for a return to the old fare structure complete with through cars and a 5¢ fare, and the Village of Forest Park, the most belligerent of the suburbs, was the first to condemn Judge Grosscup's proposal. The other municipalities then followed suit, except for the Town of Cicero. Of course, the only way that through service could be reinstated would be to replace the rails that had been removed on the day after the Judge's original decision.

Attorney Ross C. Hall, representing the Town of Cicero, was active in trying to bring order out of chaos. He said that he could not understand what the municipalities stood to gain by rejecting the truce proposal of Judge Grosscup. He also criticized the other suburbs for refusing to adopt the peace plan saying that the interests of the people of Chicago had to be considered as well as those of the suburban residents. Hall felt that there was little chance of the one fare being restored to the outlying towns until such time as the territory grew in population to make the business profitable. Officials of the other municipalities had a different opinion, but they did not see a way to improve the situation. Representatives from Oak Park,

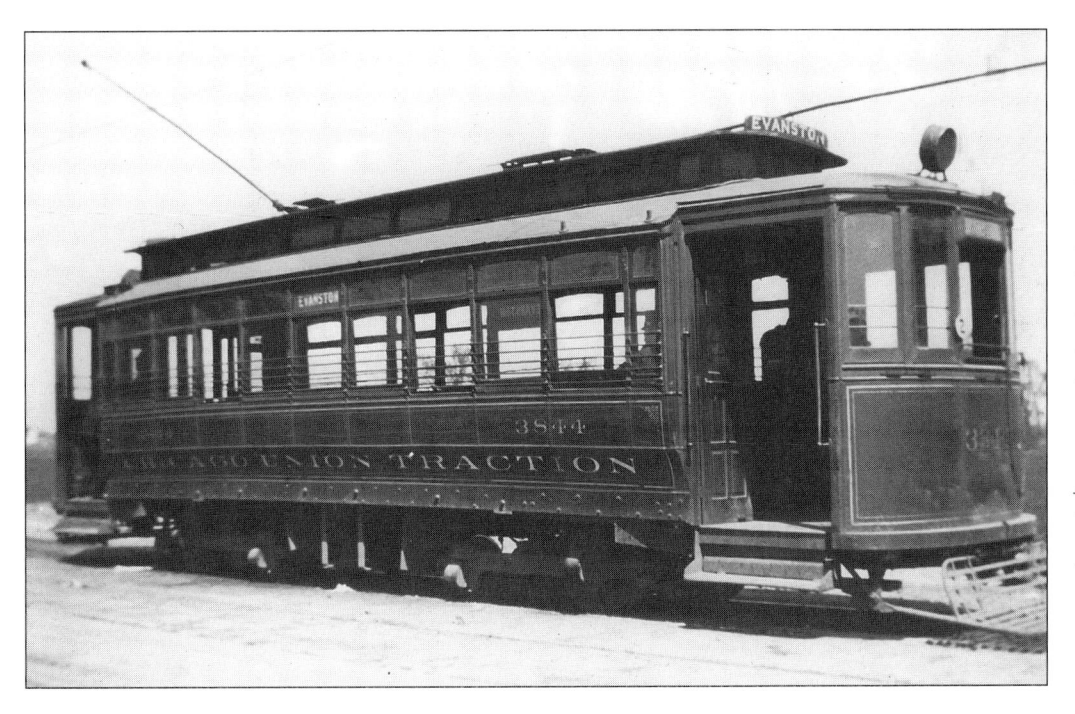

Chicago Union Traction car 3844 was photographed on Central Street near Crawford Avenue in Evanston circa 1911. The car was one of several dozen built by the American Car Company which were leased by County Traction from Chicago Railways. About a dozen of these cars saw exclusive service on the Evanston line.
Fred Borchert photo

Forest Park, River Forest, and Maywood felt that the same situation would exist on February 12, 1911 and thought it would be prudent to resolve the issue immediately.

Mr. W. W. Gurley, an attorney representing the Chicago Railways, said that the Chicago Railways would not take over and operate the County Traction routes even if they received $2 million along with the lines. He claimed that the County Traction's system was merely an illogical, fantastic collection of traditionally unprofitable stub-end streetcar lines. Many of the stub-end routes were not only isolated, but were not capable of being supplied with streetcars from car barns or electricity from power houses. Furthermore, operating franchises had been forfeited and customer boycotts were ongoing. This was a traction nightmare without precedent.

On January 2, 1911, mandamus proceedings to compel the Chicago Railways to resume through service with a single fare were brought by Oak Park, River Forest, Forest Park, and Maywood. The original order for the sale of the Chicago Consolidated Traction Company was amended by the court forcing the Chicago Railways and County Traction to make an agreement with the boards of the respective suburbs for an equitable settlement of the traction muddle. The terms of the judge's order required the two traction companies to carry out such ordinances as may be passed by the boards of the communities involved and by the Chicago City Council. Operating arrangements were left to be negotiated by the two traction companies in order to restore some through service to the suburbs. However, if the local community boards refused to compromise in the traction matter after the court and its experts had drawn plans for an agreement, then the obligation of the traction lines ceased. The judge basically told the suburbs again to resolve this matter themselves.

Two of the most important requirements of the judge's order were that the County Traction Company should accept from each community it served an ordinance imposing obligations as to service and rate of compensation. These terms were modified to allow an expert, appointed by the court, to determine if the company was receiving a reasonable compensation for services rendered. The Chicago Railways was also required to perfect traffic arrangements with the outlying system. These arrangements would need to be approved by the Chicago City Council and by an expert appointed by the court. Judge Grosscup set March 29, 1911 as the date when final action would be expected from the village boards.

What this amounted to was that if any one of the suburbs served by County Traction could prove that the 5¢ fare to and from the City of Chicago would be profitable for both transportation companies, the companies would be required to operate the service. Whether or not the terms offered by the suburbs were compensatory or not was to be determined, not by the companies, but by two experts, one appointed by Judge Grosscup and the other by the interested villages.

The main reason the villages did not

Chapter 3: County Traction Company

Leased Chicago Union Traction car 4474 was used only on the Berwyn-Lyons line. It was photographed later in its career at the Humboldt Park terminus of the Division Street line in Chicago.
Fred Borchert photo

take advantage of the judge's order is that they had to take the initiative and pass ordinances asking for service under certain terms. The villages feared that this would constitute recognition of the claim by County Traction that it was free of all the obligations assumed by its predecessors. The suburbs were anxious to do nothing that might be so construed. In order to avoid any such compromising action all municipalities, except for Cicero, refused to pass the truce ordinance.

Judge Grosscup had some things to say to the management of County Traction as well. He indicated that selling a street railway was vastly different from selling a horse or a house, and in this instance, management was dealing with a public utility in which the public had rights. The car lines needed to be maintained as best as possible, so the judge stated that not even the court had the right to destroy and sell the property for scrap. The officers of Oak Park, River Forest and Maywood then changed their minds about accepting the judge's offer of truce. Nevertheless, they still felt that the problem should be solved now, not just postponed for a couple of months. Only the officials of the Village of Forest Park still held their ground.

With some of the municipalities agreeing to Judge Grosscup's truce, partial streetcar service was reinstated. Service first resumed on Chicago Avenue from Austin Boulevard to Harlem and south to Lake Street. The Madison Street line was then reopened between Austin Boulevard and Harlem Avenue. Obviously, these two lines did not serve Forest Park.

Only the Lake Street line, which did not use the streets of Forest Park, was restored to normal operation. However, with the passenger revolt still on going, patronage was poor on both the Madison Street and Chicago Avenue lines. The company had 220 trainmen on duty and expenses were high. Many potential passengers walked to the elevated lines for their trip to Chicago rather than take the streetcar and pay the extra fare, and as would be expected, patronage was up at all the suburban elevated stations.

The lack of service in the Town of Cicero was the cause of much friction. County Traction said that a permit to install a turnout from 12th Street onto Cicero Avenue was refused, preventing cars from using Cicero Avenue. Furthermore, the Traction claimed that it could not run cars into Cicero without operating through Forest Park where police had been arresting the crews of streetcars that tried to operate within its municipal boundaries. After County Traction asked Cicero officials to use their influence to permit some equipment to be moved through Forest Park, streetcar service was restored on Cicero Avenue, after the Chicago Railways installed a temporary track connection at Cicero Avenue and Twelfth Street.

Employees of the Western Electric Company were among those most inconvenienced by all these events. Personnel who lived in the communities of Forest Park, Oak Park and the Chicago neighborhood of Austin who used the Cicero Avenue car line to get to work found that with the Cicero Avenue line being cut off at the city limits at Twelfth Street, direct access to the plant was impossible, forcing them to either walk the mile to 22nd Street or pay another fare on the Chicago Railways. Berwyn did not accept Judge Grosscup's truce so streetcars did not operate there or in the adjacent municipality of Lyons.

Aside from these issues, the major problem that County Traction faced was that it had difficulty collecting fares. Since it did not have any operating franchises it could not enforce fare collection. Further, because the municipalities involved were not happy with the service provided by County Traction, their respective police departments looked the other way at fare evasion and did not come to the aid of the trolley conductors. Fare payment became a matter of size: who was bigger — the conductor or the passenger? On Tuesday, January 24, 1911, matters really got out of hand when a conductor attempted to collect fares from a group of men who boarded the car at the American Can Company plant in Maywood. A confrontation quickly became a full-fledged riot when the mob broke all the windows in the car, even pulling the trolley pole off the roof. The result was that the crew was forced to abandon the car (which was later removed by a wrecker and service was restored). At this time, County Traction was losing about $700 per day.

More Service Restored

The residents of Maywood and Melrose Park wanted public transportation. The extra nickel fare was not relevant to many of them, however, because few rode all the way into the city. On May 1, 1911, two single-truck streetcars were dragged across the Chicago & North Western Railway's tracks at Fifth Avenue in Maywood and were placed in service on a loop using Fifth Avenue, St. Charles Road, 19th Avenue, and Madison Street. The initial trip was made at 6:00 p.m. and on May 6, 1911, service was extended east on Madison Street to Lathrop Avenue into neighboring River Forest.

Still angry at the company, the River Forest Trustees ordered their electricians to cut County Traction's feed wires at the village limits. This action resulted in the cars being unable to operate in River Forest as well as in Maywood and Melrose Park. County Traction then obtained permission from the Chicago & North Western Railway to install a feeder line across the North Western's tracks at Fifth Avenue, and when completed, service was resumed. At this time, some of the double-truck "Buffalo cars," (so-named because they had once operated in Buffalo, New York) which had seen so much service on Madison Street, were transferred to the Lake Street route.

Chicago & Southwestern Railway Company

In May 1911, County Traction President George Blanchard sent a letter to the Cicero Town Board stating that the nickel fare, a major item in Judge Grosscup's truce, would end on Tuesday, May 16th. Blanchard indicated that it would be impossible for the Chicago Railways and the City of Chicago to agree on an equitable division of fares on the 5¢ basis. He claimed that County Traction would be forced to carry all passengers originating in Chicago for nothing, and he expanded his arguments by noting that the financial reports filed by the receivers of the Chicago Consolidated Traction proved that the streetcar lines in Oak Park and the adjoining suburbs did not even earn operating expenses and taxes. The deficit on the west side lines was made up by the profit on the north side and Evanston lines. The most valuable portion of Chicago Consolidated Traction had been conveyed to the Chicago Railways.

The Town of Cicero then entered the picture. Town President George Comerford stated that steps were already taken to provide the community with its own streetcar system. A gang of fifty men, acting under order of the town board and guarded by its police, ripped up the rails of County Traction at two points. This took place at the intersection of Cicero Avenue and Twelfth Street and also at Ogden Avenue and Kenton Avenue. With these rails removed, County Traction could not operate any of its cars through Cicero, although the town tried to obtain four trolleys and power to operate the cars from the Suburban Railroad. However, the Suburban declined Cicero's offer. Comerford claimed that the tracks and right-of-way of the County Traction had been forfeited and all that Cicero needed to do was to obtain some vehicles. He stated that the town had never recognized the County Traction, and that the truce agreement

Chapter 3: County Traction Company

In 1908, double-truck car 3824 turned north onto Fifth Avenue from Madison Street in Maywood.

Barney Neuberger Collection

brokered by Judge Grosscup was only with the Chicago Railways.

A mass meeting was held in the Cicero Town Hall attended by officials and citizens of the municipalities of Berywn, Melrose Park, Forest Park, River Forest, Lyons, and Cicero. Comerford told the attendees at the meeting that a new company, the Cicero & Southwestern Railway Company was being formed. The company was chartered in Springfield, Illinois on May 31, 1911 with a capital stock of one thousand dollars. Men of substantial means in the district were going to guarantee the success of this undertaking including attorneys Emil J. Rosenthal, Lewis Coben, Augustus J. C. Timms, as well as L. E. Meyers, who was still managing the horse car line for Cicero and promised to support the nickel fare cause. Comerford reiterated that the tracks left by the County Traction belonged to the Town of Cicero and would be turned over to the new company. A tentative order was placed with the American Car Company in St. Louis for ten streetcars that were priced at $4,000 each, and a 60-day delivery was promised.

President Mohr of Forest Park was also in favor of forming a new company. He declared that his village would tear up the tracks if an injunction was approved that restrained suburbanites from interfering with its operations. The village also decided to operate a bus line on Sundays and holidays to the cemeteries.

The County Traction still hoped to obtain ordinances from the various municipalities to permit operation with a 5¢ fare within its own territory, the former Chicago Consolidated Traction lines lying outside of the limits of the City of Chicago. One plan under consideration called for streetcars to be through routed into the city, with second fare to be paid at the city limits. Such an arrangement was in effect on the south side of Chicago for many years between the Calumet & South Chicago Railway Company and the Hammond, Whiting & East Chicago Railway Company.

Blanchard said that if the suburbs wanted the 5¢ fare, the way to get it was by voting annexation to the City of Chicago. A City of Chicago ordinance, dated February 11, 1907, would permit the 5¢ fare for the Chicago Railways when it extended its lines into annexed territory. Judge Grosscup had earlier told the officers of the municipalities the same thing, but annexation, among other things, would have meant that the village officials would have been out of a job, so this idea fell on deaf ears.

In the four and one-half months since the lines were severed from the Chicago

Railways Company, County Traction had collected $22,500 in fares and had incurred $42,500 in operating expenses, and these figures did not include any return on capital. During the truce, County Traction carried 374,783 passengers who held Chicago Railways transfers. Had County Traction been compensated for this ridership at the 5¢ fare rate, this traffic would have generated more than $19,000. The Chicago Railways income would also have been reduced by over $16,000. In the four and one-half months that it exchanged transfers in Cicero, it carried 328,880 passengers on transfers. However, the $19,000 that County Traction might have earned had it received the 5¢ fare instead of a transfer would still have been insufficient to permit the Company from meeting actual operating expenses. In view of this experience, County Traction management awaited with great interest the actions of Cicero's president George Comerford to establish a municipal streetcar system.

In June of 1911, the Village Board of Lyons entered into a contract with an automobile company for the operation of buses that would carry passengers to selected points where connections could be made to a Chicago-bound streetcar for a fare of 5¢. This action was considered to be a continuation of the warfare between County Traction and the suburban municipalities. Later that summer, Emil G. Schmidt became President of County Traction after George Blanchard had resigned. Schmidt had been Operating vice-president of the Union Railway, Gas & Electric Company, a firm that controlled the street railways in Springfield, Peoria, and Rockford, Illinois. Schmidt was an experienced executive with special expertise in contract negotiation. Temporary permits to operate the trolleys were granted by the municipalities of Oak Park, River Forest, and Maywood, and could be revoked at any time without notice. As part of these negotiations, County Traction made a concession regarding fares. "Workingmen's Special Tickets" were to be sold only by conductors, priced at twelve-rides-for-one-dollar. These tickets provided the bearer with a continuous ride between Oak Park, River Forest, Maywood, Proviso, Forest Park, Cicero, Berwyn, and Lyons and Chicago with full transfer privileges. The tickets were valid between 5:00 a.m. and 8:00 a.m. each weekday morning and between 5:00 p.m. and 7:00 p.m. each weekday evening, but were not valid on Sundays and holidays.

With the issuance of the "Workingmen's Special Tickets" County Traction wanted all passengers to pay for their rides. Until this time, passengers who lived in Chicago and worked in the factories of Maywood and other western suburbs could ride County's cars for free by showing the conductor a valid transfer from the Chicago Railways Company. About 1,000 people per day were using this loophole and the company had estimated its loss from this situation at $1,000 per month.

When the municipalities granted operating permits to County Traction, its authority to collect fares was legitimized, and it moved aggressively to collect all fares due. For example, the company modified eight of its ex-Buffalo, New York cars for service on the Lake Street Line so that passengers could only enter the car by the rear door one at a time. An extra man was put on each car to assist the conductor in holding back patrons until they had paid their fare. On the first day that this arrangement was in effect — due to the element of surprise in County Traction's favor — all fares were collected. On the second day of service under the new arrangement, a mild passenger protest took place. About fifty workers presented the conductors with $2 bills for the purchase of the "Workingmen's Special Tickets." With the need to make change, there was a delay in service until County Traction responded by assigning extra men to the cars. Fare collection soon became routine and uneventful.

In September 1911, negotiations were renewed with the Town of Cicero. On November 15, 1911, following two nights of negotiations, the town board granted the company temporary permission to operate its cars within the township and stipulated that it could be revoked, without notice, at any time. This agreement was identical to those made with Oak Park, River Forest and Maywood.

During November 1911, a turnout was installed at Harlem Avenue and Madison Street that permitted the extension of the Chicago Avenue line from its terminal at Lake Street and Harlem Avenue via Harlem Avenue and Madison Street to Austin Boulevard. The new operation on Harlem Avenue created an unusual operating permit situation: County Traction cars used the east track only, which was in Oak Park, while the west track, in Forest Park, would not allow the company to run cars. This route was placed into service during the last week of the month, and the businessmen of Oak Park hailed the new route as the biggest traction improvement in the village in years.

Chapter 3: County Traction Company

At the same intersection as the preceding photo, but showing a view in the opposite direction, "Buffalo Car" 3834 has turned off Madison Street and was traveling northward on Fifth Avenue. Circa 1911.

C. R. Childs photo/Carl P. Klaus Collection

County Traction was also allowed to relay its tracks on the Laramie Avenue viaduct that spanned the Chicago, Burlington & Quincy Railroad's yards. This area, south of the Burlington on Laramie Avenue, had been without service for eleven months. County Traction's President, Emil G. Schmidt promised a 5¢ fare on all of its lines and even offered to reopen the Twelfth Street, Ogden Avenue, Cicero Avenue, and Laramie Avenue lines within a week. After the City of Berwyn granted a similar operating permit on November 22, 1911, the cars resumed service on December 1, 1911.

Lyons was the next suburb to grant an operating permit. When County Traction resumed service in Cicero and Berwyn, a few trips were also made into Lyons, but the local police stopped these cars because the village had not authorized the service. Within a week, on December 7, 1911, the Lyons Village Board granted the special permit, similar to that granted by the other suburbs. However, the Village of Forest Park continued to hold out.

As a result, a conference was held on January 11, 1912 between County Traction President Emil G. Schmidt and Frank S. Richeimer, an attorney representing the Village of Forest Park. At this meeting, Schmidt specified generous terms for inducing the village to grant the needed temporary operating permit, including the offer that County Traction would move to dismiss, without cost to the village, the injunction proceedings then pending in the Circuit Court of Cook County. County Traction would also consent to a forfeiture of the present ordinance about which the litigation had arisen. In addition, they would enter into negotiations for an ordinance permitting County Traction to operate throughout the village, and if a satisfactory ordinance was agreed upon, County Traction would pay the village the sum of $1,000 as full settlement for legal and other expenses in connection with the suit then pending in Circuit Court. If permission would be granted to operate under a temporary permit, County Traction proposed to operate the following service:

MADISON STREET:

From Austin Avenue to Maywood using the same type of double-truck cars that were operating on the Cicero and Berwyn lines (Berwyn-Lyons).

CHICAGO AVENUE:

From Austin Avenue via Chicago Avenue, Harlem Avenue, Madison Street, and Des Plaines Avenue to Twelfth Street using the same type of cars that were proposed for the Madison Street service.

TWELFTH STREET:

Cars on this route would terminate at Cicero Avenue on the east and Des Plaines Avenue on the west.

The political situation in the Village of Forest Park was still muddled. The village's refusal to grant County Traction an operating permit deprived the company of the lucrative cemetery and amusement park business, while the local real estate

The Chicago & West Towns Railways

and commercial interests suffered due to the lack of local transportation. In fact, some of the local businessmen had been trying for months to convince the village board to work out some sort of compromise. Over 500 residents signed petitions addressed to the village trustees urging that County Traction be given permission to operate in the village. The name of almost every businessman in town was on these petitions, and the documents were a clear expression of the feeling of the commercial, as well as private interests, of the community. The village board still was not convinced, however, and continued to delay taking any action. When a public referendum on the question was finally authorized, the people voted in favor of the temporary permit by a large margin. As a result, the Forest Park Village Board granted County Traction a permit to operate with the provision that it could be revoked at will. Streetcar service was resumed through Forest Park on Sunday, February 11, 1912.

County Traction Buys the Suburban

County Traction was the only bidder at the receiver's sale of February 27, 1912 for the property of the Suburban Railroad Company, and its subsidiary, the Chicago, Riverside & La Grange Railroad. At the time of the sale, County Traction operated 54 miles of track, but with the acquisition of the Suburban Railroad, 90 miles would now be operated and the two major street railway properties in Chicago's near west suburbs would be controlled by the same firm.

At the same time, County Traction President Emil Schmidt was appointed receiver of the Suburban. Prior to the receiver's sale, Schmidt had negotiated with the Yerkes estate for purchase of the debt instruments of the Suburban Railroad owned by the estate. The estate owned a majority of the First Mortgage 5% Bonds and all of the capital stock of the Suburban, and the Yerkes estate owned various notes dated prior to 1903, including 50 shares of stock in the Chicago, Riverside & La Grange, and $14,000 of notes of the Chicago, Riverside & La Grange dated 1903.

In March 1912, the court authorized Schmidt to spend $159,900 for paving, track renewal and acquisition of new pay-as-you-enter cars. Twenty cars were ordered from the McGuire-Cummings Manufacturing Company at a cost of $100,000. They were scheduled for delivery in June and would be painted in the same green color as the County Traction Company's cars. A major operational change took place with County Traction's purchase of the Suburban as well. County Traction transferred the cars required to operate the Berwyn-Lyons route to the Suburban's barn on Harlem Avenue. This action significantly reduced pull in/pull out time. Also, even though Suburban Railroad was now owned and operated by the County Traction, two sets of books were kept. Under the laws in place at that time, the companies could not be merged because the Suburban Railroad Company was chartered under steam railroad laws while County Traction was chartered under street railway laws.

During March 1912, two cars that had been leased from the Chicago Railways were destroyed in separate accidents. On March 9th, car 3819 was hit by an Illinois Central Railroad switch engine on Laramie Avenue, and although no one was injured, the rear end of the car was demolished. A couple of weeks later, on March 28th, car 3828 was wrecked at the same crossing, which frequently produced delays in service since the Illinois Central did a considerable amount of switching there. In this case, the conductor flagged the trolley through the crossing when it was clear. However, a railroad switch crew attempted a "flying switch" maneuver which sent a free-rolling caboose right into the streetcar. Both the conductor and motorman were badly hurt in the accident.

The trestle over the Des Plaines River on Madison Street proved to be another political problem for County Traction. In March 1912 the Proviso Township Board of Highway Commissioners, claiming that the trestle was unsafe, ordered it closed to both streetcar and wagon traffic. The village boards of both Maywood and Melrose Park objected to the closing. They pointed out the hardships for passengers having to walk across the trestle in bad weather to change cars, and were concerned that many potential new residents of the area would decide to live elsewhere if the public transportation was judged to be poor. However, the real issue was something quite different. The closing of the trestle was a legal maneuver by the township so that County Traction could not claim occupancy rights on the new bridge that was to be built adjacent to the trestle.

However, the riders held the upper hand in this instance. It seems that a $60,000 bond issue was required to construct the new bridge, and when the citizens of Maywood learned that County Traction was to be charged $10,000 for a 20-year franchise to use the bridge, they

Chapter 3: County Traction Company

An westbound "Buffalo Car" turned off Fifth Avene onto St. Charles Road in Maywood. The streetcar was operating on County Traction's Madison Street route, circa 1912. The Chicago & North Western's tracks are to the extreme right. The streetcar tracks on Fifth Avenue never crossed the railroad.
Charles R. Childs photo/LeRoy F. Blommaert Collection

defeated the bond issue. The highway commissioners had to reopen the trestle if they wanted the bond issue passed, and beginning on Saturday, May 19, 1912, streetcars and wagons were again allowed to use the old trestle. A special car, one of the new yellow Suburban Railroad pay-as-you-enter cars, was provided for the re-opening. The bond issue came to another vote in June 1912 and passed with the provision that streetcars would be allowed to use the new bridge. The new bridge was opened on Tuesday, November 26, 1912. At that time, the surrounding area was hardly more than a prairie, but large scale real estate development was about to begin.

With the Suburban under new ownership, the villages demanded that the two companies allow free transfers between lines. Schmidt, the great negotiator, wanted new franchises granted by the villages, although he soon relented on the matter of transfers. Effective July 1, 1912, transfers were allowed between County Traction and the Suburban Railroad cars at the following four corners: Twelfth Street and Harlem Avenue, Twelfth Street and Laramie Avenue, Laramie Avenue and 25th Street, and Cicero Avenue and 22nd Street.

In July 1912, the Suburban Railroad placed 14 of the new pay-as-you-enter streetcars (numbered 107-120) into service. Initially, the cars operated on the La Grange line, but after a trial run, the cars were judged not to be suitable for service on the La Grange route because of poor track conditions, and were transferred to the County Traction routes. The press described the cars as being the most elegant and comfortable cars to be found anywhere and were well received by the passengers.

Meanwhile, County Traction claimed that it was losing about $1,000 a month on the Cicero Avenue service and President Emil Schmidt said that the company could not continue operating the service under these conditions. A letter was sent to the Cicero town president requesting permission to discontinue service on Twelfth Street from Laramie Avenue to Cicero Avenue and on Cicero Avenue from Twelfth Street to 25th Street. The letter indicated that County Traction would agree to operate the Chicago Avenue cars east to Laramie Avenue where passengers could transfer to the Suburban Railroad, and if the passengers preferred, they could also transfer at Twelfth Street and Harlem Avenue and ride south on Harlem Avenue to connect with the Suburban's main line at 22nd Street. Needless to say, Schmidt's proposal was rejected.

Effective August 15, 1912, the Laramie Avenue route was merged with the County Traction Company's so-called Chicago Avenue line. This unusual route started at Austin Boulevard and Chicago Avenue and ran via Chicago Avenue west to Harlem Avenue, south to Madison Street, west to Des Plaines Avenue, south to Twelfth Street, east to Laramie Avenue, and south to 35th Street. The Laramie Avenue Bridge over the railroad yard between Harrison and Twelfth Streets was in terrible condition, so County Traction reduced the remaining portion of the Laramie route to only a single-truck car in shuttle service between Lake Street and Twelfth Street.

County Traction had its share of accidents during these years. On Thursday, August 29, 1912, car 506 was hit by an Illinois Central Railroad train at the Parkway crossing and was knocked over on its side. There were 12 passengers aboard at the time of the accident and three women were hurt. The motorman had stopped, but then he tried to beat the train across the tracks and failed. There had been several complaints about this crossing and village officials wanted an underpass. Other plans called for the elevation of the Illinois Central tracks and rerouting the car line underneath on Harlem Avenue, then circling back on the south side of the railroad to 26th Street. Nothing came of either of these plans.

It was the same story in Oak Park on Harrison Street. In August 1912, residents on this street complained to the Oak Park Village Board that "the cars rattle and jump to such an extent that it is impossible to sleep, rest, or sell your property on Harrison Street. The plastering of rooms has been cracking in many places." Other complaints included a problem with the switch at Pleasant Avenue, and on the right-of-way at Harlem Avenue, the paving blocks were afloat after every rain. Obviously, this trackage had not been properly maintained.

In response to the residents' complaints, Schmidt promised that the switch at Pleasant Avenue would be removed and indicated that the Illinois Railroad and Warehouse Commission had ordered his company to install an interlocking signal at the Chicago Great Western crossing. However, since this would cost at least $40,000 to install and would be expensive to operate, County Traction's only solution was to abandon the tracks west of the crossing until the village board would permit the company to relocate tracks to the north side of the railroad, crossing it on Harlem Avenue. Schmidt also raised the subject of the proposed Harlem Avenue line stating that he would like to put track in the street to fill the two gaps in the route between Madison and Harrison Streets and between 26th and 31st Streets.

In the summer of 1912, Harrison Street was paved with brick, except between the car tracks, where County Traction had placed crushed stone between the rails and covered it with tar. In September, they installed a switch at Euclid Avenue to permit turning back cars so they would not cross the Chicago Great Western. The line would be cut and service between Euclid and Harlem Avenues would not be provided. However, the Village of Oak Park claimed that the company did not have a permit to install the switch. The solution to this problem came from the City of Chicago. Columbus Park was being built between Central and Austin Boulevards on the north side of the Chicago Great Western track, and part of the planning for this park included the closure of Harrison Street. Jens Jensen, the landscape architect of the West Side Park Commission, insisted it would be impossible to make a satisfactory park unless the car tracks were kept out of the park. The city had planned to relocate the tracks along the new park's southern boundary, but Mr. Jensen got his way in spite of the protest by area businessmen. By truncating the street at the park boundaries, the street lost most of its potential for retail business traffic.

County Traction had another notable encounter with the City of Chicago in 1913. Chicago had a long-standing policy declaring that whenever it annexed a new area, all of the street railway trackage in that area was to be owned by the transportation companies serving the city, thus providing passengers with a single fare ride anywhere within its borders. So when the unincorporated neighborhood of Austin was annexed by Chicago in 1899, the policy was in effect. For some reason, over a decade lapsed before the city council passed an ordinance on January 13, 1913 authorizing the Chicago Railways Company to purchase the trackage rights of the former Suburban Railroad (now County Traction) on Harrison Street between Cicero and Austin Avenues and on Laramie Avenue between Lake and Twelfth Streets. The ordinance did not require purchase of the bridge over the Chicago Great Western, but the Chicago Railways paid $22,554.31 for the 2.87 miles of track.

Meanwhile, the Laramie Avenue car line was in terrible shape. The line was considered a public nuisance, and it was not uncommon for an occasional motorist or motorcyclist to run his vehicle down the sidewalks to bypass the worst potholes. Local residents claimed that the conditions of its franchise were so flagrantly violated that only the railway's political clout kept them in business. Service was discontinued on the line effective January 14, 1913. This segment of track was now the responsibility of the Chicago Railways Company, and on February 8, 1913, service was restored between Lake and Harrison Streets. No attempt was made to repair the bridge over the Chicago Great Western tracks, and the old structure was taken apart by junk men

Chapter 3: County Traction Company

piece by piece and finally dismantled by the City of Chicago.

On the night of Sunday, April 14, 1913, at about 10:30 p.m., the rear end of a westbound streetcar was struck by a fast moving freight train. The mishap took place at the Indiana Harbor Belt crossing, just east of La Grange when the motorman and conductor were on the front end of the trolley at the time of the accident. The conductor had just flagged the car across the tracks, but apparently did not see the headlight of the southbound freight train. One passenger was killed and another 11 required hospitalization for their injuries.

It seemed that County Traction went from one series of problems to another. Now that the franchise issues were temporarily resolved, labor troubles promptly arose. The root of the difficulty was not with the company, but between union locals. County Traction employees were represented by one division of the Amalgamated Association of Street Railway Employes (sic) of America, while the employees of the Chicago Railways were represented by another division (241) of the same union. (The term "division" is a term that was used then to describe what we call a "local" today.) Division 241 was trying to expand by representing the employees of County Traction.

The labor agreement between County Traction and its division expired on August 1, 1912. Schmidt indicated that he was perfectly willing to deal with the men and their union, but not with the union employees of another company. Schmidt wanted his men to be represented by their own division, as they had been in the past, and did not want the union representing the Chicago Railways Company to dictate affairs on his lines. The union claimed that County Traction was effectively owned by the Chicago Railways Company because County Traction was using its cars and facilities.

County Traction President Schmidt's position hardened, and he stated that he would not tolerate any interference from strangers who had nothing to do with his affairs. Schmidt knew, as did everyone else, that the lines were not making any money and the union's demands were making his task of returning the lines to profitability nearly impossible. Schmidt further stated that he was willing to suspend service and let the rails rot in the ground. On September 1912, the men approved a strike, but elected to stay at work. During this time, President Schmidt tried to sell County Traction, but prospective buyers were uninterested because the company did not hold any valid franchises from the communities it served.

While the labor situation was difficult, the legal environment was no better. The mandamus suit filed by the Villages of Oak Park and River Forest to force the exchange of transfers between County Traction and Chicago Railways was continuing. By March 1913, the evidence collection phase of the proceedings was concluded. The last witness called in this case was A. W. Harris, President of the Harris Trust & Savings Bank, who stated that operation of County Traction was still unprofitable and any action resulting in reducing the company's earnings would force the property into the hands of a receiver. In addition, the conductors were still having a hard time collecting fares since many male passengers refused to pay their fares and bullied their way onto the cars for a free ride.

In the meantime, the Town of Cicero, with the assistance of that municipality's manufacturing concerns, finally convinced the Chicago City Council that the Chicago Railways could profit by extending some of its routes into Cicero. On March 18, 1913, the Chicago City Council passed an ordinance authorizing the Chicago Railways to enter into a lease or operating agreement with the County Traction by which the companies would be allowed to share specific segments of track. Two days later, on March 20, 1913, the Board of Trustees of the Town of Cicero passed a similar ordinance. Interestingly enough, the Cicero ordinance was to be effective at the pleasure of the Board of Trustees.

Pursuant to these two ordinances, an operating agreement was executed on March 21, 1913 that provided Chicago Railways with the exclusive right to operate over the following tracks of County Traction:

TWELFTH STREET:
  South single track, Kenton Ave. to Laramie Ave.
CICERO AVENUE:
  Double track, Twelfth Street to 22nd St., 25th Street to Ogden Ave.
OGDEN AVENUE:
  Double track, Kenton Ave. to Cicero Ave.
26th STREET:
  Double track, Kenton Ave. to Cicero Ave.
This agreement also provided for joint operation on the following tracks:
TWELFTH STREET:
  South single track, Laramie Ave. to Austin Blvd.
CICERO AVENUE:
  Double track, 22nd St. to 25th St.
25th STREET:
  Double track, Cicero Ave. to Laramie Ave.

Under this track-sharing arrangement, there were some changes in maintenance responsibility. The tracks to be used by the Chicago Railways were to be maintained by them except for the south track on Twelfth Street between Laramie Avenue and Austin Boulevard. County Traction was also required to replace the 300 feet of track torn up by Cicero on Twelfth Street just west of Kenton Avenue. Chicago Railways paid no rent for the use of these tracks, but did furnish power for the south track on Twelfth Street, and this short stretch of track was used by both companies. Chicago Railways extended service on its Cicero Avenue line south to 25th Street, while County Traction discontinued its Cicero Avenue car and Chicago Railways Ogden Avenue service was extended from Kenton Avenue via Ogden Avenue, Cicero Avenue and 25th Street to Laramie Avenue. These changes became effective in April 1913.

There were additional service changes in May and June 1913 when the south track on Twelfth Street was re-laid and double track operation went into effect on that street during the last week of May 1913. County Traction's Chicago Avenue carline used Twelfth Street for the mile between Laramie Avenue and Austin Boulevard. On 26th Street, the rails also had to be re-laid and new overhead installed before service could begin and Chicago Railways provided a shuttle car for service on 26th Street in June 1913.

Labor Issues of 1913

The labor situation that had been dormant since the summer of 1912 began to smolder again in the spring of 1913 when arbitrators handed down their decision on March 30th. Wages were the obvious main issue with the union asking for a 5¢ per hour wage increase while the arbitrators granted 2¢. The union wanted a ten-hour day but were granted an eleven-hour day. There were some concessions regarding pull-out and pull-in times, but as with any good compromise, neither side was satisfied. The union called the arbitrators decision a "crushing defeat" while the company went along to keep the peace.

Incidentally, County Traction did not pay its employees as well as those who worked in Chicago. Their top wage rate was 30¢ per hour while the maximum in Chicago was 32¢. In mid-1913, the employees voted to strike, but a date for the strike was held in abeyance. On July 2nd a committee representing the employees met with President Schmidt to try to avoid the strike. This was the first meeting the union representatives had with Schmidt in six months, but his position had not changed. The lines were losing money and County Traction was opposed to having its men represented by the Chicago division. However, the company was willing to submit the wage issues to arbitration.

Schmidt told the employees that if they elected to strike, County Traction would not attempt to operate. County Traction did not want to invite riots and knew that the suburbs, not wanting any violence either, would not offer police protection to strike breakers. At midnight, July 3rd, the strike began, and Chicago Railways, which had leased twenty cars to County Traction, sent crews over to get them back before the strike took effect. Chicago Railways wanted the cars returned so that no issue could be raised in the strike negotiations that might involve them. County Traction's new cars were moved into the car houses so that they could not be vandalized, and all powerhouse and track employees were given their vacation pay. About 300 employees participated in the strike, but the union was surprised at the indifference of company officials since they had expected them to agree to arbitration.

Without any local transportation, some of the suburbs discussed purchasing the street railway and paying the men the wages they demanded so that service would be resumed, but the strike was resolved when the County Traction simply went out of business. The lines of County Traction and the Suburban Railroad were sold to a group headed by William McEwen and a new company, the Chicago & West Towns Railway, was formed.

SECTION 2
The Chicago & West Towns Railway

4 The Early Years

Left: During a December 29, 1946 snowstorm, La Grange bound car 160 had stopped at the Zoo and was approaching Salt Creek.

Robert W. Gibson photo/George E. Kanary Collection

The Chicago & West Towns Railway Company was incorporated on July 18, 1913, by a group headed by John J. Cummings, for the purpose of acquiring the west suburban lines of the County Traction and the Suburban Railroad Company. Cummings was president of the McGuire-Cummings Manufacturing Company, a well-known streetcar builder. John's younger brother, Walter J. Cummings, served as the new company's vice-president. John Cummings declined to reveal the purchase price that was paid for the railways, but he long referred to it as a "joke."

The officers of the Chicago & West Towns Railway Company were Judge William M. McEwen of Chicago, president; C. F. Probst, secretary and treasurer; and W. A. Armstrong, auditor. The directors of the company were John J. Cummings (chairman), Walter J. Cummings, C. Wilcox, A. S. Littlefield and William M. McEwen. The general office of the company was located in the Lake Street carhouse in Oak Park.

One of the new company's first actions was to hire Frank L. Butler, former receiver of the Alton, Jacksonville & Peoria Railway Company, as general manager. Butler took charge of the operation on Friday evening, July 18, 1913. He stated that schedules and fares would be the same as before the strike until an "arrangement" could be made with the municipalities. Butler also declined to discuss the price paid for the property which Andrew Cook had once offered to give away or sell as junk. The new owners expected to obtain franchises from all the various villages within six months.

Next to be resolved was the strike, which had essentially forced County Traction out of business. The new management team reached a tentative agreement with the workers giving them an increase in pay that was equal to those paid on the Chicago lines. In addition, the men were allowed back pay to August 1, 1912, also at the rate paid on the Chicago system. In the end, the employees had secured substantially everything they had asked for.

When the new owners assumed control of the company they believed they could increase patronage and profit by providing better roadbed and equipment, and eventually end the receivership. The company spent a total of $290,750 on improvements including $25,000 for paving Hillgrove Avenue in La Grange.

Partial operation was resumed on Saturday, July 19, 1913. Temporary operating permits had been obtained from all the suburbs traversed, except for Forest Park. In marked contrast to the attitude of most suburban officials, who were anxious to see the streetcar service restored, the government of Forest Park had a different opinion. Forest Park declared void all rights of the County Traction Company or any successor in the surface tracks and trolley lines in the village and ordered police to keep all cars out. They did, however, allow the company to make one equipment transfer to the Oak Park barn. This movement consisted of the 14 new cars that County Traction had leased from the Suburban Railroad.

Right: With unpaved thoroughfares, the streetcar had a clear advantage over other forms of road transportation: It could navigate through the mud. A westbound car on the Berwyn Lyons route was turning off 26th Street to travel southward on Ridgeland Avenue. The horse and buggy had to veer off to its right into the slop to allow the streetcar to pass. Circa 1920.

Richard J. Humiston, The Highball Archive

Chapter 4: The Early Years 61

One the more memorable features of the West Towns streetcars was the coal stove used to heat the cars in winter. Above the rectangular stove, was the blower which distributed the warm air throughout the car. Coal stoves were used by the West Towns because the railway's electrical power supply was not adequate to provide electricity to propel the cars and also heat them. The photo, taken in 2002, shows a completely restored stove in preserved West Towns car 141 at the Illinois Railway Museum in Union, Illinois.

Richard W. Aaron photo

Service on the Chicago Avenue and Madison Street lines was affected by Forest Park's ban on streetcar service. On the Chicago Avenue route, streetcar operation was possible on the section of the line between Austin Boulevard and Chicago Avenue (the northern terminal) and Harlem Avenue and Lake Street. Service on the south end of the Chicago Avenue line was restored from Austin Avenue via Twelfth Street and Laramie Avenue to 36th Street. Eventually, on the Madison Street line, service was resumed only between Austin Boulevard and Harlem Avenue. Passengers wishing to ride west of Harlem Avenue on Madison Street were severely inconvenienced.

Permission was received from the Chicago & North Western Railway Company to cross its tracks at Fifth Avenue in Maywood to provide service on a loop consisting of Fifth Avenue, Madison Street, 19th Avenue and St. Charles Road. It is speculated that a temporary track was laid to cross the Chicago & North Western's tracks and that the streetcars were dragged over this segment. Transfers were issued to and from the Lake Street cars which terminated at Fifth and the Chicago & North Western.

The West Towns worked diligently to overcome Forest Park's opposition. The village had a laundry list of demands for better service, including new pay-as-you-enter cars on all lines, transfers to the Suburban Railroad Company, adding three shelters on Austin Avenue, improved headways and the re-laying of track and paving of Harlem Avenue and Twelfth Street. The company gave in to all of these demands except for the transfers to the Suburban. The village relented on that point and issued a temporary permit. However, this agreement was verbal and could be revoked at any time. Streetcar service was restored on the Chicago Avenue and Madison Street lines on August 14, 1913.

Ten new pay-as-you-enter cars, similar to those already in use, were immediately ordered from McGuire-Cummings. They arrived painted in a new color scheme (yellow with maroon striping and lettering) and were equipped with stoves for heating. With the arrival of new equipment, older cars were either redeployed or returned to their lessor, the Chicago Railways Company. Whatever "Buffalo Cars" were needed were returned to service on the Madison Street and Berwyn-Lyons lines.

Fare Issues

Fare collection was a major problem for the new company. Emil Schmidt, president of County Traction Company, had been very liberal in his distribution of riding passes in an attempt to appease local politicians. Further adding to the problem, many of those bearing passes loaned them to their family and friends. In response, the passes were recalled in October 1913, and at the same time, Ohmer fare registers were installed in all the cars. Now, conductors were required to ring up each fare indicating if it was cash, transfer, or pass. As a result, revenue evasion problems were greatly reduced.

On December 30, 1913, the Suburban Railroad and the West Towns began operating under a combined management and with it came higher fares. Prior to this date, a flat fare of 5¢ was charged and transfers were exchanged between the two companies.

The new fare structure was much more complicated:

Between La Grange and Points East of Riverside:
    Cash Fare: .... 10¢
    10 ride Bearer Ticket .... 90¢
    25 ride Bearer Ticket $2.00
    60 ride Commutation Ticket $3.00

Between Brookfield and Points East of Riverside:
    Cash Fare .... 7¢
    30 ride Bearer Ticket $1.50
    60 ride Commutation Ticket $3.00

The new fare schedule increased the maximum fare charged on the La Grange line to 10¢. However, on the eastern boundary of Riverside, a 5¢ fare limit was established. For regular riders traveling beyond this point, several forms of commutation tickets (valid only for the person named on the ticket and for the month stamped) were issued. For passengers traveling between the end of the line and the 5¢ fare limit, a 7¢ single fare was charged, and commutation tickets were also available for these riders. The cash fare of 5¢ was maintained on all other lines.

On April 1, 1914, complaints about the fare increase were filed with the newly established Public Utilities Commission. Later that year, on October 15, 1914, the commission entered an order holding that the rates and fares put into effect on December 30, 1913 had not been approved by the commission (which did not come into existence until January 1, 1914). They ordered a return to the rates and charges in effect on July 1, 1913.

Obviously, the West Towns' management was not pleased with these events. The company filed a petition for a rehearing, but was overruled by the commission. The company next appealed to the Circuit Court of Sangamon County, but the order of the Public Utilities commission was again affirmed. The matter was then taken to the Supreme Court of the State of Illinois which, in a judgment delivered on October 24, 1915, reversed the order of the lower court.

Franchise Extensions

When the Chicago City Council authorized the Chicago Surface Lines to build an extension of the Division Street line from Grand Avenue to the city limits at Austin Avenue, real estate speculators urged that this line continue to Harlem Avenue. Since this segment of the street was not within the city, the Chicago Surface Lines did not have the authority to do this. It was suggested that the Chicago & West Towns abandon its Chicago Avenue line, a route that never made much money, and re-route the cars via Harlem Avenue north to Division Street and east to Austin Avenue. Of course, this routing, through largely undeveloped territory, would have lost even more money in the short run. A West Towns' spokesman said that the company was only "breaking even" and they could not get any money for improvements without additional revenue. As a result, tracks were never laid

The Ohmer fare register was hung near the ceiling at one end of the car. This mechanical device had two control rods which ran the length of the car. As the conductor passed through the car to collect fares, he would rotate the rods to record the type and amount of fare. The photo shows a completely restored fare register in West Towns car 141 at the Illinois Railway Museum in Union, Illinois.

Richard W. Aaron photo

on Division in Oak Park.

The franchise situation improved a little in 1914 when the West Towns obtained a franchise from Lyons. Work started immediately on rehabilitating the track within the village on Ogden Avenue. At that time, the company still did not have franchises for operating in Berwyn and Riverside, and Oak Park and River Forest were still stalling while litigation for restoration of the through 5¢ fare was before the Illinois Supreme Court. The company still had much work to do to get the franchises it needed.

In December 1914, Oak Park received $132,000 from the City of Chicago as a settlement of a series of claims. Some suggested that a portion of this money be used for a municipal bus line between North Avenue and Twelfth Street. At this time, there was no cross-town (north-south) rail service, except for the circuitous route of the Chicago Avenue line. The proponents of this idea claimed that this service was badly needed and that it would be impossible to obtain the needed frontage consents on any street for a car line. Recognizing an opportunity, Wilbur N. Haase of Forest Park, an agent for the General Motors Truck Company, put into service a jitney bus on Oak Park Avenue between Twelfth Street and Thomas Street on February 22, 1915. (The section of Oak Park Avenue between Thomas Street and North Avenue had yet to be developed.) The bus ran on a half-hour headway and charged a 5¢ fare, but service didn't last long.

Chapter 4: The Early Years

Chicago Strike

A strike was declared against the Chicago Surface Lines on June 13, 1915 by Division 241 of the Amalgamated Association of Street Railway Employes of America. West Towns' President Judge McEwen, fearing the strike might spread to his company's trainmen, negotiated an agreement that stated the division would not strike against the C&WT if, in exchange, the company would agree to the same terms that would be negotiated to settle the Chicago Surface Lines strike. If any local conditions needed to be resolved, they would be worked out later.

Even though the Chicago & West Towns continued to operate during the Chicago strike, the company lost much of its business from passengers who normally transferred to and from the Chicago cars. In addition, many of the Chicago-bound passengers used the suburban trains of the steam railroads to get to work.

Fortunately, this situation was resolved in three days after the Chicago trainmen agreed to arbitration on Wednesday, June 15, 1915. When issues were finalized, the trainmen received a 3¢ per hour wage increase plus some other concessions.

Five-Cent Fare Suits

When formed in 1913, the West Towns inherited the litigation over reduced fares brought against the Chicago Railways Company and the County Traction Company by Oak Park, River Forest and Maywood. The litigation claimed that County Traction was bound by street railway ordinances passed by the villages years before to carry passengers from the respective villages to the central business district of Chicago for 5¢.

In Oak Park, the 5¢ fare was stipulated in a 1903 amendment to an 1898 franchise. When the village was unable to enforce the amendment fixing the 5¢ fare from Oak Park to Chicago, it asked the Chicago & West Towns to return a portion of the fare.

This litigation continued over a period of seven years, from 1911-1917. During this period, the municipalities incurred huge legal bills.

A seven week trial was held during January and February of 1914. On March 4, 1914, Judge Charles M. Foell ruled that the County Traction Company was bound by the conditions accepted by the Chicago Consolidated Traction Company. The judge's ruling stated that the West Towns, as successor to the County Traction Company, must furnish each eastbound passenger leaving its cars at Austin Avenue with a 5¢ piece to enable him or her to continue his or her journey on the Chicago Railways Company's lines. The decree also covered westbound passengers, stating the company had to accept passengers from the Chicago Railways Company's lines at Austin Avenue and transport them anywhere in said villages without additional fare. Further, the judge said that he was not concerned by the profitableness or unprofitableness of the contract made between the villages and the Chicago Consolidated Traction Company.

Needless to say, the West Towns wished to have Judge Foell's decision set aside.

On October 27, 1915, the Illinois Su-

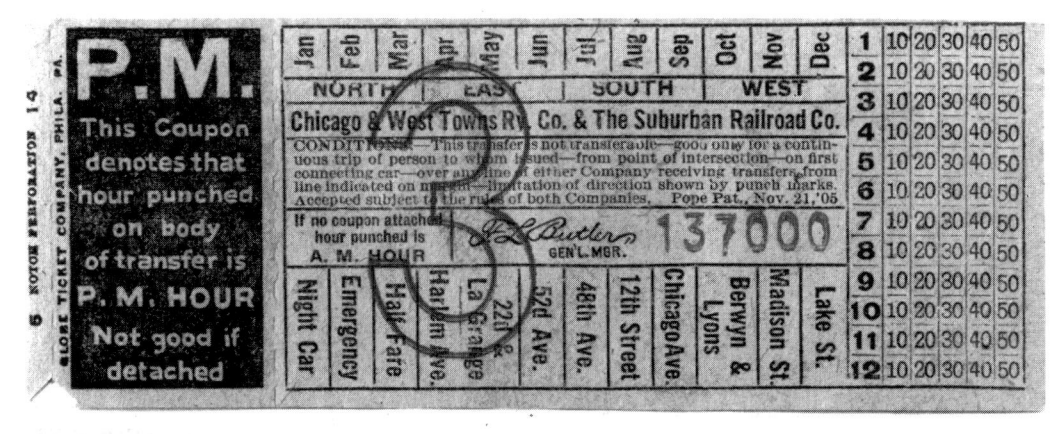

Richard R. Andrews Collection

With the demise of County Traction, transfer forms were changed to reflect the new corporation owning the system. In this 1914 form, the names of both the Chicago & West Towns Railway Company and Suburban Railroad appeared because the Suburban was being operated as a wholly owned subsidiary of the C&WT. This transfer, provided by the Globe Ticket Company of Philadelphia, Pennsylvania, was printed with black ink on several different colors of paper stock. Orange and purple transfers are known to have been used. The day of the month, in this case, the third, was overprinted on the form with red ink.

In this 1912 view of Cermak Road, looking west from Kenton Avenue, a brand new Suburban Railroad car 108 waited at its eastern terminal. Westbound Chicago City Railways car 2587 had completed its trip on the Cermak Road line. The Hawthorne Works of the Western Electric Company appeared in the background.

James J. Buckley Collection

preme Court reversed the lower court's decision. The justices simply did not believe that the villages could enforce a 5¢ fare over lines which extended beyond their corporate limits. Although the villages lost the litigation, they still had some control over the West Towns, particularly in Oak Park and River Forest, where the railway had not yet been awarded franchises to operate. In the resulting franchise negotiations, Oak Park reopened the fare issue, demanding a so-called "3½¢ fare" that would be accomplished by the sale of 15 tickets for 50¢.

Public hearings were held, but the average streetcar patron showed little interest in traction affairs and few came to these hearings. The hearings did provide a forum, however, for several area real estate developers who hoped to improve access to their subdivisions. America's entry into World War I, however, brought these hearings to a premature and inconclusive halt.

The result of the negotiations with Oak Park worked more to the benefit of the railway as the 5¢ fare was maintained. However, the West Towns agreed to reimburse the two villages for $25,000 in legal expenses incurred in the litigation.

Street Improvement Projects

During the mid-teens, many streets were improved (paved), much to the delight of the growing number of automobile owners. In 1915, Twelfth Street was re-paved with brick. At the same time streetcar track was renewed as the result of demands by Forest Park in the franchise approval process. Village officials also complained about the condition of the tracks on Des Plaines Avenue, but no action was taken to correct the situation.

The tracks of the Illinois Central Railroad through Cicero were elevated between 1915 and 1916. While work was in progress on the Laramie Avenue viaduct, service was suspended south of the underpass.

Work was also undertaken to rehabilitate the bridge carrying Laramie Avenue over the Chicago, Burlington & Quincy Railroad tracks. The "new" bridge had been used, between 1867 and 1892, to span the Mississippi River at Burlington, Iowa. The bridge was dismantled and placed into storage by the railroad until 1895, when an agreement was reached with Cicero officials to use a portion of the bridge to span the railroad's yard at Laramie Avenue. The remaining segment of the bridge was sold and erected over the Chicago & North Western Railway's tracks on Mannheim Road in Melrose Park.

The new bridge was almost 2,000 feet long, including the approaches, but only 18 feet wide from curb to curb. (The car tracks were within a foot of the curb lines.) The CB&Q was required by its agreement with Cicero to maintain the bridge; however, it elected not to do so. Furthermore, the West Towns claimed that the railroad was also required to maintain the car tracks. The resulting lack of maintenance caused several bad derailments, including a 1922 accident when a car almost went off the side of the bridge into the yard below. Fortunately, the streetcar's momentum was stopped when it hit a utility pole, thereby preventing a much more serious accident.

Ever since the leadership of Cicero convinced the Chicago City Council to require the Chicago Railways Company to extend its Cicero and Ogden Avenue lines

Chapter 4: The Early Years

A shift change was taking place at Western Electric, but the Chicago Surface Lines was on strike this day in 1915. As the photo shows, the horse drawn jitneys were the primary way to travel east from the works on Cermak Road. Five West Towns streetcars were in various stages of preparing for westbound departures.
Western Electrician

into that town, thus retaining the Chicago fare, the City of Berwyn wanted the same arrangement. A representative of Berwyn asserted that the company had discriminated against them because certain other points that were an equal distance from Chicago were accessible for a 5¢ fare. In December 1916, Berwyn forced a suspension of service on the Stanley Avenue segment of the Berwyn-Lyons route, thus depriving Lyons of service. After the company went to court and secured an injunction to resume service, Berwyn abandoned attempts to secure the 5¢ fare.

Even without Berwyn's meddling, the company found it almost impossible to keep the Berwyn-Lyons route on schedule. This was because the line's cars had to pass through the street terminals of two Chicago Railways routes. Chicago Railways terminated its Cicero Avenue line at 25th Street and its Ogden Avenue cars at 25th Street and Laramie Avenue. In both cases, Chicago cars had to change ends and lay over in the street, delaying West Towns' cars that were passing through. The bottleneck could be eliminated by rerouting the West Towns cars, but change would not come until 1916, when the West Towns installed turnouts at 22nd Street and Laramie Avenue to reroute its cars.

World War I Fare Increases

During World War I, the company was confronted by increased costs of labor and practically all materials used to maintain and operate the property. For example, the cost in 1917 over 1916 for ordinary labor, such as that used in handling coal and other materials, was up nearly 75%. In addition, wages paid to trainmen increased 10%.

At the same time costs were rising, street railway patronage decreased due to enlistments and the draft necessitated to fight the war. Travel on Saturday afternoons and Sunday, primarily to the picnic groves on the Des Plaines River, fell off greatly. The West Towns tried to cut service in response to the decrease in demand, but there were so many public complaints that the Public Utilities Commission forced the railway to reinstate some runs.

As a result, on June 22, 1917, the West Towns applied for higher fares, which were approved. The biggest increase in price was the 60 ride commutation ticket from La Grange, which was increased to $4.20. However, the financial picture remained as bleak as ever, and the railway reduced service by about one-third. Competition from the Burlington railroad was keen, particularly from La Grange, Brookfield and Riverside, which provided the La Grange line with its principal source of revenue.

On August 8, 1918, the West Towns again filed with the Illinois Public Utilities Commission asking for a new passenger tariff, which included a base street railway fare of 7¢. This would be a 40% increase over the existing 5¢ fare, and proportionally higher fares would be charged on the La Grange line. Public hearings were held in Chicago during September and October 1918, with company officials testifying that the rising cost of labor and material brought on by World War I inflation made it impossible to continue operating with the 5¢ fare. They also claimed that during the previous eight months, it had incurred an increase in wages of $66,000, an increased cost of materials of $40,000, and a lost of revenue due to a decrease in ridership of $45,000. At the time of the hearings, the railway held that it could barely meet operating expenses, let alone pay dividends.

The crux of the fare increase rested with wage costs. The existing labor contract with Division 241 of the Amalgamated Association of Street Railway Employes of America ran for three years, effective June 1, 1917. On June 1, 1918, the union filed a petition with the National Labor Board asking for higher wages because of the increased cost of living. On July 31, 1918, the board raised maximum wages for trainmen to 48¢ per hour, with wages of other employees increased by an average of 24%.

The villages complained loudly against the fare increase, wondering how the West Towns could regularly pay dividends on its $1,000,000 preferred stock if it was truly cash-strapped. The villages felt that since the company was able to pay dividends, its past financial condition should not be offered as an excuse for what the villages termed gross neglect of repairs and improper upkeep of roadbed.

On October 29, 1918, the commission decided that in fixing a reasonable fare, the entire system should be considered as a unit, not just specific lines. Further, because fare increases cause most transportation companies to lose a disproportionate amount of their profitable short-haul business, efforts should be made to encourage short-haul traffic. As a result, the commission ruled that the company was entitled to a fare increase sufficient to pay increased costs in wages and materials that had been forced upon it by causes beyond its control.

For riders, this meant a 7¢ cash fare for travel between any two municipalities served, five tickets for 30¢, and a 5¢ local fare within the limits of any one village. Fares on the La Grange line were raised to 7¢, 10¢, and 13¢, based on which zones you traversed, and commutation tickets were increased by approximately 40%.

An eastbound Lake Street car crossed Harlem Avenue in downtown Oak Park. At the time of this photograph, in the early 1920s, the Marshall Field & Company store on the northeast corner of the intersection had not yet been built. A southbound Chicago Avenue route streetcar was waiting to enter the intersection.

H. B. Brooks photo/
Carl P. Klaus Collection

Chapter 4. The Early Years 67

A Lake Street car waited for a Bowman Dairy wagon to pass before it turned south, off Lake Street, at Fifth Avenue in Maywood to reach its terminal at the Chicago & North Western tracks. Circa 1924. The absence of tracks in the foreground indicates that the photograph had been taken before November 29, 1930, the date the line was extended to 25th Avenue.

H. B. Brooks photo/
Carl P. Klaus Collection

1919 Strike and Higher Fares

The surface and elevated trainmen in Chicago went on strike on July 28, 1919, and as before, the West Towns made an agreement with Division 241 to keep the car lines operating. The strike lasted for four days, and the resolution brought a new wage scale into effect on August 6, 1919. Under the new contract, the maximum scale for trainmen was increased to 65¢ per hour.

The West Towns immediately applied to the Public Utilities Commission for a fare increase to cover the new wage rates. Effective August 8, 1919, the cash fare was increased from 7¢ to 10¢ or five tickets for 40¢, up from 30¢. Similarly, the local cash fare within any village was increased by 2¢ to 7¢. The maximum fare on the La Grange line remained at 15¢, however.

During this strike, the Baltimore & Ohio Chicago Terminal Railroad ran temporary passenger service from Forest Park and Oak Park into Chicago. One of the major beneficiaries of this service were persons commuting to Sears, Roebuck & Company's main office at Homan Avenue. This rail service was so popular that the railroad found it necessary to run trains of up to 14 cars in length.

Curiously, Charles T. Yerkes, even though deceased, was still being blamed for the higher fares. The opponents of the railway claimed that the higher fares were necessary only because of Yerkes' errors, frauds, and schemes of the past, with which the older residents were very familiar. At times, the argument was quite spirited.

In July 1920, the West Towns applied to the Public Utilities Commission for a straight 10¢ fare which would eliminate the intra-village rates. In his remarks, president William N. McEwen testified that there was no hope of his company paying dividends and the most he was asking for was enough revenue to keep operating and to pay interest on all debts. He further stated that the recent wage increases in Chicago automatically applied to his company as the men belonged to the same union. He claimed that if the West Towns paid lower wages, their best men would quit and join the Chicago system.

Effective August 4, 1920, the Public Utilities Commission granted a new fare structure. A minimum fare of 10¢ was granted and all ticket rates were abolished. This eliminated the 7¢ cash or 4 tickets for 25¢ intra-village fare rates; however, the fare to La Grange remained at 15¢.

More Fare Changes

The Illinois Commerce Commission, successor to the Public Utilities Commission, forced a reduction in the City of Chicago cash fare from 8¢ to 7¢ effective June 15, 1922. To make up for the loss, the Chicago Surface Lines immediately proposed a reduction in company wages. Top pay for trainmen was reduced to 70¢ per hour, a 12 1/2% reduction. This action triggered another strike which lasted six days, from August 1, 1922 and August 6, 1922.

The West Towns trainmen received the same wage reduction, but the company was not forced to reduce fares. Needless to say, the villages claimed that this was outrageous. The villages already were upset because the 10¢ fares its residents were paying were among the highest in the United States. No change in fares was made, as the municipal officials never mounted a consistent effort to force a fare reduction.

West Suburban Transportation Company

The West Suburban Transportation Company, a short-lived competitor to the Chicago & West Towns, was financed by Thomas S. Carey, a local brick manufacturer and politician who saw a business opportunity in providing bus service on newly paved Ogden Avenue. On February 16, 1922, the company applied to the Illinois Commerce Commission for a bus route on Ogden Avenue between Cicero and Hinsdale. Its application was approved on April 19, 1922.

On Thursday, September 26, 1922, the company initiated service on Ogden Avenue from Cicero Avenue as far west as Lyons. Five buses were required to operate the route. Ticket prices were a little cheaper than the West Towns', with a 10¢ cash fare, three tickets for a 25¢, and a 5¢ local rate within the corporate limits of any village. Eventually the company planned to purchase five additional buses and extend service to Hinsdale.

Not pleased with the new competition, the West Towns appealed the ICC's decision to the Superior Court of Cook County. The court reversed the ICC's decision, but the bus company immediately appealed this ruling to the Illinois Supreme Court.

After taking over a year to decide the case, the Illinois Supreme Court finally ruled that it was not the role of the ICC to promote competition between common carriers, but rather, it was their duty to protect them from competition. The Supreme Court thus sustained the ruling of the Superior Court, and operation of the West Suburban Transportation Company ceased in November 1923.

Bus Extensions

As new suburban communities were developed and built, the West Towns received constant demands for new service. The process to build new lines was slow, however, as the task of obtaining frontage consents was time consuming. Property owners, who held veto power over the construction of new streetcar lines, frequently objected to the laying of tracks in front of their houses. This could be frustrating for all parties concerned, as the need to connect these outlying communities with the Chicago "L" and streetcar system was as important to residents as it was to operators.

New crosstown service was especially needed on Harlem Avenue (where the West Towns had been trying to build a car line for years) and also on Oak Park Avenue. Construction of two short stretches of track on Harlem Avenue, a distance of less than one mile, would have made this possible. The first section was between Madison Street and Harrison Street while the second portion was between 26th Street and Stanley Avenue. If these tracks would have been built, continuous service on Harlem between Chicago Avenue and Ogden Avenue could have been operated, greatly facilitating travel between the communities and to the territory north of the drainage canal.

In August 1922, the Village of Maywood proposed an ordinance suggesting the following changes to the public surface transportation system:
- Extend the Lake Street car line west to the village limits at Ninth Avenue.
- Provide new bus service on Fifth Avenue from North Avenue to Roosevelt Road.
- Provide new bus service on a loop route consisting of 17th Avenue, Harrison Street, St. Charles Road, 19th Avenue and Madison Street.
- Remove car tracks on St. Charles Road and Fifth Avenue.
- Pay for the widening of Lake Street between Sixth Avenue and Ninth Avenue.
- Double track Madison Street between Fifth Avenue and 19th Avenue and 19th Avenue from Madison Street to the Chicago & North Western Railway tracks.

On Monday, December 18, 1922, Melrose Park granted a franchise to the Chicago & West Towns to extend the Lake Street car line through the village to 25th Avenue. The company wanted to do this, but could not until the franchise situation in the municipality to the east, Maywood, was resolved. As would be expected, the project did not move very fast and Maywood officials blamed the West Towns for the delays. A temporary solution was found by instituting bus service on Sunday, January 13, 1923 which connected with the Madison Street cars. The bus was routed from the Chicago & North Western Railway station via Broadway (19th Avenue is named Broadway in Melrose Park) to Lake Street and then west to 25th Avenue and vice-versa.

In May 1923, the Illinois Commerce Commission changed its bus policy in favor of the transit operators. Until this time, a permit from local authorities was all that was necessary in order to operate a bus line. Under the new policy, no local approval would be necessary. This change in policy was supposedly made to favor

Chapter 4: The Early Years

the Chicago Motor Coach Company, which was having difficulty in getting permits from the City of Chicago.

Almost immediately, the Chicago & West Towns Railway Company applied to the Illinois Commerce Commission for ten new bus routes.

CHICAGO & WEST TOWNS RAILWAY
LIST OF BUS ROUTES APPLIED FOR - MAY 1923

ROUTE	STREETS SERVED
Oak Park	Oak Park Avenue from North Avenue to 39th Street.
Ridgeland	Ridgeland Avenue from North Avenue to 39th Street.
Division	Division Street from Austin Boulevard to Harlem Avenue.
Harlem	Harlem Avenue from Chicago Avenue to Division Street.
Chicago	Chicago Avenue from Harlem Avenue to the Forest Preserve on the Des Plaines River.
Harrison	Harrison Street from Austin Boulevard to Des Plaines Avenue.
Ogden	Ogden Avenue from Austin Boulevard to Harlem Avenue.
Austin	Austin Avenue from Roosevelt Road to Ogden Avenue.
Roosevelt	Roosevelt Road from Des Plaines Avenue to Fifth Avenue on public streets and then into Hines Hospital.
Lyons	A line from the terminus of the Berwyn-Lyons car line in Lyons to La Grange.

This request would put the railway into the bus business. On April 15, 1924, the Illinois Commerce Commission granted most of the requests, although modified in some cases.

CHICAGO & WEST TOWNS RAILWAY
LIST OF BUS ROUTES AWARDED BY ILLINOIS COMMERCE COMMISSION- APRIL 1924

ROUTE	SERVICE STREETS AND COMMENTS
Oak Park	The route on Oak Park Avenue from Lake Street to 39th Street was put into service on July 1, 1924. On July 13, 1924, service was extended to Mt. Auburn Cemetery at 43rd Street.
Ridgeland	The route on Ridgeland Avenue from Lake Street to 39th Street was put into service on July 15, 1924.
39th Street	The route ran on 39th Street between Oak Park Avenue and Ridgeland. The railway's original intent was to operate a "U" shaped route connecting the Oak Park Avenue and Ridgeland Avenue lines. However, the buses did not regularly operate in this manner and the three line scheme was preferred.
Harlem	The route was awarded on Harlem Avenue between North Avenue and Chicago Avenue. However, it was not put in service at this time because Harlem Avenue had not been paved.
Chicago	The route ran on Chicago Avenue to the forest preserves on the Des Plaines River. The route was not placed in service at this time and was used only by charter buses to the forest preserve and to the picnic grounds.
Harrison	This bus line was permitted to run on Harrison Street between Austin Boulevard and Des Plaines Avenue. In fact, the line did not provide regular service. A token service was run by buses deadheading to and from the garage.
Ogden	The route ran from Kenton Avenue via 22nd Street, south on Cicero Avenue, south-west on Ogden Avenue to East Avenue in Brookfield. The route began service on June 15, 1924.
Austin	The line served Austin Avenue from Roosevelt Road to Ogden Avenue and was put into service on January 13, 1925.
Roosevelt	This short, 1.5 mile route was placed into service on January 13, 1925. The route ran on Roosevelt Road from Des Plaines Avenue to Ninth Avenue.
Lyons	The Illinois Commerce Commission awarded a route from Ogden Avenue and Lawndale Avenue in Lyons via Ogden Avenue, Mannheim Road to Burlington Avenue in La Grange. This line was never placed into service.

On September 28, 1925, the railway again filed for the following eight new routes.

CHICAGO & WEST TOWN RAILWAY
LIST OF BUS ROUTES APPLIED FOR - SEPTEMBER 1925

ROUTE	SERVICE STREETS AND COMMENTS
Lake	On Lake Street from Fifth Avenue to 19th Avenue.
Ridgeland	On Ridgeland from North Avenue to Lake Street. The West Towns presently operated on this street from Lake Street to 39th Street. Bus service on this portion of Ridgeland was being operated by Northwestern Transit Company.
Oak Park	On Oak Park Avenue between North Avenue and Lake Street. In a similar situation with the Ridgeland Avenue Line, the Chicago & West Towns was operating bus service on Oak Park Avenue from 43rd Street to Lake Street. Bus service north of Lake Street was being provided by the Northwestern Transit Company.
Division	A route on Division Street between Austin Avenue and Harlem Avenue was desired. The Railway applied for this route in its filing of May 1923, but the Illinois Commerce Commission elected not to award this route. The Company reapplied for a bus line on Division Street.
Harlem	The West Towns Company reapplied for a bus line on Harlem Avenue between North Avenue and Chicago Avenue. This route was awarded to the company in 1923, but was never operated because Harlem Avenue had not been paved. Authority to operate this route had lapsed.
Roosevelt	A westward extension of the Roosevelt Road route was desired. The extension began at Ninth Avenue and Roosevelt Road and continued west on Roosevelt Road to 17th Avenue. At this intersection, the route turned northward to Madison Street.
St. Charles	A new bus route from Austin Avenue and Washington Boulevard via Washington, Harlem Avenue, Randolph Street, 19th Avenue, St. Charles Road to Mannheim Road.
Fifth Avenue	A new line from Division Street to Roosevelt Road.

In a filing a few months later in January 1926, the company proposed even more bus service on five additional routes:

CHICAGO & WEST TOWN RAILWAY
LIST OF BUS ROUTES APPLIED FOR - JANUARY 1926

ROUTE	SERVICE STREETS AND COMMENTS
Harlem	From the Chicago & North Western Railway station at River Forest via Keystone Avenue, Chicago Avenue, Forest Street, Division Street, Thatcher Road, Grand Avenue, and Harlem Avenue. The route then ran south on Harlem to Archer.
Ogden	A southwestern extension of the existing route beginning at the East Avenue terminal in Brookfield via Ogden Avenue to Burlington Avenue to Manheim Road in La Grange.
Roosevelt	A westward extension from 17th Avenue via Roosevelt Road, Mannheim Road to a terminal at Oak Street in La Grange Park.
Cicero	A southward extension of the present Cicero Avenue route from the present terminal at Ogden Avenue to a new terminal at Archer Avenue.

On June 17, 1926, bus service on Roosevelt Road was extended per the company's request of September 28, 1925. The routing was from Ninth Avenue and Roosevelt Road westward to 17th Avenue and Madison Street. The Illinois Commerce Commission ruled that Maywood and Broadview were rapidly increasing in population and that there was a need for this service.

The Harlem Avenue route was placed in service on May 16, 1927 from the Chicago & North Western Railway station in River Forest via Keystone Avenue, Lake Street, Park Avenue, Division Street, Thatcher Road, Grand Avenue and Harlem Avenue terminating at 22nd Street. In August 1928, the route was simplified — it continued to terminate at 22nd Street, but went north on Harlem Avenue to Di-

Chapter 4: The Early Years

By the mid 1920s, the buildings had not changed much from the 1907 view, but the streetcar had. A McGuire-Cummings double truck streetcar had arrived at the Fifth Avenue, Maywood terminal of the Lake Street line. The Chicago & North Western tracks are in the foreground.

H. B. Brooks photo/
Carl P. Klaus Collection

vision Street, west to Thatcher Road, north to Grand Avenue, and east to Harlem.

The company began operation of an Ogden Avenue bus line in August 1928. The purpose of this route was to make certain that another firm would not operate an Ogden Avenue bus and thereby draw riders away from both the Berwyn-Lyons and La Grange car lines. This bus line extended the Ogden Avenue line via Ogden, Mannheim Road, Harding Avenue, to Park Avenue in La Grange Park. To hold the franchise, every two hours a bus continued up Manheim Road, Roosevelt Road, and 17th Avenue to Madison Street. On November 21, 1928, this was cut back to La Grange Park.

As of 1928, the franchise question in Maywood still had not been settled. The Illinois Commerce Commission authorized the company to provide bus service west of Fifth Avenue, reasoning that Melrose Park was made up primarily of residences with a large and growing population. Furthermore, many of the village's residents were employed in the various industries and institutions on or near the routes of the West Towns. On or about July 1, 1927, bus service was initiated on the Lake Street line via Lake Street, 18th Avenue, Railroad Avenue, 19th Avenue to the Chicago & North Western Railway's roundhouse near Wolf Road. This was a temporary routing caused by street improvements; later, the buses ran straight through on Lake Street. The local transit situation was unchanged in Bellwood, where there was still no service on St. Charles Road west of 19th Avenue.

The next service revision occured on August 19, 1927, when the Fifth Avenue line was rerouted via Fifth Avenue, Roosevelt Road, 17th Avenue, and St. Charles Road to Mannheim Road. This routing was apparently unsatisfactory and was modified on January 9, 1928, when the Roosevelt line was rerouted via 17th Avenue and St. Charles Road to Mannheim Road. The Fifth Avenue line was changed to operate via Fifth Avenue, Roosevelt Road, and Ninth Avenue to Hines Hospital. Later, on May 20, 1929, Fifth Avenue service was extended northward to North Avenue.

The Chicago & West Towns Railways

5 The Growing 1920s

During the 1920s, the company had a number of sources for ridership in addition to its commuter service. Picnic groves were a popular destination, and those located in Lyons on the Berwyn-Lyons line were so popular that it was often necessary to rent Chicago Surface Lines' cars and crews to handle the crowds. The Chicago Avenue line was also busy on Sundays carrying traffic to and from the area cemeteries. When the West Towns borrowed Chicago Surface Line equipment for this line, the Surface Lines normally provided Old Pullmans or St. Louis Rebuilds from its Kedzie depot. (The St. Louis cars were two-man, pay-as-you-enter cars.) Another source of business was from crowds going to Hawthorne Race Track. "Chicago Day" was a major event at the track, and on race days extra cars were put in service on the Chicago Avenue line.

To meet the increased business, 14 new cars of two types were ordered in 1923 from McGuire-Cummings and were placed into service on Monday, April 14, 1924. Ten of these cars were designed for service on the Madison Street and Chicago Avenue streetcar lines while the remaining four cars were suitable for use on the La Grange line. The four La Grange line cars came equipped with multiple-unit control and were used in rush hour tripper service in two-car trains. Tripper service was operated from Cermak Road and Kenton Avenue to two locations: Cermak Road and Harlem Avenue and the end of the line in La Grange. The fleet now totaled 68 cars.

Derailments in Berwyn

On August 30, 1925, a car carrying over 100 Sunday picnickers left the track and struck a building on Stanley Avenue in Berwyn. There was much fright and a few injuries, but fortunately no deaths. For a short period of time, the City of Berwyn

In the late 1920s, a West Towns streetcar proceeded eastward on Cermak Road toward its terminal at Kenton Avenue. With the tracks in the dirt portion of the thoroughfare, it was no wonder that residents of the area wanted the street repaved. The photo, from company files, was taken near Scoville Avenue. The Berwyn Theater at Ridgeland Avenue appears in the background. — Bruce G. Moffat Collection

Chapter 5: The Growing 1920s

In 1930, the Chicago Rapid Transit Company hired a photographer to record virtually every street crossing on the rapid transit system. On October 8, 1930, he was standing a few feet north of the Douglas Park "L's" grade crossing of Laramie Avenue. The view looks south and shows two streetcars on the Chicago Avenue route. The car closest to the photographer, traveling south, was stopped at the north side of Cermak Road while the streetcar in the distance was northbound.

A. F. Scholtz photo/James J. Buckley Collection

stopped all traffic on the line. Immediately upon resumption of service on September 1, 1925, there was another derailment at the same place. Berwyn then obtained an injunction against removing the wrecked car and arrested some company employees who were trying to re-rail the car. The company substituted buses.

In reaction to the accident, a committee of vigilantes comprised of local residents barricaded the bad section of track with automobiles and other obstacles. Early the next morning, a crowd tore up some of the rails. The city filed suit to prevent the removal of the car until the company repaired the street. The company, however, had already filed it's own counter suit. The matter was settled when the court enjoined the city officials from interfering with the removal of the streetcar.

The company, looking for an excuse not to spend funds to re-surface the street, stated that it could not obtain adequate financing to fix the street unless its franchise was extended beyond the 1937 expiration date. Berwyn refused to consider an extension and a verbal controversy raged for months. To make matters worse, streetcars were picketed with signs reading, "Ride at your own risk."

Eventually the city filed a complaint with the Illinois Commerce Commission, claiming that the tracks on Stanley and Harlem Avenues were "worn, bent and broken in many places." The city requested that the company be directed to repair and rehabilitate its tracks, roadway, and equipment and to pave the area between the rails.

Hearings were held and the commission largely agreed with Berwyn. While the commission found the streetcars and other equipment to be in fairly good condition, the tracks on Stanley and Harlem Avenues were in great need of rehabilitation. The West Towns immediately started the necessary track improvements. On Stanley Avenue new ties and rails were installed and the street was then paved with concrete between the rails and tracks. The paved portion of the street had a width of 28 feet from curb to curb. Harlem Avenue was also paved with concrete to a width of 20 feet between the tracks and the west curb and 15-feet between the tracks and the east curb. This construction left a 15 foot private right-of-way for the railway in Harlem Avenue.

Harlem Avenue

In the 1910s, the segment of Harlem Avenue south of 12th Street was mostly undeveloped. Since there was little demand for passenger service, the company's extension into the area was limited to only a single track in the middle of the street from Harrison Street to 22nd Street. This permitted cars to reach the Suburban Railroad carbarn on Harlem Avenue a little north of 22nd Street. To make operations easier, the company installed a turnout to permit east bound cars on Twelfth Street to turn south onto Harlem Avenue to reach the barn. Token service was operated on Harlem Avenue between 22nd Street and Harrison Street mainly for West Towns' employees going to and from the car house. In 1915, the company normally assigned streetcars 105 or 106 to this service. Later, the Suburban Railroad's 500-series cars were used here.

In 1923, the Harlem Avenue Improvement Association sponsored plans to widen and improve the street. The plan called for an 18 foot right-of-way for car tracks between Madison Street and Harrison Street and also between Stanley Avenue and 26th Street. At this time, the company had plans to operate a car line on Harlem Avenue between Chicago Avenue and Ogden Avenue. Nothing came of this plan, however. In the end, the company opted to run buses on Harlem Avenue, beginning on May 16, 1927.

Interestingly, the track on Harlem Avenue between Harrison Street and 19th Street was leased from the Baltimore & Ohio Chicago Terminal Railroad, which had purchased the Chicago & Southwestern. On September 15, 1928, the railway and the railroad filed a joint petition with the Illinois Commerce Commission to discontinue streetcar service on Harlem Avenue. The railway felt that if streetcar service were to be continued, the entire segment, which was already in poor shape, would have to be replaced.

The commission ruled that the track could be abandoned, noting that the small number of passengers using the line would not justify the cost of rehabilitation. Oak Park, Forest Park, and Berwyn, through which these tracks ran, indicated that they preferred to have Harlem Avenue be paved and the tracks removed. On September 26, 1928, the Illinois Commerce Commission granted permission to discontinue streetcar service on Harlem Avenue and to remove the tracks.

The company moved quickly, canceling its lease with the B&OCT on October 3, 1928, and promptly removing the track north of Roosevelt Road. However, the track between Roosevelt Road and the north end of the company's carhouse near 22nd Street remained in use until 1934. The abandoned center private right-of-way was finally paved over around 1940.

During the reconstruction of Cermak Road, the West Towns tracks at Oak Park Avenue were encased in brick, but the street outside the tracks was not. Westbound line car 15 stopped at this intersection in the early 1930s.

George Krambles photo/Robert H. Hansen Collection

Chapter 5: The Growing 1920s

A photo taken in 1934 shows an eastbound streetcar at the Parkway station of the Illinois Central Railroad. The conductor was "flagging" the car across the tracks of the steam railroad. This safety precaution involved the car stopping to allow the conductor to disembark to inspect the IC tracks for oncoming trains. When it was safe for the streetcar to proceed, the conductor motioned to the motorman with his flag to proceed across the tracks. After the crossing, the conductor re-boarded the car. The Parkway station, located on 26th Street, a little west of Harlem, was torn down shortly after this photo was taken.
Ed Frank, Jr. photo

New Cars

In April 1927, 10 new streetcars (numbered 152-161) were purchased and placed in service on the La Grange route, replacing cars that had been in service since the opening of the line in 1897. The arrival of new equipment allowed the company to modify its older 500-series cars for one-man service, which first appeared on the Harlem Avenue shuttle and later, in 1928, on the Lake Street route. Shortly thereafter, one-man cars were assigned to Madison Street while the Berwyn-Lyons route got its new cars in August 1931.

As with any change, there was a stir of protests in the media and among some members of the public about the introduction of one-man cars. General manager, Bert Collett, stated that it was to the company's advantage to use one-man cars and that two-man operation was a thing of the past. Obviously, the economic advantage of the one-man operation vs. two-man was overwhelming.

The Village of Forest Park, however, had a different agenda than the West Towns. For safety concerns, the village forced the company to add a conductor to all Madison Street and Chicago Avenue cars that traversed Forest Park. The "conductor" simply rode the cars; he did not collect any fares. The conductor would board the car at one village limit and ride across town to the other limit. He then would then ride the next car back.

St. Charles Road

A large number of improvements were scheduled in Maywood during 1927-1929 that would affect service on the Madison Street car line, including street work on both Fifth Avenue and Madison Street. During July 1927, while work was in progress on Fifth Avenue, no streetcar service was offered on that line and all Madison Street cars terminated at 19th Avenue and the Chicago & North Western Railway tracks. A shuttle car was operated on St. Charles Road between Fifth Avenue and 19th Avenue on a 40 minute headway.

The West Towns was conducting clearance testing at the Illinois Central Railroad overpass of Ridgeland Avenue near Stanley Avenue in Berwyn. The testing showed that there was more than enough room for trolleys 103 and 104 to pass. The narrow sidewalks, however, provided adequate space for two pedestrians to pass, even if one were pushing a perambulator, but there was not enough room for a flivver to squeeze between the streetcar and the bridge abutment. A pedestrian tunnel west of Ridgeland was later built. Circa 1920.

Richard J. Humiston, The Highball Archive

Between Monday, August 8, 1927 and Saturday, August 20, 1927, new rail was installed on Madison Street between Ninth Avenue and 19th Avenue. During the construction period, the company did not provide streetcar service west of Ninth Avenue. Since additional north-south transportation in the territory was needed, the company rerouted the Fifth Avenue bus line via Fifth Avenue, Roosevelt Road, 17th Avenue and St. Charles Road to Mannheim Road.

On April 1, 1928, the shuttle car on 19th Avenue was replaced with a temporary rerouting of the Madison Street cars around the Maywood loop. The cars alternated direction around the loop — the first car would operate via Madison Street and 19th Avenue to the Chicago & North Western Railway's Melrose Park station, and when the car returned east, it ran via St. Charles Road and Fifth Avenue back to Madison Street. The next car would proceed west on Madison Street and turn north onto Fifth Avenue to St. Charles Road and terminate at the Chicago & North Western station. It would then return east via 19th Avenue to Madison Street.

This system provided an interesting operational situation. Cars were operating on both St. Charles Road and Fifth Avenue every ten minutes, but not in the same direction. For instance, if a patron just missed a car going east at 17th Avenue and Madison Street, in ten minutes another car going westbound would appear. Transfers were provided, as usual, so that passengers could ride around the loop in either direction to get to their destinations.

The shuttle around the Maywood loop returned in the Fall of 1928. In previous years, the shuttle car would lay over between runs on Madison Street, just east of Fifth Avenue. The company now scheduled the car to lay over on Fifth Avenue, just north of Madison Street. Some local

Chapter 5: The Growing 1920s

Globe Ticket Company continued to be the supplier of transfers to the West Towns into the 1920s. Due to corporate restructuring, the above form no longer listed the name of the Suburban Railroad. Salmon and yellow paper stocks were known to be used.

One of the more unusual features of the West Towns transfer was the use of a detachable coupon to distinguish between morning and afternoon. Since it has been conventional practice among transit operators to use a 12-hour clock, a means to distinguish a.m. from p.m. is necessary. In Chicago, on the other hand, a.m. vs. p.m. was identified by the conductor's punch in the appropriate place.

Richard R. Andrews Collection

merchants felt that this change jeopardized their business, but the company viewed this move as very minor.

A long simmering controversy over the future of St. Charles Road came to a head in 1929. The Village of Maywood insisted that the streetcar service be continued, but it was the West Towns intention to discontinue streetcar service, mainly because it would be required to pay for the cost of repaving the street. Instead, the company agreed to establish bus service on St. Charles Road.

St. Charles Road was an industrial thoroughfare with the American Can Company plant being the largest occupant of the street. American Can officials stated that they did not care if transportation service was provided by streetcars or buses, just so their employees had service. American Can Company, however, did insist that the street be repaired.

A good example of how the company was losing the battle with public opinion is found in a letter written by a local doctor to the Maywood *Herald* in June 1929. The subject of the letter is the West Towns' tracks in Fifth Avenue and St. Charles Road.

I am making an appeal to the citizens of Maywood in behalf of a very poor and starving corporation. This concern is no other than our well known Chicago & West Towns Railway Company. This company has just discovered that it cannot afford to rehabilitate its tracks on St. Charles Road even after finding enough money to rehabilitate its tracks in Fifth Avenue. They can not afford to give the people of Maywood good service, are too poor to hire conductors for every car, and have no money to pave between their car tracks. They are even too dumb to understand the material value of a franchise and the sanctity of a written contract, but not dumb enough to ask the Village Board for a new franchise and have enough money to build a streetcar extension to Melrose Park. The company is prosperous as evidenced by its dividends and high priced stocks. The company collects more dimes in Maywood and immediate suburbs than in River Forest and Forest Park combined.

The doctor's advice to the company was to change its attitude toward the village and "eliminate the horse and buggy stage in its management!" He further concluded," Call off their trials and extend a hand of friendship, give the people the transportation they want. The people are the master and their wish is law!"

The repaving of St. Charles Road started in July 1929. The West Towns would not support the project unless it could remove the streetcar tracks, and threatened to use the courts to further delay the project. Streetcar service was discontinued on May 28, 1929 and no substitute service was offered while the street was under construction.

Maywood officials still preferred the restoration of streetcar service, but the cost of ripping up the newly repaved street and installing a new single track for the streetcars was estimated at $50,000. The

By the early 1930s, the West Towns was using a slightly smaller transfer form prepared by the Ansell-Simplex Company. Yellow and buff colored paper stocks were frequently used for these transfers. The document was printed in black ink with red ink used for the date and serial number overprints.

Richard R. Andrews Collection

matter was appealed to the Illinois Commerce Commission, which ruled that the expenditure was not justified because better transportation on the street could be furnished by a bus line.

Buses were placed in service from Madison Street via Fifth Avenue and St. Charles Road to Mannheim Road in November 1929. The Fifth Avenue merchants were still unhappy because they felt that the streetcar loop was more convenient for their customers. With the paving completed, St. Charles Road bus service became part of a route from Hines Hospital to Bellwood and Berkeley. The bus line was extended further in January 1930, when a Certificate of Convenience and Necessity was granted to run buses to Western Springs. The route selected began at Kenton Avenue and 22nd Street and traversed 22nd Street, Cicero Avenue, Ogden Avenue, Harlem Avenue, Joliet Road and 47th Street to Central Avenue in Western Springs. A through fare was charged on 47th Street west of the Indiana Harbor Belt tracks.

Lake Street Extension

Good public relations was never a strength of the Chicago & West Towns Railway Company, for it seems that every time a problem was solved in one village another would crop up in the next. One major irritant was the fact that the base fare was 10¢ while on the Chicago Surface Lines it was still 7¢. One newspaper editor charged that the company paid no license fees for its cars and was "a pig in the manger" on every street improvement where it could handicap progress. By this time, with all the new improved roads, many residents of the communities served by the company considered the West Towns a liability rather than an asset.

In Maywood, where the thorny St. Charles Road question had been resolved, attention turned to Lake Street. Maywood officials were holding up franchise renewal until the question of the widening and paving of Lake Street could be resolved. As was the usual case, money was the key ingredient and neither the village nor the company had much to spare.

The need for streetcars on Lake Street dates back to the turn of the twentieth century, when the area was first being developed. At that time, a real estate investor had ties spread along Lake Street and Division Street to give potential purchasers the impression that streetcar tracks were about to be laid. The question was discussed yearly, especially in connection with every political campaign, until the line was finally opened.

There was insufficient population to warrant construction west of Fifth Avenue, but as the western suburbs developed there was more need for additional transportation routes. In September 1925, the Illinois Commerce Commission granted the West Towns the right to operate a bus line on Lake Street from Fifth Avenue to 25th Avenue.

Most people viewed this as a temporary measure and preferred that the company operate streetcar service to 25th Avenue. A public debate over extending the streetcar line began in earnest in 1929, when residents expressed their preference for the convenience of a streetcar line. In addition, Melrose Park officials claimed that they had lost four potential industries because of the lack of good public transportation. Company officials stated that they too would like a streetcar extension, but it needed to be built in conjunction with a street paving project and a suitable franchise agreement with Maywood.

The first action towards the extension was made in April 1929 when a report was presented to the local Kiwanis Club by a

Chapter 5: The Growing 1920s

As bus operations expanded, the West Towns needed a new transfer form. Ansell-Simplex provided a transfer similar to that used for the streetcar routes with the word "bus" overprinted, along with the serial number and date of issue.
Richard R. Andrews Collection

public affairs committee. At the outset, the greatest difficulty encountered was due to the ill will that existed by the residents of Maywood toward the company. This animosity prevented the elected village officials from taking any action with the company for fear of repercussions at the polls. Furthermore, there were objections to the extension from the businessmen on Fifth Avenue, who claimed that the loss of the terminal on Lake Street at Fifth Avenue would reduce the foot traffic there and could directly translate to lost business.

After years of bickering, the turning point in changing public opinion was accomplished after several months of intense meetings, both official and unofficial, to sell the streetcar extension project to the citizens of Maywood. The meetings were chaired by village officials, executives of local businesses, and other community leaders. The public eventually accepted the reality that if their leaders thought that the streetcar extension was important, they had better support it.

Progress soon became more rapid, and in the Summer of 1929 a petition was filed with the Illinois Commerce Commission. Public hearings began on October 29, 1929, where the company agreed to construct the extension as soon as a suitable franchise was granted by Maywood. As would be expected, Maywood officials stalled until after the elections of April 1930.

The issue was finally resolved in May and June of 1930. Initially, in May 1930, the matter was officially presented to the Maywood village board. But sensing opposition from the business and political interests in the town, the board called for a referendum to resolve the matter by the voters. On June 21, 1930, Maywood residents voted almost five to one in favor.

In the meantime, because of the constant political delays that were taking place, contractors had already moved ahead with the paving of Lake Street. However, the contractors did allow space in the middle of the street for the later installation of car tracks, which the West Towns would be responsible for.

The company completed its part of the agreement and opened the streetcar line extension on November 28, 1930 with great fanfare. Several hundred people braved the sub-zero weather of the day to witness the opening ceremony, and village officials called the extension the greatest improvement in Melrose Park in the last 25 years. As would be expected, free rides over the new extension were provided to the public on opening day.

Other Changes Affecting Streetcar Service

On August 23, 1928, the Cicero Town Board passed an ordinance authorizing the construction of a double-track streetcar line on 35th Street running one mile west from Laramie Avenue to Austin Avenue. It was built and paid for by the real estate development firm which had subdivided the land adjacent to the new streetcar line. Unfortunately for the real estate firm, the Great Depression eliminated the demand for homes in the subdivision and the property remained virtually vacant until after World War II. The one-mile extension was placed into service during 1931 and became the last streetcar line extension in the West Towns' system.

The most important revenue producer for the company in the area of 35th Street and Laramie Avenue was the race tracks. The racetrack business, which was always strong, expanded in 1928 when a second track, Sportsman's Park, opened adjacent to Hawthorne Park. The company maintained a spur on Laramie Avenue, between 35th Street and 36th Street, for racetrack specials. To handle the crowds when the races were over, the company diverted some cars from service on the Chicago Avenue route. The crews greatly enjoyed this because not only did they miss a trip, but the management of the racetracks allowed them into the parks for free to watch the last few races. Starting in September 1931, the company substituted buses for the streetcars, operating directly from the Douglas Park "L."

Contracts were awarded in June 1930 to widen and repave Ogden Avenue from Lawndale Avenue in Lyons to Aurora. The work was completed to Western Springs by October 1930 and to Aurora in December 1930, with the exception of one overpass and one set of underpasses. The former carried Ogden Avenue above the Indiana Harbor Belt Railway while the latter permitted Ogden Avenue to pass under both the Chicago, Burlington & Quincy Railroad Company's tracks and those of the Chicago and West Towns' line in La Grange.

These bridges had been the subject of much debate for the previous ten years, mostly because the Chicago, Burlington & Quincy Railroad had vigorously fought the overpass plan. The railroad had both a small yard at Congress Park as well as an important interchange with the Indiana Harbor Belt Railway in La Grange. To accomplish the overpass, the Burlington thought that it would have to elevate its tracks and there was much concern whether or not the West Towns had the resources to pay for its share of the project. Further concern was voiced about who would finance the necessary land acquisition. The county wanted the Villages of Brookfield and La Grange to file the necessary condemnation suits and purchase the required property. (These bridges were a joint project of the railroads, the West Towns, the County of Cook and the State of Illinois.)

Hearings on the overpasses were held before the Illinois Commerce Commission on September 30, 1930. The commission ruled that the State of Illinois, the Burlington, and the West Towns should split the cost of the project equally. A little later, the State of Illinois had to resolve other issues including labor disagreements over the approaches to the viaduct over the Indiana Harbor Belt. The obstacles to the construction of the viaducts were resolved later in the year and on Saturday, October 1, 1932, the half-million dollar project was completed.

But there still remained one incomplete portion of the Ogden Avenue improvement project — the section of the street between Harlem Avenue and Lawndale Avenue in Lyons. At that time, the Berwyn-Lyons car line operated over private right-of-way parallel to the south side of the street. Since it was desired that the street be widened, the company's tracks would either have to be removed or relocated, and this controversy held up the street widening for several years.

The state highway department eventually completed its plans for the street widening in June 1933, and all that remained to be done was to reach an agreement with the West Towns and to award the contracts. In September 1933, the federal government, under the National Industrial Recovery Act, agreed to finance the project and final approval was completed in October 1933.

Permission to discontinue streetcar service west of Harlem Avenue was sought from the Illinois Commerce Commission because West Town's management considered this section of track to be in poor condition. Further, paralleling bus service had been operating over this portion of Ogden Avenue since 1924. At the hearing, representatives from the Villages of Riverside and Lyons did not object to the removal of the tracks. The State of Illinois agreed to pay the West Towns $20,000 for its right-of-way, and the commission granted permission for the discontinuance of streetcar service on October 26, 1933.

At the same time, bids were accepted by the State of Illinois for the widening of Ogden Avenue between Harlem Avenue and Lawndale Avenue and for the construction of a new four-lane highway bridge over the Des Plaines River. Work began almost immediately, and the completed road was opened to the public, as far as the river, in May 1934. The bridge was completed and placed in service the next month.

In spite of all the problems and difficulties, the 1920's found the West Towns to be a modern and progressive firm. Gradually, the network of bus lines had been developed, additional buses were purchased, and a large storage garage was built on the company's property at Harlem Avenue and Cermak Road. Many people look back at the early 1920's and recall that the building boom of the era was due in part to the rapid expansion of the West Towns.

Chapter 5: The Growing 1920s

September, 1925 — ELECTRIC TRACTION — 21

Cummings Motor Coaches and Bodies

Fleet of Motor Coaches with Cummings Bodies Recently Put in Service by Chicago and West Towns Railway Co.

OUR transportation experience, our modern plant facilities and our well established reputation as good car builders, places us in an exceptionally strong position to build MOTOR COACHES that will give long-life service, with inviting appearance and great riding comfort.

CUMMINGS BODIES

mean careful design, strength combined with lightness, durability resulting in long life, careful attention to detail, and good trim with lasting finish.

PERSONAL ATTENTION to these details, combined with *Personal Service* to the purchaser, make it to your advantage to specify *Cummings Bodies*.

Large Modern Plant located at Paris, Ill.

Cummings Car & Coach Company

Successor to McGuire-Cummings Mfg. Co.

GENERAL OFFICES

111 W. Monroe St. . . . Chicago, Ill.

The Chicago & West Towns began experimenting with motor buses in 1922 with the purchase of one from Mack and another from Reo. Because of the common ownership of the street railway and the car manufacturer, many of the West Towns early buses were either built totally by Cummings or built by other firms with Cummings bodies. In 1925, 10 buses were ordered from Reo with bus bodies by Cummings. Cummings Car & Coach Company used this order to advertise its bus building expertise to the transit industry. This full page ad appeared in the September 1925 issue of Electric Traction *magazine.*

Roy G. Benedict Collection

6 Buses to Hines Hospital

The Speedway Auto Bus Company was incorporated on July 1, 1921 and its directors included J.D. Galvin of Maywood, who served as president of the bus company, C. P. Apelt, who was the company's treasurer, and J. P. Flanagan. Speedway applied to the Illinois Commerce Commission to operate a bus line connecting the Forest Park terminal of the Garfield Park "L" with the Speedway Government Hospital, then under construction, a route that would also provide service to Broadview and Maywood.

Speedway Hospital, which later became known as the Veterans Administration Hospital, opened in phases, with the initial opening on Monday, August 9, 1921. After the first construction phases of the project were completed, the hospital was comprised of seven buildings, with four buildings for patients and three for personnel. The hospital employed a staff of 450, including 100 nurses, and provided beds for 849 patients. This facility, along with the V.A. Hospital in Chicago located near Lake Michigan on Erie Street at Farbanks Court, were built to provide Chicago area veterans with health care during the post-war years. The hospital was renamed almost immediately, and at its formal dedication on Sunday, October 31, 1921, became known as the Edward Hines, Jr. Hospital, in honor of a former first lieutenant in the military.

The Illinois Commerce Commission held hearings on the Speedway Auto Bus Company's application in July and August 1921. At the hearings, the only objector to granting Speedway's request was the Chicago & West Towns Railway Company. Obviously, the new firm would compete directly with the West Towns service on Roosevelt Road, but the Commission granted the bus line a required Certificate of Convenience and Necessity anyway.

Local transportation companies were well aware of the potential business that the hospital could produce, and, in fact, the Illinois Central Railroad built a new station there on its Addison suburban line, appropriately named, "Speedway." In addition, the West Towns operated a bus line on Roosevelt Road with an eastern terminal at Des Plaines Avenue, but the route was not as convenient because it did not directly serve the hospital grounds nor did it pass the Des Plaines Avenue "L" station.

Speedway Auto Bus Company began operations soon after receiving Illinois Commerce Commission approval, and

Regional Transportation Authority "new look" bus 8037 was operating on West Towns Route 308, Hines Loyola Hospital during the construction of the new Forest Park Transit Center. Route 308 is the eastern portion of the former Speedway bus line. Because the line is short, running between the hospital and Forest Park, one bus can easily provide a half-hourly headway. The northern portion of the former Speedway route, utilizing Fifth Avenue between the hospital and the Chicago & North Western's Maywood station, is part of Route 331, Cumberland-Fifth Avenue. Bus 8037 was one of 51 new buses furnished to the West Towns by the RTA in 1976. October 1978.

Richard W. Aaron photo

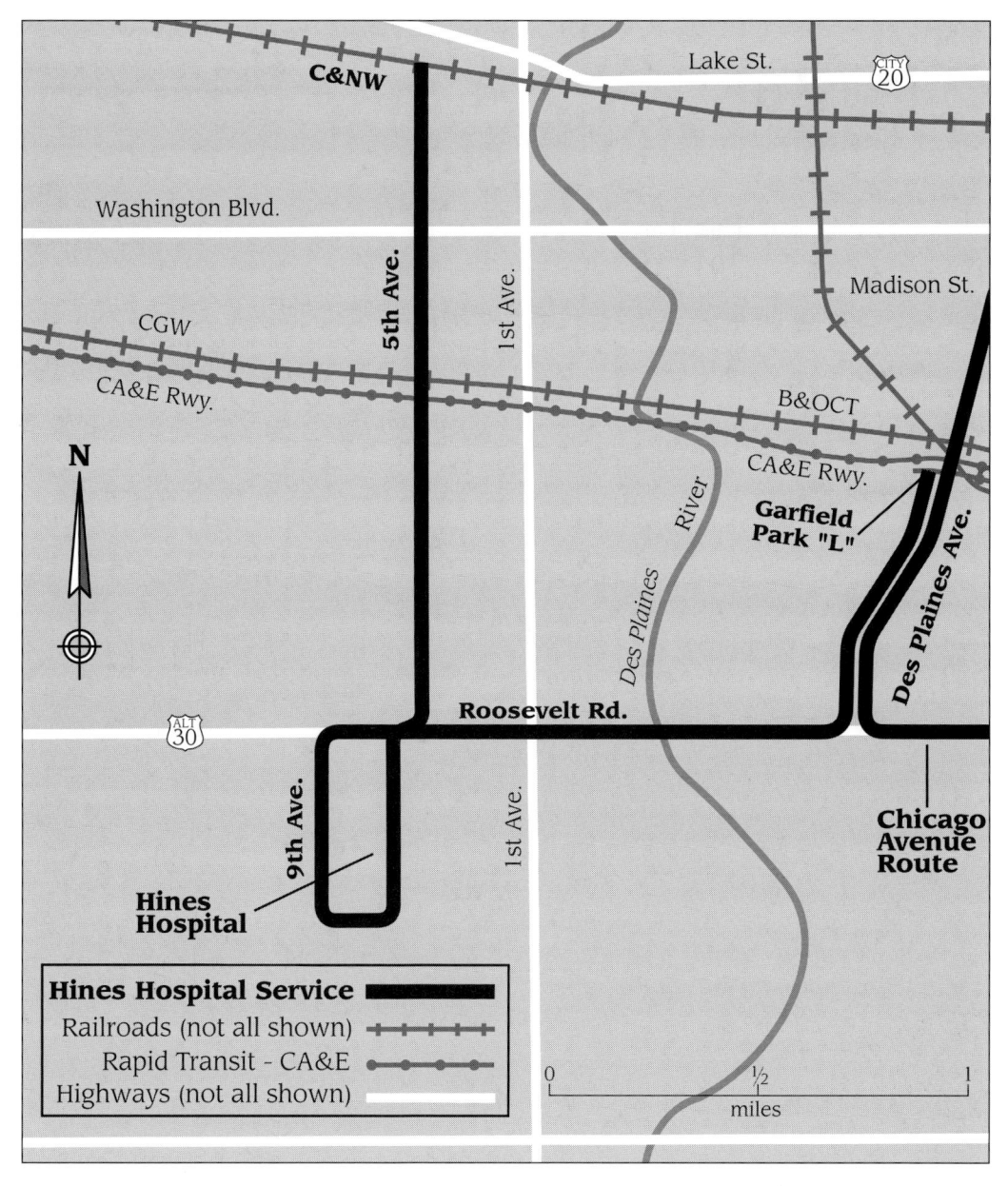

eventually rostered three buses purchased from the White Motor Company. A garage and office were established on South Fifth Avenue in Maywood.

On September 9, 1921, service was initiated along a "U" shaped route that operated from the Garfield Park "L" station in Forest Park via Des Plaines Avenue, Roosevelt Road, and Ninth Avenue onto the hospital grounds. The route then continued back out Roosevelt Road to Fifth Avenue to the Chicago & North Western Railway's station in Maywood. Service on this line was initially provided by a Ford touring car, with a cash fare of 10¢ and the option to purchase three tickets for a quarter. Speedway could not pick up or let off passengers on Des Plaines Avenue because service on this thoroughfare was provided by Chicago Avenue route streetcars.

In June 1922, Speedway extended service to Hillside, including the Oak Ridge and Mt. Carmel cemeteries, and the buses were routed via Fifth Avenue, Lake Street, 19th Avenue, Butterfield Road, Hillside Avenue, and Harrison Street. Speedway elected to begin service on this line after it had filed an application with the Illinois Commerce Commission, but before the commission awarded a Certificate of Convenience and Necessity. Needless to say, Speedway's application was contested. In the hearing before the Illinois Commerce Commission, a major objector to the granting of the Hillside route was the Aurora, Elgin & Chicago Railroad and its successor, the Chicago, Aurora & Elgin Railroad. The Chicago, Aurora & Elgin purchased the third rail operations of the Aurora, Elgin & Chicago on March 16, 1922, and the railroad operated a spur from its Bellwood Station to the Oak Ridge and Mount Carmel

The Chicago & West Towns Railways

Pace bus 6069 was providing service on Route 308 on Saturday, October 9, 2004. The bus was photographed at 17th Street and First Avenue with the Outpatient Clinic of Loyola University Hospital in the background. The Loyola medical campus is directly east of Hines Hospital.

Richard W. Aaron photo

cemeteries, with a shuttle car providing half-hourly service on the spur that connected with all main line trains.

At the hearing, representatives of the Chicago, Aurora & Elgin testified that for ten months of the year this service was in excess of the actual needs and requirements of the public. Most of the time, they argued, travel to the cemeteries was negligible, and the only time of the year that service could be operated so that it paid operating costs and expenses were the three or four Sundays prior to and following Memorial Day. On these days, the railroad carried 20,000 to 25,000 passengers per day and did not have sufficient equipment to operate this service, needing to rent Metropolitan "L" cars to meet the demand. The railroad's representatives further testified that, with but a few exceptions, there had not been any serious delay or interruption in its regular service.

According to the railroad, if the Speedway Auto Bus Company were granted the permission it sought, it would serve people of substantially the same communities and territories that were served by the Chicago, Aurora & Elgin and some of the bus routes of the Chicago & West Towns Railway. Speedway now had nine buses, averaging in capacity from 10 to 25 passengers which would add little in terms of the transportation of passengers on the day preceding and following Memorial Day. The railroad's management claimed that placing an additional public utility, such as a bus line, in this territory would divide the present patronage of the railroad and West Towns. As it was, the existing service was more than was really needed.

Furthermore, the CA&E asserted that Speedway had little experience in the operation of public utilities and was not

Speedway Auto Bus Company, Inc.
Selected Operating and Financial Results

Year Ending	Gross Earnings	Operating Expenses	Net Earnings	Fixed Charges	Surplus/ Deficit	Passengers Carried	Number of Buses
12/31/21*	$ 3,561	$ 3,351	$ 210	$ 147	$ 63	35,612	3
12/21/22	$37,004	$36,082	- $672	$1,810	- $1,560	403,000	9
12/31/23	$46,198	$54,076	- $7,399	$1,340	- $8,698	---------	6
12/31/24	$36,245	$35,714	$530	$1,608	-$3,544	360,784	4
12/31/25	$38,169	$36,277	$1,891	$ 703	$1,054	393,407	5
12/31/26	$40,157	$39,620	-$140	$ 737	-$239	402,957	6
12/31/27	$41,868	$40,524	$747	$ 726	$557	388,388	7
12/31/28	$42,193	$39,177	$1,183	$ 495	$986	527,407	7
12/31/29	$40,268	$37,756	$1,745	$1,128	$1,743	423,880	8
6/30/30	$20,177	$24,302			-$4,125	209,325	8

*From July 1, 1921   Capital Stock carried at $3,500

Chapter 6: Buses to Hines Hospital

Speedway Auto Bus Company, Inc. Roster of Buses

Buses	Year and Model	
1-3	White 10-1921, Model 20	20 Passenger, #2 sold 1924
4	White	
5-6	White 5-1922, Model 20-45	20 Passenger
(2)	White 1926, Model 50	Sold 5/1930 to C&WT, became # 45 and 46, off roster before 1936.
(1)	Yellow, 1927, Type X	21 Passenger, sold 5/30 to C&WT, became #43, off roster before 1936.
(1)	Pierce Arrow, 1927	25 Passenger, sold 5/30 to C&WT, became #44, off roster before 1936.
(1)	Pierce Arrow, 1929	29 Passenger, sold 5/30 to C&WT, became #42, sold 1941.
12	White 10-1922	13 passenger, sold 1924.

Speedway extended regular service north on Fifth Avenue to North Avenue, but service on North Fifth Avenue was discontinued in response to the same ICC ruling that closed the Hillside bus line. In February 1923, Speedway petitioned the ICC for four new bus routes, three of which would originate at the Forest Park terminus. The lines were:

Via Des Plaines Avenue, Washington Boulevard, 17th Avenue, St. Charles Road, 19th Avenue, and Lake Street to Elmhurst.

Via Des Plaines Avenue, Washington Boulevard, and Fifth Avenue north to River Grove and Franklin Park.

Via Des Plaines Avenue, Washington Boulevard, Fifth Avenue, and Lake Street to Elmhurst.

From the Aurora, Elgin & Chicago Railroad's 17th Avenue Station via 17th Avenue, St. Charles Road, 19th Avenue, and Lake Street to 25th Avenue.

The Illinois Commerce Commission also denied Speedway's request to operate these routes.

On December 13, 1928, Speedway applied for a bus route from the Riverside Station of the Chicago, Burlington & Quincy Railroad through North Riverside via Des Plaines Avenue to the Forest Park terminal of the Garfield Park "L." The Commerce Commission also denied this request. In the meantime, John P. Flanagan acquired J. D. Galvin's interest in Speedway. Flanagan then became president of Speedway with C.R. McEldowney joining the key officers as secretary and C. P. Apelt continuing to serve as treasurer. Fifteen months later, on May 5, 1930, the company was sold to the Chicago & West Towns Railway for the sum of $13,500. The West Towns took over operation of the routes on July 1, 1930.

With the purchase of Speedway, the West Towns slightly realigned its bus routes. Since the West Towns had been serving Hines Hospital with its Roosevelt Road and Fifth Avenue lines, bus service on the east end of the Speedway line was abandoned. The St. Charles Road/Berkeley service now originated at Hines Hospital, with buses running via Ninth Avenue, Roosevelt Road, Fifth Avenue, St. Charles Road, and Taft Avenue to the Chicago, Aurora & Elgin Railroad station in Berkeley.

well informed as to what the cost of the operation or the probable income would be from such a service. If the railroad were forced to discontinue service, there was not any way in which Speedway could furnish it on a busy day. On the other hand, the railroad had ample equipment and means for procuring more equipment, when necessary, as well as the means to expand service as conditions warranted and as the area grew.

The Commission was apparently concerned with the financial condition of the Speedway Auto Bus Company, especially when balance sheets and detailed income statements that had been requested were not produced. Permission to operate the route was denied on May 16, 1923 at which time the service ceased.

The Speedway Auto Bus Company also held charter rights, the privilege to operate vehicles for private parties, to serve the Cook County Fairgrounds. The fairgrounds were located at the intersection of North Avenue and Fifth Avenue in Maywood, and when the fair was held in August 1922, 11 buses were leased to provide service which connected with the Chicago & North Western Railway's Maywood Station and the Forest Park "L" terminal. On Monday, October 16, 1922,

7 Crosstown Bus Service in Oak Park

Northwestern Transit Company was a small firm providing local bus transportation in Oak Park from 1921 to 1935. In late 1921, Northwestern Transit purchased Oak Park Motor Transit, a company that had begun operating buses only a few months earlier, in June 1921.

Oak Park Motor Transit

On June 22, 1921, Oak Park granted a franchise to the Oak Park Motor Transit Company. The company, supported by local businessmen, had agreed to adopt an initial 5¢ fare with the option to raise the fare as high as 10¢ if the lower fares proved to be unprofitable. Headways would be 30 minutes or less, and a franchise was granted for the streets listed in the table appearing at the top of the next page entitled "Routes Awarded to Oak Park Motor Transit." The list included all major streets across the length and width of the village which were not served by the Chicago & West Towns Railway Company.

Even though the principal backer of the Oak Park Motor Transit was a prominent auto dealer, many village board members thought that the venture was just a stock selling scheme. However, real estate speculators interested in developing property in north Oak Park were also investors, and, at this time, the area north of Augusta Boulevard was entirely unimproved. Temporary bus service was provided on Ridgeland Avenue.

A photo was taken of coach 513 at the Lake Street car barn shortly after the bus was acquired from Marigold in 1935. This bus, along with sister units 511 and 512, were manufactured in 1927 by Yellow.
Bruce G. Moffat Collection

Chapter 7: Crosstown Bus Service in Oak Park 87

Routes Awarded to Oak Park Motor Transit

Street	Route Boundaries	Street	Route Boundaries
Ridgeland	Thomas to Roosevelt	Harrison	Austin to Harlem
Oak Park	Thomas to Roosevelt	South Boulevard	Austin to Scoville
Wisconsin and Marion	Thomas to Roosevelt	North Boulevard	Scoville to Harlem
Fillmore	Austin to Harlem	Thomas	Austin to Harlem
Harrison Place (Garfield)	Austin to Harlem	Humphrey	Thomas to Roosevelt

Northwestern Transit Company

On September 21, 1921, the Northwestern Transit Company started a limited bus operation on Oak Park Avenue. The bus was scheduled on a 25-minute headway between Thomas and Harrison Streets, and connected with the Garfield Park "L" line at Harrison. Service was operated only on weekday mornings from 9:00 a.m. to 11:00 a.m. and in the afternoons from 4:00 p.m. to 6:00 p.m. The cash fare was 10¢ with twelve tickets for $1 and 25 tickets for $2.

Northwestern Transit purchased the Oak Park Motor Transit Company in late 1921 and acquired three buses in the deal. On December 1, 1921, the two routes were consolidated with the new route beginning at the Lake Street "L" station on

Bus 41 was one of eight Yellow Model Z coaches owned by the Marigold Lines. The stubby buses were built in 1926-7 and seated 21 passengers. Marigold Lines was the trade name for the Metropolitan Motor Coach Company.
Bruce G. Moffat Collection

Ridgeland Avenue and running to the Garfield Park "L" station at Oak Park Avenue. The buses were routed over Ridgeland Avenue, Thomas Street, and Oak Park Avenue.

When the Illinois Commerce Commission changed its policy of granting bus routes in May 1923, the Northwestern Transit had a difficult time getting the required Certificate of Convenience and Necessity, since both Oak Park and the West Towns objected to Northwestern's new route request. The village attorney stated that service on Ridgeland Avenue and Oak Park Avenue would be satisfactory, but objected to extending bus service to the other streets.

Northwestern Transit then amended its petition to include only two routes: the first route originated at the Oak Park Avenue Garfield Park "L" station and ran via Oak Park Avenue, Chicago Avenue, Grove Avenue, Division Street, East Avenue, and Augusta Boulevard, then returning south via Oak Park Avenue; the second route began at the Ridgeland Avenue Chicago & North Western Railway station and ran via Ridgeland Avenue, Berkshire Avenue, Mapleton Avenue, and Thomas Street before returning south via Ridgeland. After eleven months, on April 20, 1924, the Illinois Commerce Commission finally granted Northwestern Transit route rights north of Lake Street while the Chicago & West Towns received rights south of Lake Street. To complicate matters further, the north side fare was 5¢ while the south side fare was 10¢.

In November 1924, the Insull interests indirectly acquired control of Northwestern Transit. At this time, the company was using only three buses, but added four new Yellow Type-X buses to the system in October 1926. Routes were modified slightly at this time to eliminate the need to loop via the local side streets, with both routes operating via Ridgeland Avenue, North Avenue, and Oak Park Avenue.

On July 1, 1928, the Metropolitan Motor Coach Company, an Insull company known as the "Marigold Lines," began to assemble a network of bus lines operating around Chicago, including Northwestern Transit. Insull wanted to develop a system of feeder bus lines to his elevated system, and in conjunction with this, Metropolitan Motor Coach wanted to extend the Ridgeland Avenue route south to Ogden Avenue and to open a new route on Augusta Boulevard to River Forest.

During this period, the population in Oak Park increased from about 30,000 to almost 65,000 residents. Most of this increase occurred on the north side of Oak Park where many of the residents were employed in the municipalities lying north and west of the village, territories served by the West Towns. In addition, large shopping districts had been built in these towns and many residents of north Oak

Observation Coach 516 was photographed southbound on Lake Shore Drive adjacent to the downtown campus of Northwestern University. The 1-1/2 deck bus seated 29 passengers and was built by ACF in 1927.

Bruce G. Moffat Collection

Chapter 7: Crosstown Bus Service in Oak Park

Park traveled to these areas to shop.

On January 17, 1929, the Illinois Commerce Commission granted the West Towns a Certificate of Convenience and Necessity to extend its Ridgeland Avenue and Oak Park Avenue bus lines up to North Avenue. The commission ruled that the service given on these streets by Northwestern Transit was purely local while the service granted to the West Towns would be through service. Any duplication in service would be purely incidental and the decision of the ICC served as the death knell for Northwestern Transit.

On February 14, 1929, Northwestern Transit filed a petition for a rehearing on the matter and on March 5, 1929, the commission granted the request. The rehearing was short, however, after evidence was presented which showed that Northwestern had lost only 1-1/2 to 3% of its business on Ridgeland and Oak Park Avenues to the West Towns. The question before the commission then became which company would provide the through service. On July 24, 1929, the ICC ruled in favor of the West Towns.

These routes never earned a profit for Metropolitan anyway, and during this time, the company was selling off or leasing some of its routes to other operators. On April 25, 1935, both companies went before the commission seeking approval of a merger agreement. The Ridgeland Avenue and Oak Park Avenue routes, along with 20 buses, were purchased by the West Towns on September 5, 1935.

Bus 12 was one of the buses acquired by the West Towns as part of the purchase of Marigold routes.
Bruce G. Moffat Collection

8 The Depressing 1930s

The Chicago & West Towns Railway Company defaulted on three bond issues that were due on July 1, 1932. On October 1, 1932, the Harris Trust & Savings Bank of Chicago, representing the bondholders, filed suit in the Superior Court of Cook County to place the company in receivership. The court promptly granted this request and the property was then sold on December 8, 1932 and reorganized as the "Chicago & West Towns Railways, Inc." The new firm was formally incorporated on November 23, 1932 and the sale was completed on December 22, 1932.

One early service improvement was the establishment of bus service on 16th Street on December 15, 1932. The route, the sole purpose of which was to transport Western Electric Company employees to and from work, ran weekday rush hours only from Kenton Avenue via Cermak Road, Cicero Avenue, 16th Street to Harlem Avenue.

As part of a street improvement project, the Harlem Avenue bridge at Argo was replaced by a wider one. On August 11, 1933, the West Towns' Harlem Avenue bus route was extended to Argo via Harlem Avenue and Archer Avenue, through Summit to 63rd Street at Argo. Connections could be made here with the Chicago Surface Lines' Argo streetcar line, and for a short time, connections could also have been made with the electric cars of the Chicago & Joliet Electric Railway. Unfortunately, the interurban's railcars were replaced with buses on November 16, 1933.

Brookfield Zoo

The Brookfield Zoo was developed because Lincoln Park Zoo, the other zoo in the metropolitan Chicago area, was considered to be limited by its small size. In 1920, Mrs. Edith Rockefeller McCormick donated 83 acres of land in Riverside and Brookfield, 14 miles west of Chicago's loop, to the Forest Preserve District under the condition that a modern zoo would be built there. In February 1921, the Chicago Zoological Society was incorporated to carry out development, and in 1926, a formal contract was executed between the society and the forest preserve that included

The West Towns provided riders with directions to reach the fair, A Century of Progress, being presented on Chicago's lake shore slightly south of the Loop. The ad appeared in the August 15, 1933 issue (Volume 1, Number 4) of "Traction Topics," the company's new official publication.
John F. Humiston Collection

an additional 103 acres of land. In the meantime, the design of the zoo was being formulated, with the highlight being a new type of outdoor enclosure where the

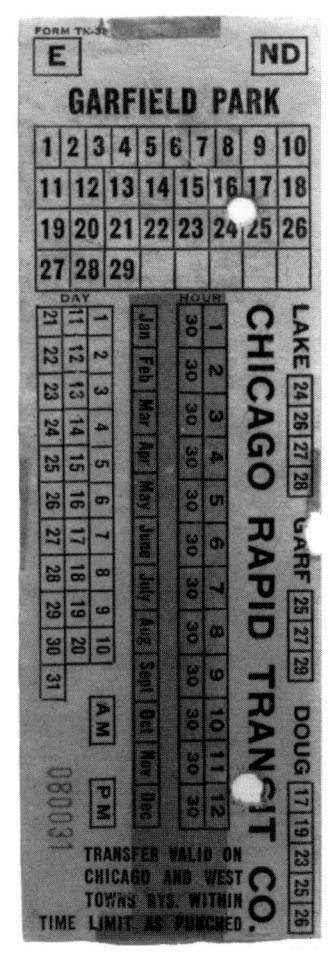

The Chicago Rapid Transit Company's transfer to the Chicago & West Towns was printed with black ink on salmon colored paper stock. It was valid as long as it was presented for transportation before the time punched into the form.

Both transfers:
Richard R. Andrews Collection

The West Towns transfer to the Chicago Rapid Transit Company was also printed with black ink on salmon colored paper stock.

animals would be surrounded by moats rather than the more typical iron bars.

Construction of the zoo began in 1927 with an opening anticipated for 1933 to coincide with the opening of the Chicago World's Fair. For some time, there was not enough tax revenue to continue construction, but the deed that Mrs. McCormick gave to the Forest Preserve District specified that the zoo would be in operation no later than July 31, 1934. The impact of the Great Depression caused the opening date to be delayed, but on July 1, 1934 Brookfield Zoo was opened to the public.

The opening of the zoo was a bonanza for the Chicago & West Towns. While the north gate of the zoo was on 31st Street, the south gate was on the West Towns' La Grange line, and the zoo brought back pleasure patronage to the railway that had not been seen since the demise of the picnic business. The zoo also caused several traffic and automobile problems that the West Towns was more than glad to solve. A switchback was installed at the zoo, and numerous extra "zoo" cars were operated to meet the demand for service on the weekends and on "free" days.

In addition, to alleviate some of the automobile congestion near the zoo, 26th Street was extended west from Harlem Avenue to Des Plaines Avenue. This project was not completed until 1937 because of delay in condemning the necessary land. Bordering the new 20-foot pavement to the south was the 30-foot right-of-way of the La Grange car line.

Elevated Transfers

On May 19, 1935, the municipalities of Berwyn, Stickney, Forest View, Oak Park and Brookfield petitioned the Illinois Commerce Commission to require the Chicago Rapid Transit Company and the West Towns to exchange transfers. It was estimated that 300,000 residents of the area could benefit from the reduced fare generated by the transfer privilege.

Through the efforts of Chicago's Mayor Kelly, the Chicago Rapid Transit Company and the Chicago Surface Lines began exchanging transfers on September 22, 1935. In order to obtain a transfer, a Chicago Surface Lines rider had to pay an additional 3¢. This amount was the difference between the 7¢ Chicago Surface Lines fare and the 10¢ Chicago Rapid Transit Company fare. Historically, the Surface Lines had objected to the transfer arrangement while the Rapid Transit, always looking to increase its market penetration, had supported it.

The merits of the transfer plan were debated before the ICC. The Chicago Rapid Transit Company in this case, however, did not approve of the plan and claimed that the proposed 15¢ fare did not cover the cost of the service, noting that their research indicated very little demand for the transfer. However, the commission ordered that it be put into effect as an experiment for a six-month period beginning January 16, 1938 and ending July 15, 1938. West Towns General Manager, Bert Collett said:

> This company feels that the new transfer system will serve as a material benefit to the people of the communities in which our lines operate. We have not in any way made any objection to the commission's order and together with the Rapid

Transit Company have worked out details and plans for specific working of the new system with the one thought of supplying our patrons with a better transportation system.

In fact, West Towns issued special transfers which were valid at the following Chicago Rapid Transit Company stations:

Lake Street Division:
Austin, Ridgeland, Oak Park, Marion, and Harlem.
Garfield Park Branch:
Oak Park, Harlem, and Des Plaines.
Douglas Park Branch:
Cicero, Laramie, Austin, Ridgeland, and Oak Park.

These transfers were acceptable for transportation at all points on the rapid transit within the 10¢ fare zone.

There were some limitations of the use of Chicago Rapid Transit Company transfers on the West Towns. On the Lake Street line, transfers were valid westbound only at Austin Boulevard and Harlem Avenue, while on the Berwyn-Lyons route, transfers for westbound travel were valid only at Laramie Avenue and Cermak Road. Similarly, on the La Grange line, a passenger could only transfer from the rapid transit at Oak Park Avenue and Cermak Road, and on the Ogden Avenue bus, transfers were accepted only at Cicero Avenue and Cermak Road. These limitations were not considered to be too severe, however, and on July 1, 1938, the commission granted an extension to the inter-company transfer privilege, noting it did not have the necessary data to evaluate the transfer plan.

When the survey data was finally assembled, the results were discouraging. During the 6-month trial period, from January 16, 1938 to July 15, 1938, passengers riding on the "L" trains and transferring to the West Towns totaled 318,129. The number of passengers paying fares on the West Towns, and then transferring to the elevated trains, totaled 323,145. Counsel for the West Towns testified before the Illinois Commerce Commission that the figures were most disappointing and that twice that number of passengers would have to be carried in order to make the project successful.

In response to the data, the commission authorized the discontinuance of the transfer privilege effective August 14, 1938. The survey work on the project indicated that, prior to the joint transfers, about 2,400 passengers were transferring daily between the two systems and were, of course, paying two fares. The inter-company transfer plan increased the number transferring to a figure that varied between 2,500 and 3,900 daily — only an average daily increase of 900 passengers — such a small increase in the number of passengers using the two systems that it did not justify the continuation of the arrangement.

Although never expressed, neither company was particularly comfortable with the possible revenue-sharing arrangement, and the need to maintain detailed records to calculate the amount of shared revenue was an additional effort and expense. In reality, each company preferred to keep all the fares it collected.

Oak Park Carbarn Fire

A fire swept through the Lake Street carbarn about 2:00 a.m. on December 2, 1936. The cause of the fire was not determined with certainty, but a stove in one of the cars was regarded as the probable cause. The Oak Park Fire Department,

The massive fire damage to the Lake Street carbarn is revealed in this photograph taken on December 6, 1936, just four days after the blaze. The four cars shown in this view of the center of the east bay of the barn were a total loss.

John F. Humiston photo

Chapter 8: The Depressing 1930s

Car 142 was between runs at the Lake Street carbarn on May 8, 1937. Five months after the carbarn fire, the barn tracks were usable; some of the walls and roof were not yet rebuilt.

John F. Humiston photo

which had three pieces of apparatus fighting the flames, was aided by four pieces from Chicago. A total of 45 men battled the blaze, and succeeded in limiting the fire to the carbarn, but the roof and south wall were almost wholly burned away.

In addition to the building's damage, eighteen passenger cars and seven service cars were totally destroyed. Ten other passenger cars were damaged (eventually repaired and returned to service). There were 30 employees in the barn at the time the fire started, and they were able to drive 30 buses out to safety. According to eyewitnesses, flames shot up 150 feet into the air. As a result of the fire, operations were severely curtailed. Some buses filled in on the car lines, and streetcars in storage at the Harlem Avenue barn were returned to service. Six two-man cars were leased from the Chicago Surface Lines for Madison Street service, and were returned on March 14, 1937. Rebuilding the carbarn took a little longer, and by June 1937, the repairs and reconstruction of the car house had been completed. Damage from the fire was estimated at more than $400,000.

Abandonment of the Chicago Avenue Line

On May 29, 1935, the municipalities of Oak Park, Cicero, Berwyn, and Forest Park filed a petition with the Illinois Commerce Commission against the West Towns. They charged that the condition of the tracks constituted a serious hazard, especially to motorists, and that the suburbs considered the streetcars obsolete, a nuisance, and a relic of the horse and buggy epoch.

The Roosevelt Road tracks were noted as being in particularly poor shape. The roadway had been paved by the state in 1935, but the portion of the street occupied by the tracks did not match the grade of the new pavement. The petitioners wanted the company either to replace the tracks or (preferably) substitute buses. Hearings began on this matter in November 1935, and as would be expected, the company claimed that the tracks were perfectly safe. The Village of Oak Park wanted buses to replace the trolleys not only on the Chicago Avenue line, but also on the Lake Street and Madison Street lines as well. Even after seven years of service, the village explained, it was still not comfortable with the use of one-man cars, testifying:

> **[The motorman] is a harassed man who collects fares, made change, and answered questions. His hands, hardened by years on the controller handle, fumbled coins and bills. He was not a past cashier and was in an uncomfortable position to do his work!**

In July 1936, the Illinois Commerce Commission ordered the company to repair its tracks on Roosevelt Road. There were many loose, broken and low rail joints on the street that were considered unsafe and hazardous to the operation of motor vehicles. The commission also held that if the company was financially unable to make the improvements ordered, street railway operation should be abandoned, the tracks removed, and steps be taken to substitute buses. Clearly, the commission

Chicago Surface Lines car 1381 was one of six Chicago cars rented by the West Towns after the fire. The car, now called either a "small St. Louis car" or a "matchbox," was photographed at the 19th Avenue terminal of the Madison Street route.

Ed Frank, Jr. photo/Joe L. Diaz Collection

favored the use of buses, forecasting that they would be faster, more convenient and safer.

The company was given 90 days to comply with the order, but General Manager Collett stated the company did not have the $125,000 needed to comply with the directive. Furthermore, he pointed out that since the streetcar system was in good operating condition, there was no need to remove the streetcars and to substitute buses. He said that the streetcar was faster than the bus, could make exactly the same schedule, and could carry 125 people compared to 50 on a bus. The company estimated that during rush hours it would take five buses to carry the same number of people that could be carried on two streetcars. Finally, Collett claimed that removing the streetcars would mean the scrapping of more than $4 million dollars worth of equipment and the expenditure of more than $760,000 for new buses.

Many of the residents of the communities served by the West Towns were dissatisfied with the streetcar service. Some viewed the streetcar as out-of-date as a Hansom cab. Community leaders pointed out that new buses could be purchased with just a small down payment and that there was no excuse for retaining the streetcars. All this was underscored by the demand of the Cicero Association of Commerce, which claimed that the same Illinois Commerce Commission order that applied to Roosevelt Road should apply to Cermak Road as well, unless quicker relief could be obtained through other channels than by litigation.

The company management appealed for a new hearing, declaring that the commission's order was unreasonable, arbitrary, and not supported by the evidence. Part of the order even forbade the operation of streetcars on Roosevelt Road between Harlem Avenue and Austin Boulevard, a directive the company claimed would prevent it from moving cars around the system.

If the company had to repair Roosevelt Road, management wanted the state to absorb some of the cost of the repaving. The railway would purchase new rail and ties and install this material on a concrete foundation poured for the highway department, which would then contract to pave over the tracks. This was a similar arrangement to what had been done on Des Plaines Avenue between Madison Street and Roosevelt Road and on Harlem Avenue between Chicago Avenue and Lake Street. However, all the Highway Department would agree to was to have the rails removed and to pave over the area where the tracks had been located.

All of this debate prompted the company to do what it could to improve track conditions on Roosevelt Road. Repairs were made to some, but not all, of the track, and motormen were ordered to reduce operating speed to less than 10 miles-per-hour over the worst sections of track.

However, another bad derailment occurred on the Laramie Avenue bridge over the Chicago, Burlington & Quincy on May 11, 1936. Again, as in 1922, the streetcar nearly fell off the side of the viaduct and the bridge was subsequently closed for six weeks for repairs during October and December 1936. During this period, street-

Chapter 8: The Depressing 1930s

During 1938, a construction project to widen Ogden Avenue resulted in the temporary closing of the Laramie Avenue bridge over the Chicago, Burlington & Quincy Railroad's Clyde Yard. A walkway was constructed so that passengers could reach the temporary streetcar terminal at the south end of the bridge. A Chicago Avenue route car was awaiting its departure time on April 22, 1938.

John F. Humiston photo

cars terminated their runs north of the bridge and shuttle buses were operated on the route segment south of the bridge.

During 1937, the West Towns found itself subjected to new competition. Goldblatt Brothers had been a long-time Chicago department store chain and operated a major store on State Street in the Loop as well as many smaller stores in the neighborhoods. The store at 26th Street and Pulaski Road in Chicago attempted to build its business by offering potential customers free bus rides. The Goldblatt's bus, which served residents of Cicero, Berywn, Brookfield, Lyons and La Grange, ran on some of the same streets as did the West Towns, although Goldblatt Brothers soon cut the free bus service back to Laramie Avenue where connections were made with the West Towns' Berwyn-Lyons and Chicago Avenue cars.

Also in 1937, another new form of transportation, the jitney, began to compete with the company. In Oak Park, the Blue Cab Company, in cooperation with village officials, inaugurated jitney service on both Oak Park Avenue and Ridgeland Avenue from North Avenue to the "L" stations. Service was provided during the morning and evening rush hours and a 10¢ fare was charged, but neither of these two services was economically viable. However, in Maywood, the Maywood Cab Company was also permitted to furnish jitney service that lasted until World War II. Obviously, the jitneys did not take much business away from the West Towns.

When the Lake Street carbarn was partially destroyed by fire on December 2, 1936, the villages started a major drive to force the abandonment of the streetcar lines. Officials of the municipalities of Cicero, Berwyn, Oak Park, and North Riverside even appropriated funds to employ an attorney and a traction engineer. This resulted in the expansion of the case before the Illinois Commerce Commission, and by March 1937, more than 2,500 pages of testimony, containing 750,000 words, and 125 exhibits were filed.

There was false hope for those communities wanting buses when, in May 1937, 10 buses were ordered from American Car & Foundry for June delivery and another eighteen from Available. The *Oak Leaves* overreacted to the news by stating that the tracks on Roosevelt Road would be removed as the commission had ordered and, in all probability, the entire Chicago Avenue line would be converted to buses. The newspaper further predicted the collapse of the trolley car system in

A sea of humanity moved in and out of the Telephone Apparatus Building at Western Electric's Hawthorne Works during shift changes. In this 1931 view looking southeast, passengers boarded a single Cermak Road streetcar for their trip west while a second West Towns car approached the car stop. Around the corner on Cicero Avenue, five Chicago Surface Lines streetcars were headed north.
Roy G. Benedict Collection

Oak Park and River Forest in the near future, claiming that it was now less expensive and more profitable for the company to switch to buses rather than to fight to preserve the tracks, trolley wires, poles, and "ancient" streetcars. In a report to the commission, it was estimated that the cost to replace the rails on Roosevelt Road was over $100,000, even if the cost of paving was paid by the State of Illinois, but for $1,000 down, the West Towns could obtain a new bus. This material made for wonderful reading and wishful thinking, because the new buses were purchased only to replace older buses, some of which were placed in service in 1923.

Another event that occurred in 1937 was a serious attempt at the formation of a metropolitan transportation district in the Chicago area. Chicago's Mayor Kelly invited the officials of all interested municipalities to a meeting to discuss area transportation needs. The laws of the State of Illinois permitted formation of a transportation district to include all territory within 30 miles of the City of Chicago, and the mayor's plan was to consolidate transportation facilities and then regulate operation through a committee of three men to be appointed by him. Needless to say, the officials of the suburban communities were not willing to abdicate their responsibility and yield their power to the Mayor of the City of Chicago.

With the possibility of a government purchase, the company saw no incentive to make large capital expenditures. The testimony before the Illinois Commerce Commission centered on numerous minor matters, such as proving that Twelfth

Chapter 8: The Depressing 1930s

A broken axle caused a collision between two West Towns streetcars on February 9, 1940, on Roosevelt Road near Kenilworth Avenue in Berwyn. The accident was a watershed event on the Chicago Avenue route as it triggered a series of actions which ended in the substitution of buses for streetcars.
James J. Buckley Collection

The accident of February 9, 1940 required the operator of each trolley to complete a Disabled Car Report. With damage so severe and obvious, the "Nature of Trouble" column would be easy to fill out. The report was primarily designed for much less apparent car problems.
Robert H. Hansen Collection

Form 36 5M 6-45 MCP

CHICAGO & WEST TOWNS RAILWAYS, INC.
DISABLED CAR REPORT

STATION_____ DATE_____194___

No. Car Disabled	No. Car Relief	Car Given to Crew at	ROUTE	RUN No.	NATURE OF TROUBLE

SIGNED_____

The Chicago & West Towns Railways

Berwyn policeman Kronquist parked city squad car one across the tracks to issue a citation to West Towns motorman M. A. Mead for "piloting his streetcar at the excessive rate of fifteen miles per hour." In response to a rash of accidents, the Berwyn City Council passed a new ordinance limiting streetcar speeds to 10 miles per hour.

Chicago Herald-American photo/LeRoy F. Blommaert Collection

Street was now Roosevelt Road. The company resisted the proceedings and stated that the streetcar system was in good condition and that it saw no need to substitute buses. The attorney representing the railways stated that if the commission ruled against it, the case would be appealed to the courts. Village officials knew this could drag on and on for years, so they raised $12,000 to continue the fight.

In December 1938, in an effort to improve its image, the company adopted a new paint scheme for its vehicles. Actually, all they really did was repaint the fleet into the same blue and white livery that had been used on the ten ACF buses purchased in May 1937. The first streetcar repainted in blue and white, car 144, appeared on the streets in December 1938, and the local press described the repainting as a "big deal" and reported:

> [As this] new stream-line-like painted car worked its way through traffic, many people thought it was a new car. However, the stove in the car burned merrily away and the operator was busier than a one-armed paper-hanger. Everyone who observed the car agrees it was a fine example of the painter's art and a nice Christmas present to the community by the company.

The paper also noted that Oak Park, besides being the largest village in the world, also had the oldest streetcars. The

When a vehicle was involved in an accident, West Towns personnel would request each passenger to complete a witness card so that they could be contacted at a later time.

Robert H. Hansen Collection

newspaper whimsically remarked that antique collectors had their eyes on the cars even though the new paint scheme reduced the value of the car as a collector's item. The newspaper did not report that there were hundreds of streetcars in Chicago that had been placed in service even earlier than car 144. By March 1940, all the cars and buses were repainted in blue and white and the interiors were renovated. Later versions of the blue and white livery were modified to paint the sloping area under the front headlight blue rather than white. Streetcars 105 and 106 were the exception to this and they were out-of-service by July 1940.

Chapter 8: The Depressing 1930s

At a temporary terminal of the Chicago Avenue route at Harlem Avenue and Roosevelt Road, car 103 waited for a shuttle bus to arrive before beginning its journey to Austin Boulevard and Chicago Avenue. The West Towns operated a bus on 12th Street between Laramie and Harlem Avenues, after March 19, 1940, in response to the Illinois Commerce Commission ruling that streetcar service on Roosevelt Road be abandoned. Behind the streetcar, 12th Street was closed to facilitate removal of the car tracks and a steam shovel was resting on the eastbound track. Enough motor coaches were on hand by July 7, 1940 to permit the entire Chicago Avenue route to be operated by bus. Spring 1940.
Charles A. Brown photo/Joe L. Diaz collection

Roosevelt Road Problems

Time was running out for streetcars on Roosevelt Road and for the Chicago Avenue line that served the street. In July 1939, the merchants along the Roosevelt Road portion of the line petitioned the company to remedy the "deplorable condition" of the street. They also declared that the condition of the street was a menace to health and safety, besides being a decided detriment to their businesses.

On Friday morning, February 10, 1940, eastbound car 107 derailed due to a broken axle at Kenilworth Avenue and was rammed broadside by a westbound car 101. Two persons were severely injured and 30 other passengers were badly shaken up in the crash. Although there had been many derailments in recent years, including as many as three in one day at Elmwood Avenue alone, this was the first time in many months that any severe injuries resulted.

This accident prompted the Berwyn City Council to enact an ordinance on February 20, 1940, limiting the speed of streetcars to 10 miles-per-hour. With Roosevelt Road being the northern boundary of Berwyn, this ordinance applied not only to the Roosevelt Road streetcars, but also to the cars of the La Grange and Berwyn-Lyons routes on Cermak Road. This action, designed to stop any repetition of streetcar mishaps, came with an ultimatum to either repair the tracks and equipment or to substitute buses. The chief of police was even instructed to arrest any motormen who exceeded the speed limit. Police squads actively patrolled the routes looking for violators. One motorman was arrested three times before the company obtained a temporary restraining order in federal court.

Early Saturday morning, March 9, 1940, a westbound car derailed on Roosevelt Road just west of Lyman Avenue where the streetcars normally turned back on a Chicago Surface Lines-owned crossover. The car skidded across the street, crashing into a bakery at 6111 W. Roosevelt Road. Fortunately, there was only one passenger on board at the time and neither the passenger nor the motorman was injured.

The Illinois Commerce Commission immediately issued an order forcing the company to cease streetcar operations on Roosevelt Road between Austin Boulevard and Harlem Avenue. The Chicago Avenue line was now truncated with streetcars operating on the two outer ends and a shuttle bus running the 1-1/2 mile distance in the middle. On the north segment, streetcars turned back at the existing crossover on Roosevelt Road, slightly west of Harlem Avenue. On the southern segment, trolleys now terminated at Roosevelt Road and Laramie Avenue. On March 19, 1940, as a result of conferences with the commission, company and representatives of the municipalities of Oak Park, Cicero, and Berwyn, the parties agreed to substitute buses on the Chicago Avenue route. Arrangements were also made for the purchase of 25 buses to cost about $200,000, with an anticipated delivery within 60 to 90 days.

This concluded the hearings asking for the abandonment of streetcar service on the Chicago Avenue line. The substitution of buses for the blue trolleys was considered the initial step in the betterment of transportation service in the western suburbs, and although the buses followed the identical route as did the streetcars, several special services were inaugurated. An additional bus route was operated on Sundays and holidays on Roosevelt Road, west from Laramie Avenue to the Hines Hospital, and a second bus line was operated on Sundays and holidays from the hospital to Madison Street via Roosevelt Road and Des Plaines Avenue.

The 25 new buses arrived during July and ten were needed to maintain headway on the 10-mile long Chicago Avenue route that was converted on Sunday, July 7, 1940. The buses maintained the same running times and headways as did the streetcars, but the detours caused by the repaving of Roosevelt Road handicapped operations. The new buses were well received by most of the patrons on the route and indications were that introduction of buses increased patronage on the line.

Abandonment of the Berwyn-Lyons Streetcar Route

The governments of Cicero and Berwyn wanted the conversion of the Berwyn-Lyons route from streetcars to buses, and the officials from Cicero protested most vigorously against the condition of the cars, wires, and roadbed. Cicero representatives described the track as in a "most dangerous and deplorable condition, unsafe and unfit for travel." Officials even claimed that the streetcars were so bad that they were an insult to the riders, but then the officials had a change of heart. They objected to the substitution of buses because the abandonment of the Berwyn-Lyons line would necessitate the repaving of all streets in the municipality over which the car line operated and funds were not available for this project.

In the background of these events was the plan to unify public surface transportation in the Chicago metropolitan area. Cicero had great hopes that this plan would provide the town with many benefits, including better funding and the through routing of some of the lines of the Chicago system. A wait-and-see attitude developed because no one was sure whether the latest plan was just another political football. The policy of unification was achieved in Chicago, but not the suburbs, when the Chicago Transit Authority assumed operation of the "L" and surface lines in the city on October 1, 1947. Com-

West Towns car 115 was going to Brookfield Zoo on September 3, 1944, when it traveled westbound on Cermak Road at Lyman Avenue. The car was traversing the construction area in which the street level was raised and new rail was imbedded in concrete. The 115 was traveling westbound on the normal eastbound track.

Robert W. Gibson photo/George E. Kanary Collection

Chapter 8: The Depressing 1930s

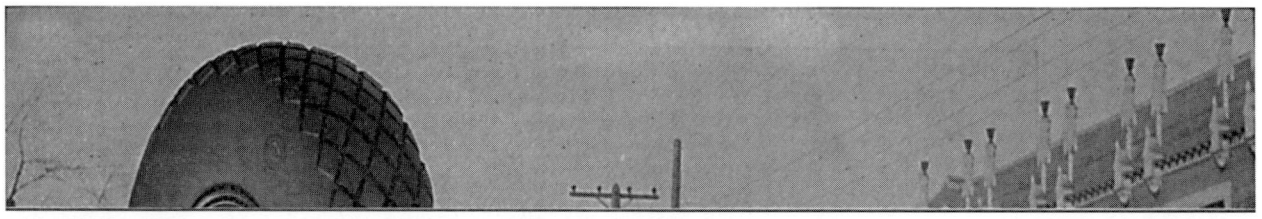

"Gladly recommend them to anyone using tires"

One of the 100%-Goodyear-equipped motorbus fleet of Chicago and West Towns Railway Company

West Towns buses were also used in advertising by component manufacturers. In this ad appearing in the February 10, 1927 issue of Operation & Maintenance magazine, the reader is advised that the West Towns bus fleet is 100% equipped with Goodyear pneumatic bus tires. Featured in the ad is bus 9, one of a lot of 10 buses built in 1924 by Mack with Cummings bodies.

Roy G. Benedict Collection

bination of the suburban lines would require three more decades to create a Regional Transportation Authority and another decade to actually amalgamate the service.

Berwyn and company negotiators reached an agreement in August 1941 allowing for abandonment of the car line, substitution of buses, and resurfacing of Ridgeland Avenue. The Berwyn-Lyons car line operated on Ridgeland Avenue from 26th Street on the north to Stanley Avenue, on the south (about 31st Street), a distance of less than three-quarter's of a mile. Implementation of this agreement required the approval of the Illinois Commerce Commission, In the proceedings before the commission, Cicero again voiced its objection to the change. Apparently, if Cicero had not objected, buses would have replaced trolleys almost immediately after its August 1941 meeting. However, now the commissioners needed to study the issue. On November 27, 1941, they concurred that buses could replace streetcars on the Berwyn-Lyons route.

The change took place on November 30, 1941. Buses followed the same route as did the streetcars — via Cermak Road, Laramie Avenue, 25th Street, Central Avenue, 26th Street, Ridgeland Avenue, Stanley Avenue, and Harlem Avenue to Ogden Avenue. (The portion of the streetcar line west of Harlem Avenue on Ogden Avenue had been abandoned in 1933.) The normal running time from Kenton Avenue and Cermak Road to Harlem Avenue and Ogden Avenue was 25 minutes.

Removal of the tracks was left to the municipalities, county or state, depending on which jurisdiction was responsible for roadway maintenance. The company was directed to collect the rails when they were removed and to take down all poles, wires, and overhead structures, but since the La Grange streetcar line would still be in operation, the tracks and wires would remain intact on Cermak Road.

The Cicero attorney's office announced they would file a petition for a rehearing of the evidence in an attempt to "protect the town against a situation expected to crop up with the discontinued use of streetcar right-of-way property." The West Towns claimed when the company removed the streetcars from the

Berwyn-Lyons route, it was relieved of all responsibility for the maintenance of roadbed. (At this time, the track on Central Avenue had not yet been encased in paving.) Cicero's petition for a rehearing was prompted by the fact that it could neither finance the removal of the tracks and the repaving of the right-of-way, as authorized by the Illinois Commerce Commission, nor let the tracks remain and keep the gravel ballast area in an acceptable state of repair without financial assistance.

By early 1942, the dispute reached a conclusion. In January 1942, Cicero's petition for a rehearing was denied by the Illinois Commerce Commission, and since World War II had started, a new federal bureau, the Office of Defense Transportation, had jurisdiction in the case. However, the new office did not provide Cicero relief either, declining to intercede in the matter.

In October 1942, negotiations between the West Towns and the War Production Board's salvage section resulted in the removal of almost 3,300 tons of now unused rails from the streets of River Forest, Oak Park, Maywood, Forest Park, Cicero, and Berwyn. Approximately 180 tons from the long idle tracks of the Chicago & Joliet Electric Railway were also salvaged from the streets of Lyons Township. About one-third of the rail was used for other street railway uses, but the majority was melted down to produce new steel for the war effort.

LaGrange Line Improvements

The management of the West Towns made a concerted effort to improve the La Grange line over the years. In 1937, work began to lower the elevation of tracks in Brookfield by 15 inches to conform to the grade of adjacent streets, and eleven new waiting shelters were installed to protect waiting passengers from the elements. Wartime passenger loads provided some of the much-needed funds to complete this and other work. Rail replacement continued throughout the war, with some of the work done by local high school students.

In 1942, the line was converted to one-man operation to further enhance productivity. In order to reduce some of the protests over this, a flagman was stationed at the busy Indiana Harbor Belt

Ford bus 264, purchased in 1941, paused in front of the Harlem Avenue entrance of Marshall Field & Company's Oak Park store, circa 1945.

Bruce G. Moffat Collection

Chapter 8: The Depressing 1930s

The Available Bus

A NEWCOMER to the bus field is the new 25-passenger two-door transit design recently developed by the Available Truck Company. This new design is built on a flat frame chassis with the engine, a 263 cu.in. six-cylinder Waukeshaw at the front and driver's position offset to the side. This design employs six standard units, has a three-speed Spicer transmission and clutch. Lockheed hydraulic chassis known as Model WS-175-SB has a 141-in. wheelbase and is fitted with 9.00-18 tires on the front and 7.00-20 tires dual on rear, American Cable emergency, Timken axles, Ross steering, Budd wheels and Leece-Neville 500-watt gear driven generator.

The body is of formed steel throughout with side panels screwed in place. The roof panel is of aluminum. The only wood in the body is on the floor. This latter is covered by heavy duty linoleum. Shatter-proof glass is used throughout and sashes are of lift type with brass mounting. Seats and lights were furnished by the Brill Company.

A newcomer to the bus field—a 25-passenger transit type design by the Available Truck Company.

BUS TRANSPORTATION ✦ December, 1937   583

Bus Transportation magazine ran a news item in its December 1937 issue about the Available Truck Company's entry into the transit bus market. The West Towns had purchased a lot of 18 of Available's 25 passenger model WS-175-SB in 1937.

Roy G. Benedict Collection

crossing. With the introduction of one-man service, the through fare to La Grange was reduced from 15¢ to a dime, and on the Western Springs bus line the fare was reduced for travel through the former fare zone boundary at the Indiana Harbor Belt Railroad crossing. In August 1946, new rail was laid on Des Plaines Avenue and its Woodside Drive continuation, with the entire right-of-way paved curb to curb from Park Place north to 31st Street.

There were two noteworthy accidents on the La Grange line in the 1940s. In 1943, car 123 was destroyed when it was hit by an Indiana Harbor Belt train. The car so badly damaged that it was scrapped on the spot. On May 30, 1946, car 114 was badly damaged when it rear-ended car 138 on 26th Street near Hainsworth Street in Riverside. The motorman on car 114 claimed that the brakes had failed. Unfortunately, for everyone concerned, both cars were crowded with zoo visitors and picnickers totaling over 70 passengers aboard each car. Thirty passengers were hurt, 19 severely. As a result of the accident, the line was closed for hours. Car 114 was never repaired.

For years, Hillgrove Avenue in La Grange and the streetcar tracks on it had needed major repair. One way to accomplish this work, at a time when neither the village nor the streetcar company had the funds, was to arrange to bury a storm sewer in the street. The new design for Hillgrove specified the removal of the streetcar tracks, the widening of the street from 36-feet to 40-feet, and the removal of a Chicago, Burlington & Quincy Railroad freight spur into a lumberyard at Spring Street.

On December 1, 1946, the West Towns revised its routes for the construction project. The La Grange streetcars continued to operate on regular schedules, but turned back at La Grange Road and a switch was installed there to permit the cars to change direction. Shuttle bus service, with a half-hour headway, was initiated west of La Grange Road, but since Hillgrove Avenue was impassable, the bus ran on Burlington Avenue between La Grange Road and Gilbert Avenue in Western Springs. Almost immediately, the West Towns realized that operation would be simpler if the shuttle bus service was replaced with an extension of the Ogden Avenue bus route to Gilbert Avenue, and every other Ogden bus made the trip to Western Springs. The sewer project itself was completed in 1948.

Additional Bus Service

From 1938 to 1945, there were a large number of changes to the Chicago & West Towns bus system. On October 25, 1938, the Illinois Commerce Commission ordered that the Ogden Avenue bus line be rerouted via Cicero Avenue, 31st Street, and Ogden Avenue, a route that had previously been operated over Cicero to Ogden. The Commission stated that "hundreds" of residents of the Hawthorne dis-

West Town bus 530 was southbound on Wolf Road, near the Eisenhower Expressway, in Hillside, Illinois on November 24, 1963. The vehicle was purchased in 1947, in a lot of 40, to permit the retirement of streetcars on the Madison and Lake Street lines.

Michael M. McGowan photo

trict had to walk a half-mile either to Ogden Avenue or to 35th Street in order to reach bus transportation, and this re-routing would afford a necessary and convenient service to these people. In addition, on August 5, 1940, rush hour service was inaugurated on North Avenue from Narragansett Avenue to Wolf Road, with full-time service on this route beginning eleven months later on July 5, 1941. (In November 1941, the route was extended into Elmhurst.)

On April 22, 1941, the new Broadway route was placed into service to provide transportation to a Buick automobile plant that had opened at North Avenue and Mannheim Road. The bus line was operated from Mannheim Road via North Avenue, Broadway, 19th Avenue, Madison Street, and 17th Avenue to the "L" station at 17th Avenue, and, in 1942, this route was combined with the Broadview bus line.

The Defense Plant Corporation began construction of an aluminum rolling mill in McCook at the southwest corner of 47th Street and First Avenue. When it opened on June 18, 1943, it was one of the three largest aluminum rolling mills in the world. Although the federal government owned the mill, the Aluminum Company of America, better known as ALCOA, operated it. The facility was built primarily to provide aluminum sheets for aircraft production, and although initial employment at the plant was 600, ALCOA expected the plant to eventually employ 4,500. At the request of ALCOA, the ICC ordered service extended to the rolling mill to aid the war effort. The company complied, and the south end of the Broadview bus line was extended from Prairie Avenue and Ogden Avenue via Ogden Avenue, First Avenue, and 47th Street to the plant.

Also on the South Side, the Electro-Motive Corporation requested service to its plant at McCook, Illinois. On April 30, 1941, the ICC authorized the company to operate a shuttle bus from Ogden Avenue via East Avenue and 55th Street to Electro-Motive, but this service proved unsatisfactory. On February 16, 1944, the Commission authorized the replacement of the shuttle bus with a new bus line from the Westchester "L" terminal at 22nd Street and Mannheim Road to the plant. From the "L" station, the bus line ran south over Mannheim and La Grange Roads and east on 55th Street to the plant. This route was inaugurated on May 1, 1944 and provided hourly service along with a few rush-hour trippers.

On May 27, 1942, the ICC authorized the West Towns to establish bus service to the Clearing Industrial District in Bedford Park. The new bus line operated between a western terminal at Archer Avenue and 63rd Street and an eastern terminal at 65th Street and Cicero Avenue via 63rd, Harlem Avenue, and 65th. Since 65th Street was a major thoroughfare in the district, the ICC considered service on this street, between Central and Cicero Av-

Chapter 8: The Depressing 1930s

105

The West Towns purchased a lot of 20 Mack buses in 1948 to replace trolleys on the La Grange line. One of these buses, number 611, was traveling eastward on Lake Street in charter duty at Humphrey Avenue on July 22, 1961.

Michael M. McGowan photo

enues, to be more convenient than that provided by the Chicago Surface lines two blocks away on 63rd Street.

The Office of Defense Transportation ordered the West Towns to eliminate 37% of the stops on its bus routes on October 18, 1942. Under this directive, which was part of a national policy to reduce fuel and rubber consumption, stops would be no less than 600 feet apart. Appropriate signs were provided at all the closed bus stops.

On April 13, 1944, the ICC authorized the West Towns to extend bus service to Hillside. The company instituted bus service, weekday rush hours only, on a route from Des Plaines Avenue via Roosevelt Road to York Road in Elmhurst, then the route returned east via Roosevelt Road, Buck Road, Harrison Street, Wolf Road, and Roosevelt Road to Des Plaines Avenue.

As the war drew to its conclusion, the West Towns fleet of buses was suffering from deferred maintenance. The problem was a lack of personnel — in 1945 it employed only seven mechanics to keep a fleet of 147 buses in repair, resulting in as many as 40 buses being out of service at any given time. Obviously, when this occurred the company could not maintain scheduled service. Adding to the problem, many of the Ford buses required new engines, but during the war engines were difficult to obtain. Finally, through the efforts of Bert Collett and a committee representing some of the villages, the Office of Defense Transportation allocated 20 new General Motors buses to the West Towns, and they arrived in February 1945.

After the war, the equipment fleet was overhauled and modernized as replacement parts and the manpower to install them became more available. Matters were further improved when a new, 75-bus garage was erected on the company's property facing Cermak Road at Harlem Avenue.

Much needed new housing development began in the area at the end of the war, and the West Towns provided additional service capacity to one of the new subdivisions being built west of First Avenue in North Riverside. The company instituted bus service on Cermak Road from Harlem Avenue to 17th Avenue on October 17, 1946, and service was extended west to Wolf Road later in that month. Brookfield Zoo trippers were operated via Cermak Road and First Avenue to the zoo's 31st Street Gate, and the Cermak Road bus line connected with the La Grange streetcar line at the eastern terminal of the bus line at Harlem Avenue and Cermak Road.

9 Competition from Bluebird

In July 1934, the Bluebird Coach System, Inc. purchased the two Chicago to Joliet bus routes of the Chicago & Joliet Transportation Company from the Central Illinois Public Service Company of Springfield. The $15,000 purchase price included all franchise rights and rolling stock. One of the routes served Chicago and Joliet via Joliet Road, Harlem Avenue, and Ogden Avenue while the other, operating on the other side of the Des Plaines River, primarily ran via Archer Avenue. The franchise for these routes did not include carrying local traffic in either Cicero or Berwyn.

On July 8, 1936, Bluebird applied for an express route between Berwyn, Cicero, and Chicago. In anticipation of approval of its application, Bluebird rented terminal space in downtown Chicago at the Trailways Depot at 20 E. Randolph Street. However, Bluebird's petition was contested by the Chicago & West Towns Railways, the Chicago Rapid Transit Company, and the Chicago, Burlington & Quincy Railroad. In response to these objections, in September 1937, Bluebird Coach System amended its petition by changing the proposed route and this led to the Illinois Commerce Commission approving Bluebird's application on July 27, 1938.

Both the West Towns and Chicago Rapid Transit Company filed petitions for a rehearing, and following the debate the Commission found that the service and headways of the West Towns were primarily designed to meet the local traffic requirements, based on data collected in a transfer exchange experiment. Thus, Bluebird was allowed to place the route in service in October 1938. The line operated on an hourly headway beginning at Stanley Avenue via Oak Park Avenue, Riverside Drive, Cermak Road, Ogden Avenue, Washington Boulevard, Wacker Drive, State Street, and Randolph Street to the bus terminal. In September 1940, the route was extended southwestward via Oak Park Avenue and Ogden Avenue to Harlem Avenue and operated on a 15-minute headway. Eventually, the successful line was further extended via Ogden Avenue, Harlem Avenue, and Joliet Road to 45th Street in Lyons.

After the ICC denied the petition filed by the Chicago Rapid Transit Company and the West Towns, both companies filed an appeal with the Circuit Court of Cook County. However, the judge ruled that the Commission was justified in permitting the Bluebird system to operate this service. In fact, the possibility of the discontinuance of the Bluebird express bus service caused a furor among residents in both Berwyn and Lyons. Residents even took the unusual step of preparing petitions to the court expressing the belief that the Bluebird express bus service was essential. However, the judge ruled that the municipalities could not enter the suit or file appearances in favor of Bluebird.

On appeal to the Illinois Supreme Court, the judgment of the Circuit Court was reversed and the case remanded to the Circuit Court of Cook County. The high court's order also included directions to send the matter back to the ICC. Further hearings were held on numerous dates between June 30, 1943 and March 7, 1945, resulting in the ICC giving its final approval for the Bluebird route on June 14, 1945.

While the legality of the Cicero - Berwyn express bus route was being determined, Bluebird filed a petition in 1939 for an express bus route from Maywood to the Loop. The list of objectors not only included the West Towns and the Chicago

In later years, Bluebird operated its Chicago-Joliet service from Chicago's Greyhound bus terminal. A Chicago-bound bus entered the Greyhound terminal, on Clark Street between Randolph and Lake Streets, from lower Wacker Drive.

Bruce G. Moffat Collection

Chapter 9: Competition from Bluebird   107

At the other end of the route, Bluebird bus 380 had arrived at the Joliet, Illinois bus station. The vehicle, a GMC model TDH-4509, was photographed on December 21, 1962.

Michael M. McGowan photo

Rapid Transit Company, but also the Chicago & North Western Railway, the Chicago, Aurora & Elgin Railroad, and the Chicago Motor Coach Company. These companies argued that, as a result of their investment and effort, the customer base for those routes had already been built, and if Bluebird skimmed off some of the business, it would hurt their profitability. However, the ICC approved Bluebird's request on June 23, 1942.

The Maywood express bus route was opened on June 26, 1942, operating from 20th Avenue and Washington Boulevard to the bus depot at 20 E. Randolph in Chicago. In short order service was extended into Bellwood via 24th Avenue, 21st Street, 25th Avenue and back to Washington Boulevard following ICC approval (with the proviso that local traffic could not be carried).

By ruling in favor of Bluebird, the ICC gave a verbal slap in the face to the West Towns. The Commission determined that the West Towns was not qualified to render the service because the company had a deficit of over $1 million and was not profitable. Further, the Commission felt that the West Towns would not be able to redeem its $2.1 million first mortgage bonds due in five years, and concluded that the company would not have the financial resources to operate the route at all.

Meanwhile, Bluebird continued to expand. On May 5, 1941, it requested rights for a route to serve Brookfield Zoo. For reasons unclear the approval process took almost five years, coming on October 17, 1946. The line was placed into service on November 9, 1946 with the normal proviso that the company could not pick up local passengers in either Cicero or Berwyn. (On October 28, 1947, permission was granted to extend this route into La Grange.) On March 28, 1945, they applied for a route from connecting Stone Park to downtown Chicago. The Commission denied Bluebird's request for many reasons, but mainly because they saw no real need for the service.

In the background of this bus route expansion, legal activity was ongoing. In March 1947, the Illinois Supreme Court rendered a decision to remand the express bus service cases back to the Circuit Court for a rehearing. Bluebird then announced that it would petition the high court for a rehearing and would continue to operate the routes until it was held. West Towns' Vice President Bert Collett publicly stated that his company would supply an equivalent or better service the day that Bluebird stopped.

The high court determined that the Illinois Commerce Commission was without the authority to issue a Certificate of Convenience and Necessity to Bluebird. At the rehearing held in May 1947, the company provided an impressive list of statistics to describe its operations and results. At the time, Bluebird Coach served 6.5 million passengers annually and supporters claimed that Bluebird's service was better and faster to the Loop than that of the West Towns, mainly because the West Towns' routes only connected with surface or elevated lines at the city limits. In September 1947, the Illinois Supreme Court ruled that the case again be returned to the ICC for additional findings.

Realizing that the ICC had always looked favorably on Bluebird's service, the West Towns filed another suit against the commission in the Circuit Court of Cook County. The West Towns also continued its fight before the ICC to gain the right to provide express bus service to the Loop, while Bluebird maintained its claim that the West Towns was unable to provide the service.

At this time, the West Towns had three cases pending before the commission: the Berwyn route, the Maywood route and the Brookfield route. In both the Maywood and Brookfield route cases, the Circuit Court of Cook County reversed the ICC's approval to operate the express bus service. In the Maywood case, the Illinois Supreme Court had twice reversed the approval to Bluebird. The legal wrangling came to a conclusion before the Illinois Supreme Court when the high court heard arguments from the West Towns, Bluebird and the ICC. Finally, in October 1947, the Illinois Supreme Court ruled in favor of Bluebird.

10 The End of Streetcar Service

During the final years of World War II, many residents of the western suburbs were complaining about the continued presence of streetcars. They claimed that the cars were old, not as fast as they would like, and that the poor track conditions disrupted automobile traffic. Because of the war, strict regulations precluded the West Towns management from acquiring as many buses as they would have liked. When new buses were finally received, the West Towns management thought that they could be better utilized on existing bus lines as opposed to replacing streetcars.

Even though the Lake Street and Madison Street car lines were the most profitable of the West Towns' routes, there was no hope of preserving streetcar service on them. On September 13, 1945, the Illinois Commerce Commission entered a citation against the West Towns directing it to show cause why the present streetcar operations on its Lake Street and Madison Street car lines should not be abandoned and motor coach operation substituted. The commission held intermittent hearings from October 9, 1945 until September 9, 1946.

In spring 1946, an event occurred which further shortened the life of the West Towns' streetcar operations. John L. Lewis, President of the United Mine Workers of America, led his coal miners on strike and the area's utility companies, which used coal as the primary fuel to power their plants, saw their supplies dwindle. In May 1946, the Public Service Company of Northern Illinois was forced to drastically reduce the amount of power that it could provide to its customers and businesses were limited to only four hours a day of operation.

As a result, on May 8, 1946, the ICC ordered the West Towns to temporarily substitute buses for streetcars on its owl, Sunday and holiday runs on Madison and Lake Streets. There were immediate public complaints about buses using side streets to turnaround. This was especially true on the east end of the Madison Street line where the buses looped using Austin Boulevard, Adams Street, and Humphrey Avenue. The coal strike was not settled until the first week of June 1946.

At the public hearings held to examine the wisdom of substituting buses for the trolleys, evidence was presented which showed that the streetcar system needed to be rehabilitated. Officials from Forest Park were particularly unhappy with the condition of the track on Madison Street, claiming that the 25-year-old streetcars were less comfortable to ride and less efficient to operate than new buses. What was left unsaid, however, was that the passenger comfort afforded by the bus ride depended on the condition of the streets on which they operated, while the comfort of the streetcar ride was determined by the condition of the tracks.

In the early 1940s, the West Towns provided service to Sportsman's and Hawthorn race tracks with both buses and streetcars. Streetcar 104 and bus 244 waited on the storage tracks on Laramie Avenue, south of 35th Street, for the races to finish. Bus 244, an ACF Model 31-S, was purchased in 1940.

Robert H. Hansen Collection

Chapter 10: The End of Streetcar Service

109

The railways, in an instance of providing effective communications, had banners prepared informing the public of the replacement of streetcars by buses on Lake Street. Then, a bus and trolley were posed, front to front, to provide the newspapers with a photograph to run in the local editions.
Robert H. Hansen Collection

In this case, the streets were in much better shape than were the tracks.

At the public hearings, the West Towns relied on Charles W. Chase, President of the American Transit Association, as an expert witness to help support its position. He testified that, in the west suburban area, there were three widely dispersed locations for which adequate transportation service could only be maintained by the continued use of streetcars: Brookfield Zoo, the Lake-Harlem business district of River Forest and Oak Park, and the Western Electric Hawthorne Works. At Hawthorne, 5,000 workers used the facilities of the West Towns each working day, while the zoo, on good summer Sundays, was attracting between 40,000 and 60,000 visitors. Many of the visitors used the La Grange streetcars for transportation and, on certain "free days," it was estimated that the blue and white streetcars carried over 15,000 visitors to and from the city limits. Mr. Chase also stated that, in his opinion, the track and operating equipment of the West Towns was in excellent condition and that service schedules were maintained on a satisfactory basis.

While the municipalities involved had wanted a move from streetcars to buses for many years, there was always the question of who was going to pay for the change. The municipalities wanted the West Towns to remove the tracks and pave the right-of-way at its own expense. In the end, the company agreed to contribute $30,000 towards the resurfacing of the streets in Oak Park, River Forest, Maywood, Melrose Park, and Forest Park.

The ICC was clearly aware of the recently settled coal miners' strike, and the fact that buses did a satisfactory job of replacing streetcars on the Madison Street and Lake Street routes was not lost on its members. In spite of objections from property owners, the ICC ruled that the only feasible and practical turnaround for buses was at the east end of the Madison Street line, a loop used during the coal miners' strike emergency via Austin Boulevard, Adams Street and Humphrey Avenue. (The Chicago Surface Lines would not let the West Towns buses use its Madison Street and Austin Boulevard loop.)

Another point of controversy was the

Streetcar Assignments
1940-1947

Lake Street Barn	Suburban Barn
100-104	105-108
	111-112, 114-116, 119
124, 126-128	122-123
130, 132-136	138-139
142, 145	140-141
151	152-159
163-165	160-161
16-19	5-9, 12, 15

Cars 124, 126-128 were transferred from the Suburban carbarn in 1943. Cars 105 and 106 were scrapped in 1943. Car 123 destroyed in 1943. Cars 16-19 and 5-9 were snow sweepers. Car 12 is a work motor while car 15 is a line car.
Electric Railway Historical Society

The fleet of buses ordered to replace the streetcars on Lake Street were parked near the carbarn for a publicity photo.
Bruce G. Moffat Collection

proposed consolidation of all transit operators in metropolitan Chicagoland. In 1945, after the failure of six separate attempts to reorganize the Chicago Surface Lines and the Chicago Rapid Transit Company with the aid of private capital, Chicago's Mayor Kelly and Illinois' Governor Green proposed the establishment of a public authority to acquire, own, and operate the city's local transit facilities. The proposal, endorsed by civic, commercial, financial, and industrial leaders, as well as by business and community organizations, led to the passage of the Metropolitan Transit Authority Act on April 23, 1945.

The Metropolitan Transit Authority Act also permitted the inclusion of the suburban transit companies into the combined system. In spite of all the pro-bus propaganda being generated by the suburban municipalities, some thought it was logical and now possible to join the Chicago Surface Lines' Madison Street and Lake Street streetcar routes with those of the West Towns; and after all these years, it would mean a one-seat ride at a single fare as well as permit the substitution of modern streetcars (instead of modern buses) for the Chicago & West Towns' older generation trolleys. When the Chicago Transit Authority began operating the Chicago surface system and "L" lines on October 1, 1947, the suburban carriers were excluded, and, in fact, the management of the CTA had little interest in serving suburban areas, although the CTA did study the issue from time to time.

The ICC entered an order, dated Tuesday, September 24, 1946, for the West Towns to replace streetcars with buses on both the Lake Street and Madison Street lines. The bus service was to start within 30 days after the delivery of enough buses to serve either street. The commission allowed the company to decide which street would first begin bus service and how to best deploy the equipment. The West Towns had earlier placed an order for forty 32-passenger buses from General Motors and there were expectations that the buses would be delivered in November 1946. However, that turned out to be a little optimistic, since the vehicles were not delivered until early 1947.

On Valentines Day, with twenty of the new buses on-hand, officials of Maywood, Melrose Park, Forest Park, River Forest, Oak Park, and Bellwood, as well as representatives of the chamber of commerce of each village, were guests of the company for a ceremonial first ride on Friday, February 14, 1947. On the following Sunday, sixteen buses were assigned to Madison Street replacing the cars.

The use of buses on Madison Street allowed the West Towns to slightly modify the route to better meet the needs of its passengers. The line was divided into two routes, with the first one running from Austin Boulevard and Madison Street via Madison and 19th Avenue to a terminal at 19th and Lake Street. The second route was extended further west via Madison Street, 25th Avenue, Washington Boulevard, and Butterfield Road to York Road in Elmhurst. Several weeks later, on February 27, 1947, the first route was changed so that instead of traveling on 19th Avenue to Lake Street, buses continued west on Madison Street and used 25th Avenue and Washington

Chapter 10: The End of Streetcar Service

CENTRAL ELECTRIC RAILFANS' ASSOCIATION
P.O. Box 503, Chicago 90, Ill.

***

March 23, 1948.

Dear Railfan:

SUBJECT: CERA TRIP No. 49 - APRIL ~~4th (or~~ 11th), 1948.
CHICAGO AND WEST TOWNS RAILWAY
Account Abandonment of Street Car Service.

    This trip will be a final inspection of the last street railway line of the West Towns, and will cover the entire remaining tracks of the LaGrange Line, thru Cicero, Berwyn, Riverside, Brookfield and LaGrange, Illinois.

    It will be held the Sunday AFTER conversion of regular service to buses, which it is now believed will be April 4th. However, this may be delayed to April 11th - therefore, if you want final information send us a self-addressed, stamped, envelope. Advance reservation will be appreciated.

    Our cars will be the only ones on the line. Any equipment that can roll will be available. We will meet at 1:30 P.M. at Kenton Ave. & 22nd Street - accessible from Douglas Park "L" or Cermak Road street cars. Absolutely your last chance to see the WEST TOWNS as a street car line. COST $1.00 per person.

Theo. A. Kawol
Theo. A. Kawol
Registration Officer

The last day of scheduled service for the La Grange line was Saturday, April 10, 1948. The railway allowed Central Electric Railfans' Association to operate a post-abandonment excursion on Sunday, April 11th. The $1 fare covered the association's publicity and administrative costs because the railway did not charge CERA for the excursion.
Robert H. Hansen Collection

MCERA Bob Hansen had purchased a ticket for the April 11th fantrip for himself. As the date of the trip approached, his father wanted to join and Bob bought ticket 224 for his dad.
Robert H. Hansen Collection

TRIP 49
Pass ROBERT HANSEN No. 224
CENTRAL ELECTRIC RAILFANS' ASSOCIATION
FINAL TRIP—CHICAGO & WEST TOWNS RAILWAY
22nd & Kenton, 1:30 P.M.
Sunday, April 11, 1948

112   *The Chicago & West Towns Railways*

3 OLD TROLLEYS END CAREERS IN CLANG OF GLORY

Haul 100 Pall Bearers on Last Mile

BY WARD WALKER

With many a wheeze, a rattle and a valiant shriek of the old air whistle--and perhaps a tear or two from the Railfans who were the passengers--three old trolleys made the last run over the LaGrange st. car line yesterday.

As the trolleys rocked along the meandering route they've followed from Cermak rd. and Kenton av. to LaGrange since 1893, the modern streamlined buses that have replaced them were picking up pay loads at the different stops.

But members of the Central Electric Railfans association--more than 100 strong, including members from New York, Philadelphia and Cincinnati--had nothing but sneers for the fume-spewing buses which sped almost silently past.

Dark Hints Of Politics

"Sure, trolleys are on their way out," admitted F. M. Smith, of 8332 S. Sangamon st., a sales engineer and chairman of the Railfans. "But they shouldn't be. We think that politics must be mixed up in it someway," he hinted, darkly.

Smith and George Krambles, of 2244 Cleveland av., a director of the Railfans and an engineer for the Chicago Transit authority, said that passengers along the route would regret the switch when winter comes.

"Who ever heard of a bus with a coal burning stove?" asked Krambles. "On a cold winter's night when the trolley stove was going good, nothing could beat it."

It was only occasionally, they said, that something would go wrong with the fan and fill the car with smoke; "Even then," Smith added, "it smelled kind of like grandma's kitchen used to when the wind was blowing the wrong way and the chimney wouldn't draw."

Old Whistle "Comfortable"

Hugh Ewald, a supervisor for the Chicago and West Towns Railways, Inc., which has abandoned the trolley line, admitted that after 42 years of working with the trolleys it was hard to see them go.

"That old air whistle was a comfortable, familiar sound along the route," he said. Lots of people going to miss it, and the honk of a bus isn't going to replace it."

But if nothing else, the death of the trolleys gave the Railfans--an organization dedicated to collecting data on disappearing electric roads --a chance for an outing.

Members of the Central Electric Railfans' Association took last ride yestersay on old trolleys of Chicago and West Towns Railways which had been abandoned on LaGrange line.
SUN-TIMES Photo

150 fans take last ride' on W. Side line

The West Town Railway made its last trolley car run on the Berwyn-Brookfield-La Grange route, loaded with 150 electric railway fans.

They were members of the Central Electric Railfans Assn. with headquarters in Chicago.

Armed with cameras, the association members scrambled aboard the three-car train at 22d St. and Kenton Ave. for the trip to La Grange. The railway fans had come from all over the country to take the "last ride."

The rail fan group was formed in Chicago 10 years ago and is composed of men and women whose hobbies are studying and compiling data on electric powered transportation.

Motorman for the final run was Hugh P. Ewald, 60, of 1142 Holly Ct., Oak Park, one of the oldest employes with the railway. The company replaced the trolleys Monday with buses.

When West Town Railway runs last trolley, rail fans click shutters to record the event. Buses replace suburban street cars.
SUN-TIMES Photo

Several of the fans in the bottom photo have been identified. At the extreme right is MCERA Richard N. Lukin. MCERA Wendell Dillinger, focusing his bellows camera and wearing a dark suit, is also in the front row. Partially obscured in the back row on the far left, is MCERA Charles E. Able.

Chapter 10: The End of Streetcar Service

With the closing of both the Madison and Lake Street car lines, the surplus streetcars were moved from the Lake Street facility to provide storage space for new buses. Two special movements were made. In February 1947, former Madison Street equipment was transferred to the Suburban barn for scrapping. About a month later, immediately after the closing of the Lake Street car line, the remaining street railway equipment was transferred to the Suburban barn.

Since the West Towns track connection between the carbarns was severed with the abandonment of the Chicago Avenue line, these equipment moves were made using the tracks of the Chicago Surface Lines. For the final equipment move, temporary rails were positioned to connect the tracks of the West Towns with those of the CSL at Lake Street and Austin Boulevard. Once on CSL tracks, the cars were routed on a round-a-bout path (via Lake Street, Pulaski Road, Ogden Avenue and Cermak Road), that necessitated changing direction at several points.

The final equipment move was an event in which the West Towns allowed the train buffs to participate simply for the payment of a fare. Eleven passenger cars and two snow sweepers made this trip early Sunday morning on March 30, 1947. To complicate matters that evening, car 151 derailed and line car 15 was summoned to tow it back onto the track. That night, Bob Gibson arranged to be the last person to pay a fare on a West Towns Lake Street streetcar.

Robert W. Gibson photo/George E. Kanary Collection

Boulevard to a terminal at La Grange Road. Every other bus terminated in Elmhurst.

The remainder of the new buses were delivered on Sunday, March 30, 1947, thus permitting the changeover of the Lake Street line. A celebration was held to commemorate the substitution, and included a large parade featuring the new vehicles. The parade also included civic and business leaders from Oak Park, River Forest, Forest Park, Maywood, Bellwood, Elmhurst, and River Grove. The Oak Park *Oak Leaves* wrote, "The buses took over (from) the street cars with their coal burning stoves and other vestiges of a by-gone era. They will limp off to pasture or whatever fate awaited them after long and honorable careers." It was estimated that between 16,000 and 17,000 passengers took last streetcar rides on the preceding Thursday.

As a bus line, Lake Street service was provided from Austin Boulevard on the east and York Road on the west via Lake Street, North Avenue, Michigan Street, Third Avenue, and York Road back to North Avenue. This routing eliminated the need for passengers to transfer back and forth from streetcar to bus at 25th Avenue. Every other bus was short-turned at 25th Avenue in Melrose Park. However, twenty buses were required to operate the line providing a 7-minute base headway on weekdays and a 12-minute headway on Sundays and holidays. About 4,000 passengers were using the Lake Street bus line daily.

There remained but one streetcar line — the La Grange route — the scenic ride to the zoo. When Lake Street was converted, the West Towns transferred the remaining street railway equipment and some personnel from the Lake Street car barn to the Suburban car barn. West Towns General Manager Bert Collett then told the transferred employees that the streetcars could last for another 15 years, but the line that had been formally opened on July 3, 1897 by the Suburban Railroad would only survive just over a year. The barn on Lake Street was converted into a bus facility.

The war years had been profitable for the West Towns, but after the conflict, the railway's finances resumed their downward trend. In fact, the company could not pay principal and interest on its cumulative income bonds due July 1, 1947. The Harris Trust & Savings Bank of Chicago filed a petition for reorganization in the federal court in Chicago, and on July 1, 1947, Judge Walter J. LaBuy appointed Raymond P. Drymalski and Bert Collett trustees for the company. Shortly thereafter, on November 11, 1947, the La Grange line's principal proponent Bert Collett passed away in Presbyterian Hospital in Oak Park after a short battle with pneumonia.

On February 4, 1948, a petition was filed in both the federal court and with the ICC to substitute buses for streetcars. In the same month, Judge Walter J. LaBuy authorized bankruptcy trustee Raymond P. Drymalski to purchase the necessary buses, with payment partially financed by the $140,000 expected from the salvage of the car line and its equipment.

The ICC gave its approval for the conversion on March 11, 1948. In testimony before the Commission, it was explained that costs for operating the line exceeded the derived revenue. The Commission also believed that the line would need substantial repair. Since a large portion of the line was on private right-of-way, buses could not be put into service on exactly the same route and needed to use existing parallel or nearby streets. Although suggestions had been made to convert some of the right-of-way into a busway, nothing came of this idea. The chosen bus route began at Kenton Avenue and proceeded via Cermak Road, Harlem Avenue, 26th Street, Des Plaines Avenue, 31st Street, First Avenue, Forest Avenue, Washington Avenue, Harding Avenue, and La Grange Road to Burlington Avenue in La Grange. (Forest Avenue, Washington Avenue, and Harding Avenue are the continuation of the same street in the municipalities of Riverside, Brookfield, and La Grange Park, respectively.)

The West Towns awarded a purchase order to Mack Trucks, Inc. for 20 Model C-45 buses in February 1948, based on Mack's promise of almost immediate delivery. Even though the C-45 design could provide seating for 45 passengers, the West Towns selected a version with seating for 38, thereby increasing the "crush" capacity of the vehicle by providing more standing room. The company was in such a hurry to obtain these buses that they flew personnel to the factory at Allentown, Pennsylvania to drive them back.

A parade and civic celebration was held on Monday, April 6, 1948, marking the transition from streetcars to buses in Cicero, Berwyn, Riverside, Brookfield, and La Grange. Eight of the new Mack buses were used to provide local officials and other dignitaries with a free ride on the new bus line, which was followed by the customary special luncheon. At the event, West Towns officials predicted that company's buses would provide the main local transportation to the zoo in spite of the fact that the La Grange bus line followed a less direct route and that Bluebird buses were competing with them at the 31st Street gate.

Motor 12 was the last piece of West Towns equipment to perform any major function on the railway. It was leased to the firm doing the demolition to haul salvaged rail components. Motor 12 was carrying a load of spikes and tie plates near Salt Creek early in Summer 1948. Once the components of the track were removed, the power was turned off and motor 12's career was completed.

Donald N. Idarius photo/George E. Kanary Collection

Chapter 10: The End of Streetcar Service

On May 28, 1942, motor 12 moved a box car from the Parkway interchange to the Suburban barn. The box car, New Haven 69739, carried a load of bagged hard coal used to fuel the heating stoves on the passenger cars.

James J. Buckley photo

The End of an Era

Buses replaced the La Grange streetcars on Sunday, April 11, 1948. As a goodwill gesture, the company permitted a post-abandonment charter sponsored by the Central Electric Railfans' Association. Line Car 15 joined cars 138 and 161 to transport over 100 rail buffs for the last time.

Salvage operations began immediately on the private right-of-way section west of Harlem Avenue. Instead of using a locomotive to pull up the rails, the scrap firm leased West Towns work car 12. When the scrapping of the tracks was completed, power was turned off for the final time on May 28, 1948 so that the overhead could be removed. The scrap firm took almost six weeks to complete the dismantling.

The La Grange line was now just a pleasant memory. Gone were the blue and white trolleys that carried so many to the zoo. Gone were the streetcars with their piercing air whistles that disturbed the peace. Gone were the coal stoves that kept the cars so warm during Chicago winters, yet were criticized so often by the local press. Gone too, was Bert Collett's dream of preserving the La Grange line.

With the wisdom of hindsight, the economic recession that began in 1949 would have most certainly led to the abandonment of the La Grange line. Post-war economics were highly unfavorable to the continued use of streetcars nationwide, and with the massive layoffs at Western Electric and other heavy industries in Cicero, passenger traffic would have sunk to uneconomical levels. In the long term, there was no way the line could have been saved.

Financial Woes

Despite all the negotiations and activity that were necessary to reequip the streetcar lines with buses, there still were major economic problems for the West Towns. During 1948, the company instituted a rash of fare increases designed to bring revenue in line with escalating expenses. First, an 11¢ fare went into effect on Thursday, January 15, 1948, which lasted for 90 days while the ICC considered the company's petition for a permanent fare of 12¢. The penny increase was expected to generate additional $24,000 revenue per month, but the company stated that it was not enough to meet the increased cost of operation. At midnight, July 1, 1948, the West Towns again temporarily increased adult fares another 1¢ while the ICC studied the matter, claiming that it could not meet the current payroll even with the fare increase. On Sunday, October 3, 1948, another temporary increase establishing a 13¢ adult fare, with the West Towns citing a 2¢ per hour wage increase that would take effect on December 1, 1948.

Finally, a few weeks later, the West Towns petitioned for a 15¢ fare, explaining that the funds were needed to initiate a depreciation fund. The company stated that it had been operating at a financial loss, but had been able to make up the difference with funds obtained from the sale of salvaged streetcar rails.

As would be expected, the villages protested the fare increases. Some claimed that all the increases were merely a means of fattening up the company for sale to the Chicago Transit Authority. Then, with the CTA in full control, fares would be further increased. Elected officials, even if they didn't perceive the reality of the situation, knew that their political interests were best served by keeping bus fares low and by bashing the company at every opportunity.

At the public hearings over the 15¢ fare, the West Towns claimed that the increased fare was its only solution, stating that at the present fare level, it could not even meet its weekly payroll. At the same time, however, the railways knew that a large fare increase would be risky, because the ridership loss would also decrease revenue. The ICC ordered a temporary 15¢ adult fare effective April 21, 1949, but also required the company to provide a plan to put the firm back on a sound economic footing.

Transition to Buses

Even though the La Grange streetcar route was now abandoned, the West Towns still had unfinished business to settle with Cicero and Berwyn in order to remove the rail on Cermak Road. The West Towns had purchased Mack buses in anticipation that a July 1, 1948 payment could be made with funds from the salvage operation. The two municipalities, however, were delaying the work, and $30,000 of the amount required to pay Mack was affected by this.

The replacement of trolleys with buses on Cermak Road gave the local officials an opportunity to upgrade the thoroughfare. A parkway was proposed in the center of Cermak Road, and numerous stoplights were also being considered as a means to better control automobile traffic. The municipalities had requested motor fuel tax funds from the State of Illinois for this project, but were refused. Eventually, the state and the municipalities finally agreed on a plan for the parkway that permitted the removal of the final two miles of streetcar track from Cermak Road. The rail, connecting plates, and other hardware were sold to the Sand Springs Railway Company of Oklahoma during July 1948.

In June 1948, the La Grange route buses were rerouted to serve residents of Woodside Road who had lost transit service with the abandonment of the La Grange streetcar line. As a result, a schedule was developed so that buses were operated in both directions on Woodside Road between 31st Street and Park Avenue.

The West Towns now operated 246 buses serving 32 west suburban communities with a population of approximately 450,000. On March 1, 1948, the CTA began negotiations for the purchase of the Chicago Motor Coach Company and four suburban operators, and both the West Towns and Bluebird Coach System supported this idea. The CTA finally did acquire the Chicago Motor Coach Company on October 1, 1952 after on-and-off negotiations lasting almost four years.

Freight Service

Freight operations on the West Towns were quite limited. The company's key steam railroad connection was located near the old Suburban Railroad barn, where it received shipments of the normal supplies needed to operate a street railway, such as rails and ties. In addition, the West Towns operated two powerhouses, both of which burned coal, with one located at the Suburban Railroad barn

After returning the last revenue freight car ever handled by the West Towns to the Illinois Central for pick-up, motor 12 moved back onto the La Grange streetcar line to return to the Suburban barn. Motor 12 needed to wait for westbound car 158 to pass because, due to the configuration of switches, the motor would operate eastbound (north) on the normal westbound track. April 10, 1948.

Donald N. Idarius photo/George E. Kanary Collection

Chapter 10: The End of Streetcar Service

By 1947, significant changes began to appear on transfer forms. The copy was repositioned on the form. Also, the morning or afternoon designation was specified by a punch rather than a tear off coupon. The date of issue was identified by a one or two letter code rather than an overprinted numeral. Transfers were printed on yellow, salmon, or purple paper stock with black ink.

With three streetcar lines operating in early 1947, this was one of the last streetcar only transfer forms that was used.

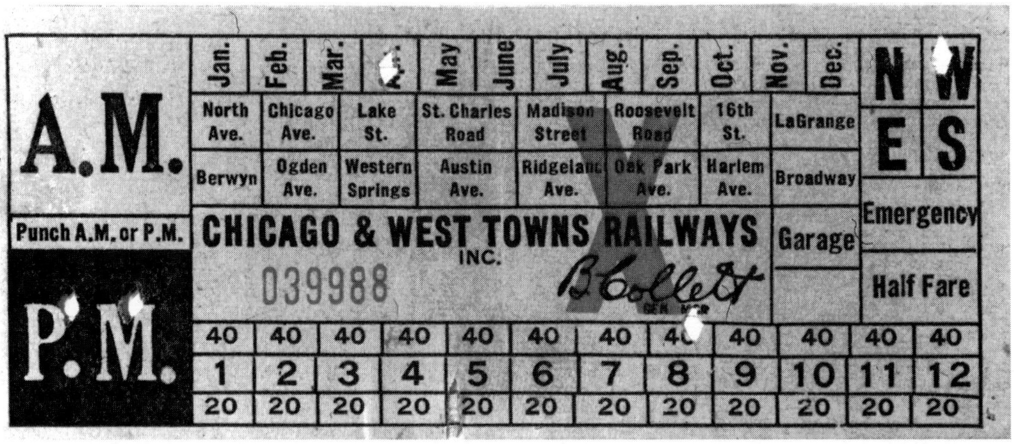

In 1947, the same basic form was used for both buses and streetcars, but was overprinted for bus service. When the final trolley route was converted to bus in 1948, identifying the transfer as one originating on a bus line was unnecessary.

Another form was for half fare on the La Grange Line. This document was printed on yellow paper stock with black ink.

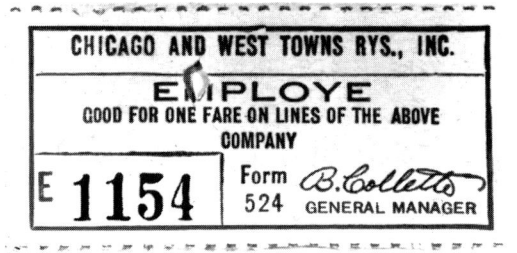

The company also issued a coupon for employees to use as fare when riding on company streetcars and buses. This one was printed on yellow paper stock with red ink.

at Cermak Road and Harlem Avenue and the other at the Oak Park barn at Lake Street and Harvey Avenue.

Information about how freight was handled at the Oak Park car barn is not known. Before the Chicago & North Western Railway elevated its tracks through Oak Park in the mid-1910's, one might expect that a siding or team track existed which the West Towns used. However, this

All: Richard R. Andrews Collection

was not the case, as coal was supplied by rail via the Chicago Railways from its Lake Street Coal Yard. At the time that County Traction was formed, track connections between the city and suburban systems were severed and this necessitated trucking the coal to the plant from Chicago. After the Chicago & North Western's tracks were elevated, it is possible that the West Towns used an elevated freight spur into the adjacent Borden dairy and W. G. Davis Coal Company, to the west of the car barn complex, for coal delivery. After the power plant stopped generating electricity, the boilers producing steam for heating continued to use coal, but it is unknown how this coal was received.

Behind the Oak Park barn on North Boulevard, the company had a short spur track to store ash cars. Ash Cars X-1, X-2 and X-3 were a familiar sight here during the winter months and Utility Car 12, the "maid-of-all-work," would shuttle the cinder cars back and forth between the two car barns. The West Towns was not known to waste material and it used the cinders for ballast on the La Grange line.

Parkway

The major freight connection for the West Towns was located due south at a place known as Parkway, where the La Grange carline crossed the Illinois Central near 26th Street. The IC had a station there for its fairly modest west suburban service until 1931. The freight connection was about five city blocks away from the car barn and Utility Car 12 was used to haul freight cars between the interchange and the barn.

Coal used to generate electricity at the Suburban powerhouse was received at Parkway, which was also used to fuel the heating stoves on the streetcars. The hard coal was delivered to the West Towns by boxcar, while a shipment of new rail or ties would be received on flat cars. Whenever the company sold used rail, it would be reloaded on these flat cars and brought to the Parkway interchange. Also, during scrapping operations, gondolas destined for the steel mills left the property via the Parkway interchange.

The railway's only public freight customer, Oechslin Florist Company, was located on the northwest side of the Suburban car house property and its siding was connected to the car barn's trackage. The greenhouse was heated by oil delivered in railroad tank cars and the florist occasionally received shipments of flowers delivered in refrigerator cars.

To house system maps, the West Towns printed a heavy paper stock cover to protect a paper map. The map appeared on one side of the insert while a list of locations served by the company was printed on the reverse.

Krambles-Peterson Archive

Chapter 10: The End of Streetcar Service   *119*

SECTION 3

Streetcar Lines of the Chicago & West Towns

11 Berwyn-Lyons

The six-mile Berwyn-Lyons streetcar line, which ran over nine different streets to reach the Village of Lyons, was built by the Ogden Street Railway and operated by the West Chicago Street Railroad and its successor, Chicago Consolidated Traction. The original eastern terminal of the route was at Madison Street and Springfield Avenue until July 2, 1897, when a second eastern terminal was opened at Pulaski Road and Ogden Avenue. The line, which was utilized until 1910, traversed Ogden Avenue until Cicero Avenue, turned north to 25th Street, and then followed the more familiar routing on 25th Street, Central Avenue, 26th Street, Ridgeland Avenue, Stanley Avenue, Harlem Avenue, and Ogden Avenue to a terminal at Lawndale and Ogden in Lyons.

When County Traction took over the service, all operations within Chicago became the responsibility of the Chicago Railways Company. The Berwyn-Lyons route was modified so that the eastern terminal of the line became 46th Avenue and Cermak Road and operated via Cermak Road and Laramie Avenue to reach 25th Street.

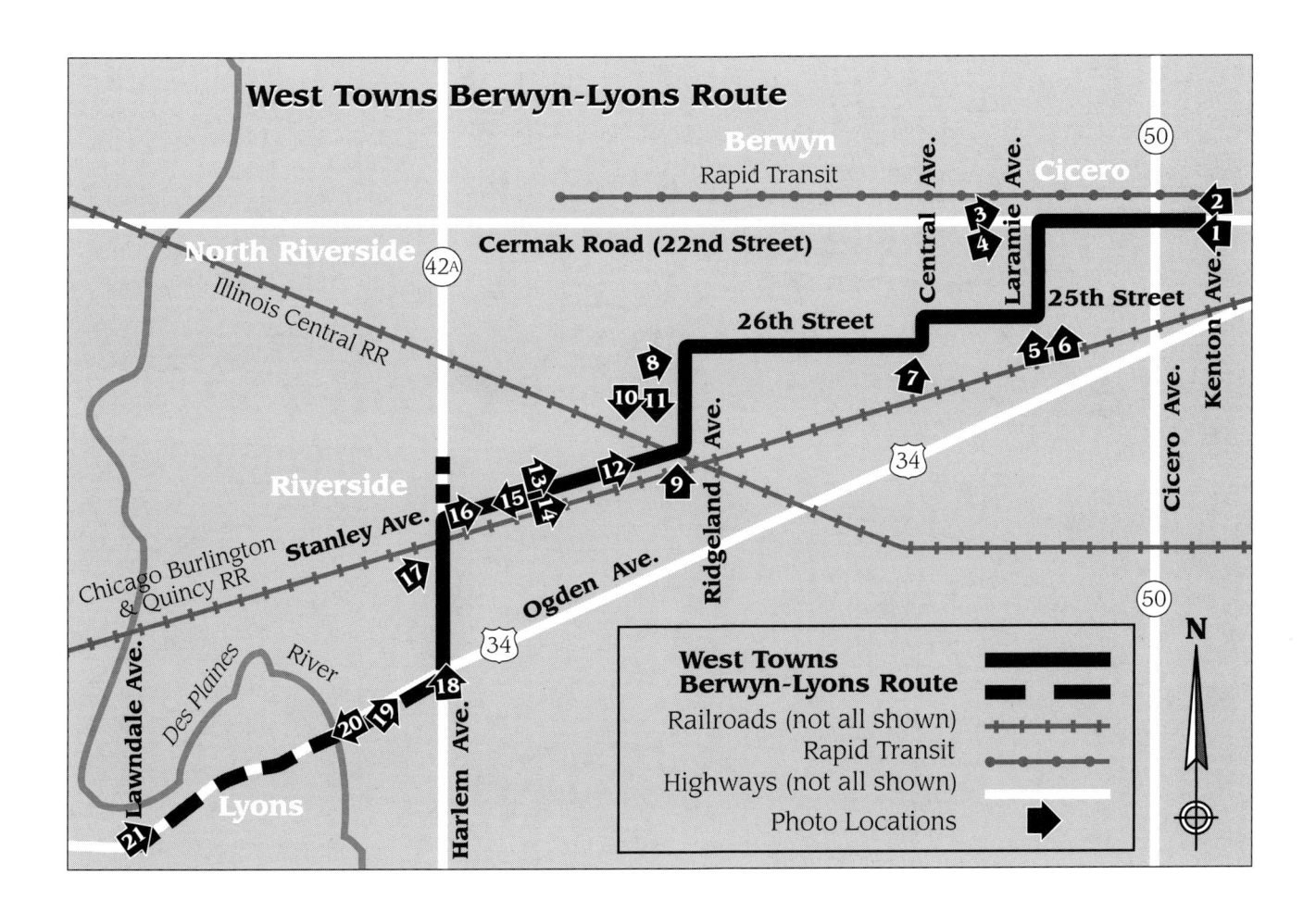

Left: Although this photo may suggest that the classic race between a trolley car and train on an adjacent steam railroad was in progress, this was not the case. On April 11, 1948, La Grange bound line car 15 had stopped for photos on a railfan charter commemorating the abandonment of the streetcar line. After the line car had crossed the Indiana Harbor Belt in La Grange Park, near the intersection of Lincoln and Beach Avenues, the steam hauled transfer run resumed its southward journey.
Joe L. Diaz photo

Chapter 11: Berwyn-Lyons 121

1 *Cermak Road and Kenton Avenue was the eastern terminal for both the La Grange and Berwyn-Lyons lines. At this intersection, passengers could board Chicago Surface Lines' Cermak Road cars or, by getting off at the Cicero Avenue stop, interchange with the Douglas Park line of the Chicago Rapid Transit Company and the Chicago Surface Lines Cicero Avenue streetcars. In the left of the photograph was a major passenger generator, the Hawthorne Works of the Western Electric Company. During World War II, this facility employed about 50,000 people, most of whom used public transportation to reach work. This site had 2-1/2 million square feet of floor space. At this major point on the West Towns, there never was a shortage of streetcars arriving, leaving, or waiting.*

Joe L. Diaz photo

2 *As communication technologies advanced, the older facilities at the Hawthorne Works were no longer cost competitive. By July 1985, the works employed about 1,000 people and it was obvious that the facility would close. The works was purchased by a real estate developer on June 23, 1986. Wrecking and construction of a shopping center began immediately and the first phase of the shopping center opened on July 4, 1988.*

With the closing of Hawthorne Works, public transportation was reorganized with most east-west bus routes terminating further west at the off street terminal of the CTA's Cermak Blue Line "L" at Laramie Avenue. In this photograph taken on March 12, 2004, bus 6024 was operating eastbound on the Cicero-Berwyn line at Cermak Road and Kenton to provide hourly Pace service to this intersection. Where once stood an industrial giant, now fast food restaurants stand. The major stores in the shopping center are out of view to the left.

Richard W. Aaron photo

3 Car 112 is westbound on Cermak Road at Laramie Avenue on June 29, 1941. This intersection was a major junction on the West Towns. Car 112, in service on the Berwyn-Lyons route, will turn off Cermak to proceed southward on Laramie. La Grange line cars ran through this intersection on Cermak while Chicago Avenue cars operated north and south on Laramie.

Donald N. Idarius photo

4 Sixty-four years later, on February 26, 2004, Pace bus 6066 was traveling westward on Cermak Road at Laramie Avenue. The bus was operating on Route 302, Ogden/Stanley, and was preparing to turn southward, just as the streetcars before it had done. In the background, the building on the northeast corner of the intersection in the 1941 view no longer stands. However, the second and third buildings from the corner were still in use in 2004. The large empty lot east of the three-story building was occupied in 2004 by an automobile dealership.

Richard W. Aaron photo

Chapter 11: Berwyn-Lyons

123

5 *The intersection of Laramie Avenue and 25th Street was an important transit location. On September 1, 1941, cars 111 and 112 passed on Laramie there. Chicago Avenue route cars, and later buses, operated on Laramie between Roosevelt Road and 35th Street. The tracks shown in the foreground, south on Laramie, were used for this purpose. In earlier days, Cicero-Berwyn cars crossed this intersection on 25th Street to reach a secondary terminal at Pulaski Road and Ogden Avenue. At the time of this photo, the Chicago Surface Lines' Ogden Avenue route terminated at Laramie on 25th Street.*

Robert W. Gibson photo

6 *By 2004, the intersection of Laramie Avenue and 25th Street was no longer as commercially important as it was in 1941. One of the reasons for this was the closure of the Hawthorne Works of the Western Electric Company and the subsequent redevelopment of this site for shopping. Pace bus 6071 was preparing to turn westward onto 25th Street on February 26, 2004. The former bank building now housed a dry goods store and a currency exchange. The United States Post Office to the north of the former bank building was virtually unchanged from its 1941 appearance.*

Richard W. Aaron photo

124   *The Chicago & West Towns Railways*

7 *Once leaving Laramie Avenue, Berwyn-Lyons cars would snake their way through Cicero and Berwyn on a series of streets. Car 108 was southbound on Central Avenue and was preparing to turn westward onto 26th Street. July 21, 1941.*
James J. Buckley photo

8 *A little later on the same day, July 21, 1941, car 108 was photographed again about a mile further west on 26th Street at Ridgeland Avenue.*
James J. Buckley photo

9 *Car 111 was operating southbound on Ridgeland Avenue through a sparsely inhabited section of Berwyn. On September 1, 1941, the photographer was standing on the Illinois Central Railroad viaduct which crossed over the street slightly north of Stanley Avenue.*
Robert W. Gibson photo

Chapter 11: Berwyn-Lyons   125

10 *The intersection of Stanley and Ridgeland Avenues provided great contrasts over the years. About 1940, a West Towns car trundled southwest on Stanley from Ridgeland with the Lavergne station of the Chicago, Burlington & Quincy Railroad in the background. Please refer to page 45 for a 1910 view of this location.*
Joe L. Diaz photo

11 *In February 2004, Pace bus 6057 was operating westward on Stanley.*
Richard W. Aaron photo

The Chicago & West Towns Railways

12 *In 1941, car 107 had rounded the curve off Ridgeland with the overpass of the Illinois Central Railroad in the background.*
John F. Humiston photo

13 *Photographer John Humiston grew up in Berwyn, not far from the Harlem Avenue station on the Burlington. On Sunday, November 16, 1941, he walked several blocks east to the intersection of Grove and Stanley Avenues and composed this photograph of westbound car 108 in a magnificent pre-World War II Berwyn streetscape.*
John F. Humiston photo

14 *A little more than 60 years later, in December 2003, Pace bus 2207 stopped at Grove and Stanley Avenues to discharge a passenger. Most of the block between Grove and Oak Park Avenue had been redeveloped and a branch office of a downtown bank now occupied the site. The building on the northwest corner of Oak Park and Stanley, containing a restaurant on the ground floor, was all that remained from the 1941 view.*
Richard W. Aaron photo

Chapter 11: Berwyn-Lyons

15 *Snow sweeper number 9 was eastbound on Stanley Avenue on February 19, 1938, having crossed the tracks of the Chicago, Burlington & Quincy Railroad. The signal is in the "up" position indicating that a westbound car should stop. When the sweeper rejoined the double track railway a few feet ahead, the signal would revert to the "down" position providing the Burlington tracks were clear.*

John F. Humiston photo

16 *The agreement made in 1896, under which the Ogden Street Railroad crossed the Chicago, Burlington & Quincy Railroad at Harlem and Stanley Avenues, stayed unchanged throughout the life of the streetcar line. The agreement called for a single track crossing of the main line railroad protected with full interlocking signals. When a streetcar crossed the Burlington, signals on the railroad would turn "red" and, vice-versa, when a Burlington train approached the intersection, the signals on the street railway would turn "red." The Burlington towerman not only controlled the crossing gates at this location, but also was responsible for streetcar operation. With the single track, it was necessary to protect a streetcar traveling in one direction from a streetcar coming from the other direction. The towerman would manually set the signal allowing the streetcar to proceed. Car 107 approached Harlem and Stanley on July 27, 1941. The signal on the pole to the right of the streetcar is "down" indicating the track is clear for the trolley to cross the Burlington.*

John F. Humiston photo

128   *The Chicago & West Towns Railways*

17 On January 31, 1939, a winter storm had interrupted service on the Berwyn-Lyons route. Car 127 was stranded in a snow drift at Harlem and Windsor Avenues, at the south switch of the single track crossing of the Burlington.

John F. Humiston photo

18 Harlem and Ogden Avenues was the terminal of the Berwyn-Lyons streetcar route after the line was shortened. In 1941, Car 112 was waiting for its scheduled time to begin a northbound trip. Back then, one could have purchased a tank of ethyl gasoline for his or her car for a mere 16¢ per gallon.

Donald N. Idarius photo

19 Between Harlem Avenue and the Des Plaines River, the Berwyn-Lyons streetcar line was built on private right-of-way on the south side of Ogden Avenue. It was abandoned on October 26, 1933 because the land was wanted to widen Ogden Avenue. The railway here was single track with two passing sidings. Car 133 was photographed on the passing siding near the Des Plaines River in October 1933, a few days before abandonment.

Ed Frank, Jr. photo

Chapter 11: Berwyn-Lyons

20 *Circa 1925, the single track wooden trestle, adjacent to Ogden Avenue, permitted an eastbound double truck car to cross the Des Plaines River. West of the river in Lyons, the railway was double tracked and built in Ogden Avenue.*

Fred Borchert photo

21 *In the days when this trackage was operated by Chicago Consolidated Traction, a trolley approached the Lyons terminal of the route at Lawndale Avenue. The terminal was about a mile west of the river.*
Roy G. Benedict Collection

130 *The Chicago & West Towns Railways*

12 Chicago Avenue

From the exclusive residential sections of Oak Park to the factories of Cicero, the Chicago Avenue streetcar line served many types of passengers as it twisted and turned over 10-3/4 miles of streets in the western suburbs. The route was a combination of three former Chicago Consolidated Traction lines - Chicago Avenue, Twelfth Street, Pulaski Road and one Suburban Railroad line - Laramie Avenue.

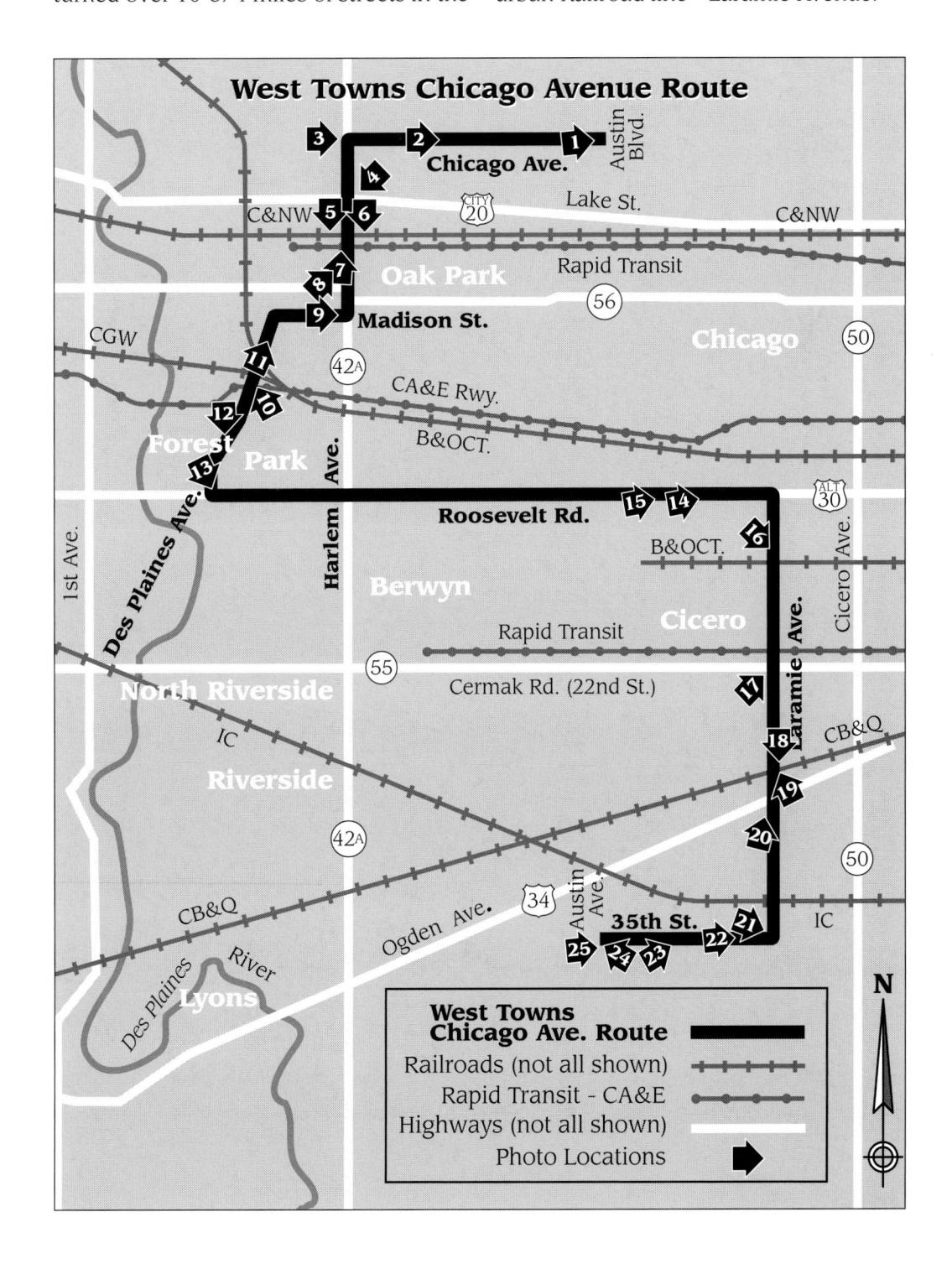

Chapter 12: Chicago Avenue

131

1 *At the Chicago Avenue and Austin Boulevard terminal of the Chicago Avenue line, West Towns car 102 waited for its departure on April 20, 1940. Chicago Surface Lines car 1964, nicknamed a "flexible flyer," waited for its eastbound departure.*

Donald N. Idarius photo

2 *West Towns car 114 journeyed westward on Chicago Avenue at Euclid Avenue on April 14, 1940. On this section of track, the railway erected wooden poles to support its trolley wire. The architecturally pleasing street lights were installed well after the railway was built.*

John F. Humiston photo

132   The Chicago & West Towns Railways

3 Car 132 was westbound on Chicago Avenue at Harlem Avenue in 1940. The car would turn south for its trip down Harlem to Madison Street.

Ed Frank, Jr. photo

4 Resplendent in its yellow-orange with bright red striping livery, car 103 crossed Lake Street while traveling north on Harlem Avenue. Wiebolts, on the southwest corner, and Marshall Field & Company, on the northeast corner of the intersection anchored what was then the largest retail shopping center in the western suburbs. July 6, 1940.
Fielding Kunecke photo/George E. Kanary Collection

Chapter 12: Chicago Avenue 133

5 *After the abandonment of the Chicago Avenue line, the track segment on Harlem Avenue between Lake and Madison Streets was retained to link the Madison Street route with the Lake Street carbarn. On February 15, 1947, car 132 traveled southbound to enter service on the Madison Street line. The photographer's vantage point was Oak Park station platform of the Chicago & North Western Railway.*
Donald N. Idarius photo

6 *In the late 1990s, a northbound Pace bus, manufactured by Orion, stopped at South Boulevard and Harlem Avenue to discharge and pick up passengers. In the 50 years between these two photos, the streetcar wires have been removed and the street has been resurfaced. A few of the buildings shown in the 1947 photograph still stand.*
Melvin A. Bernero photo

134 *The Chicago & West Towns Railways*

7 *The street scene just below the photographer's location in the previous photographs is just as interesting. Car 101 was operating southbound under the Chicago & North Western Railway and was crossing the Lake Street"L". The nearest "L" station was a short walk east at Marion Street. When the "L" tracks were moved to the North Western's embankment in 1962, the rapid transit station was relocated to Harlem.*
Robert W. Gibson photo/George E. Kanary Collection

8 *Car 135 was photographed on Harlem Avenue at Randolph Street on November 12, 1946. The car was one of many daily equipment moves from the Lake Street barn to the Madison Street line.*
James J. Buckley photo

Chapter 12: Chicago Avenue

9 Car 134 turned off Harlem Avenue to proceed west on Madison Street. The equipment move made the turn which was also made by cars on the Chicago Avenue route. The Chicago Avenue line traversed Madison Street between Harlem and Des Plaines Avenues, a distance a little less than a half mile.
Robert W. Gibson photo

10 This Chicago Avenue run was being filled by car 102. It was operating southbound on Des Plaines Avenue and was crossing the tracks owned by the Chicago, Aurora & Elgin Railway. The trains of the Chicago Rapid Transit Company also shared these tracks. To the left of the streetcar was a tower controlling the Des Plaines Avenue yard and crossing gates. The Soo's Forest Park station appeared behind the tower. July 4, 1940.
Fielding Kunecke photo/George E. Kanary Collection

11 An "owl-eyed" West Towns bus posed at the viaduct which carries the Congress branch of Chicago Transit Authority's Blue Line over Des Plaines Avenue. Bus 717, built by General Motors Coach, was one of 20 identical units added to the West Towns' fleet in 1949. The photo was taken on March 3, 1962.
Michael M. McGowan photo/
David S. Stanley Collection

12 In August 1937, car 119 was operating northbound at the triple intersection of Des Plaines Avenue, Harrison Street and Dunlop Street. Since the time this photograph was taken, Des Plaines Avenue has been widened and the beautiful Victorian building has been demolished. The location of the photograph is slightly south of the Eisenhower Expressway.

Ed Frank, Jr. photo

13 During June 1940, car 130 had just turned off Roosevelt Road and was northbound on Des Plaines Avenue. The Chicago Avenue streetcar line was routed on Des Plaines between Roosevelt Road and Madison Street, a distance of a little more than a mile.

Fielding Kunecke photo/
George E. Kanary
Collection

Chapter 12: Chicago Avenue

14 *Car 112 operated westbound on Roosevelt Road at Central Avenue in this 1940 photo. The land to the north of the streetcar would later be developed for industrial and warehouse uses. The photo also shows an early version of what is now known as Knute Rockne Stadium, a high school football field named after the legendary coach of the University of Notre Dame.*
William H. Baier photo

15 *One of the more unusual features of the Chicago Avenue route was the joint operation of West Towns and Chicago streetcars on Roosevelt Road. Eastbound West Towns car 128 passed Chicago Surface Lines "Big Pullman" 254 at Mayfield Avenue in 1940. The joint operation was created because the companies had operating territories defined by geography. Where the joint operation occurred, on Roosevelt Road between Laramie and Austin Avenues, was a boundary between Chicago and Cicero.*
William H. Baier photo

138   *The Chicago & West Towns Railways*

16 Car 108 was running northbound on Laramie Avenue at 15th Street in June 1940. Behind the car, at 16th Street, was the grade crossing with the Baltimore & Ohio Chicago Terminal Railroad, successor to the Chicago & Southwestern Railroad.

Fielding Kunecke photo/
George E. Kanary Collection

17 The corner of Cermak Road and Laramie Avenue was a busy rail junction. Car 108, in service on the Chicago Avenue line, was operating southbound through the intersection. On Cermak, La Grange line car 158 waited for its turn to proceed through the junction. Circa 1940.

James J. Buckley photo/Robert H. Hansen Collection

18 The west track of the Laramie Avenue bridge over the Chicago, Burlington & Quincy Railroad required maintenance during early 1936. To accomplish this, the track was taken out of service and cars used the east track to traverse the bridge in both directions. To change tracks, car 102 was preparing to negotiate a temporary crossover at the north end of the bridge.

Ed Frank, Jr. photo

Chapter 12: Chicago Avenue

19 *The Laramie Avenue bridge over Clyde Yard of the Chicago, Burlington & Quincy Railroad was quite narrow. The roadway was wide enough for two streetcars to pass, but not much more. Car 108, freshly repainted in the blue and white livery, crossed the bridge southbound in 1940.*
Ed Frank, Jr. photo/Joe L. Diaz Collection

20 *In a society dependant on the automobile for personal transportation, the narrow bridge over Clyde Yard and Ogden Avenue was not acceptable. Pace bus 6052 was southbound across the new four-lane viaduct, at Laramie Avenue and 31st Street, on March 12, 2004. The viaduct, known as the Cicero Centennial Bridge, was dedicated and opened for traffic on October 3, 1956. It was also extensively renovated in 1999.*
Richard W. Aaron photo

21 *Another freshly painted car, number 128 turned west onto 35th Street from Laramie Avenue on July 4, 1940. The West Towns operated Hawthorne Race Track specials from Cermak Road and Kenton Avenue to this point. After the cars unloaded their passengers, they continued southward on Laramie to be stored for their return trip. The storage tracks ran as far south as 36th Street.*

Fielding Kunecke photo/
George E. Kanary Collection

22 *Pace operates Route 305, Cicero-River Forest as a replacement for the Chicago Avenue streetcar line. On February 27, 2004, bus 6068 had turned off Laramie Avenue and was proceeding westward on 35th Street. In the background, to the left is the grandstand and track of the Chicago Motor Speedway while south of 35th Street is Sportsman's Park. A second horse track, the Hawthorne Race Track is south of Sportsman's.*

Richard W. Aaron photo

Chapter 12: Chicago Avenue

23 In 1940, 35th Street had been paved, but most of the adjacent land had not been developed. Car 134 was traveling westward on 35th Street, not far from its terminal at Austin Avenue.

William H. Baier photo

24 On September 10, 1935, Don Idarius found car 133 at the south terminal of the Chicago Avenue line at 35th Street and Austin Avenue. The car was waiting its scheduled time to begin the return trip north. At this time, 35th Street was unpaved and uncurbed behind the streetcar.

Donald N. Idarius photo

25 By the middle 1950s, the land adjacent to 35th Street, between Laramie and Austin Avenues, had been developed with low rise commercial buildings. Pace bus 2243, operating westward on 35th Street on February 27, 2004, had reached the end of the former streetcar line at Austin Avenue. The bus would turn southward on Austin and then eastward on 39th Street to reach a terminal at 39th Street and Central Avenue on the grounds of Morton College.

Richard W. Aaron photo

13 Lake Street

The Lake Street line carried the highest passenger loads of any of the West Towns' routes. Its geometry was also the simplest — the line ran on Lake Street beginning at Austin Boulevard and ending at 25th Avenue. Covering 4-1/2 miles, this line traversed the major business street in Oak Park, River Forest, Maywood, and Melrose Park. Since the shopping district centered at Lake Street and Harlem Avenue was, up to the time of the opening of the Oak Brook Center, the busiest in all of suburban Chicagoland, the line provided the means for many residents to reach the prominent stores. Further west, the line carried workers to their jobs in the factories of Melrose Park.

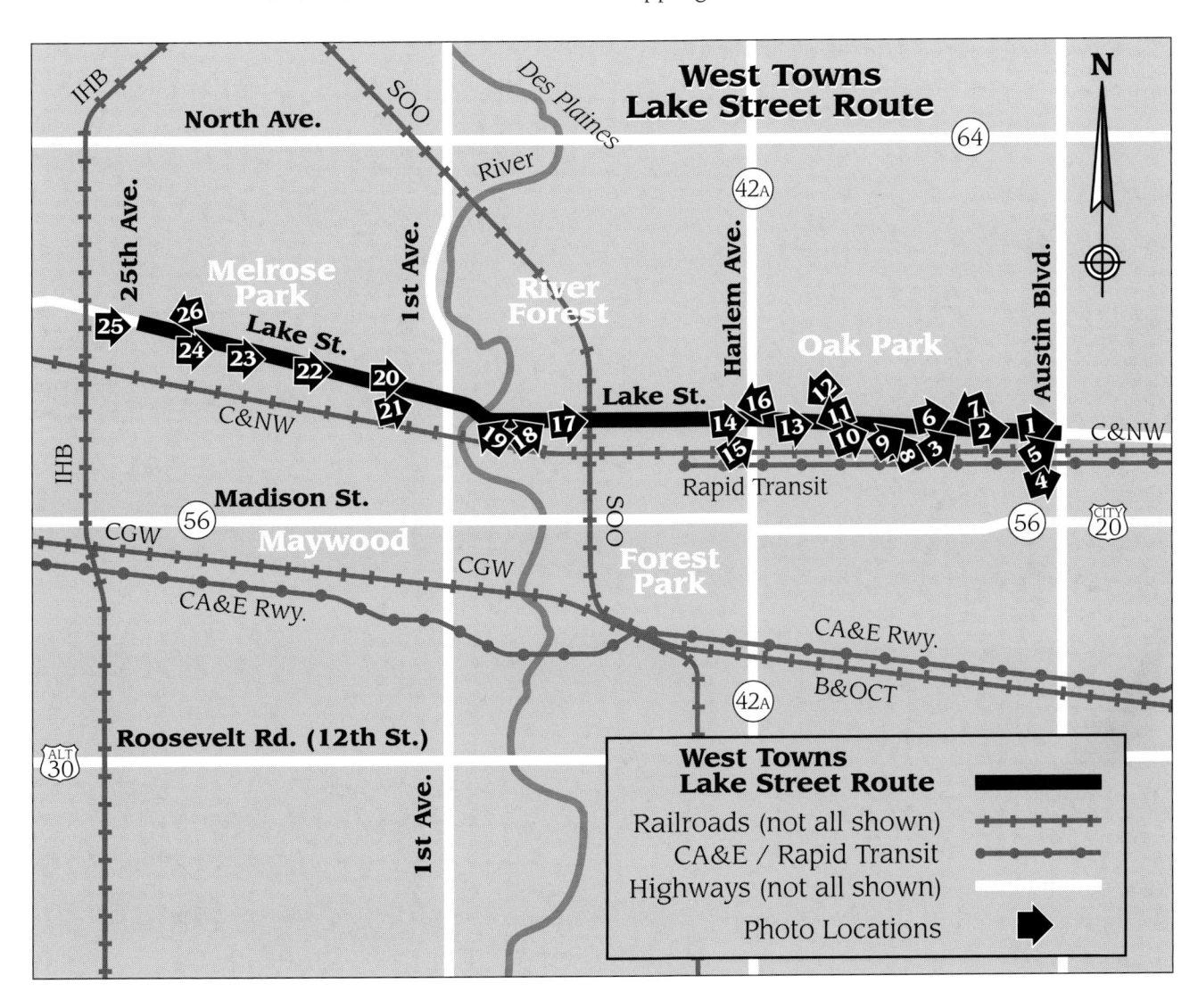

Chapter 13: Lake Street   143

1 *The eastern terminal of the West Towns' Lake Street line was at Austin Boulevard, the city limit. This intersection also was the western terminal of the Chicago Surface Lines' Lake Street route. In this view looking east, car 144 was waiting for its scheduled time to begin its westward trip. Chicago Surface Lines car 1588 was in the background. Circa 1946.*
Robert W. Gibson photo

2 *During 1946, Lake Street route car 132 had just begun its journey through Oak Park, River Forest, Maywood, and Melrose Park, when it passed Humphrey Street in Oak Park.*
George E. Kanary Collection

3 *Sweeper 18 had been clearing the streets of snow and had returned to its home at the Lake Street carbarn. The sweeper was photographed near Harvey Street on Lake in 1947.*
William H. Baier photo

The Chicago & West Towns Railways

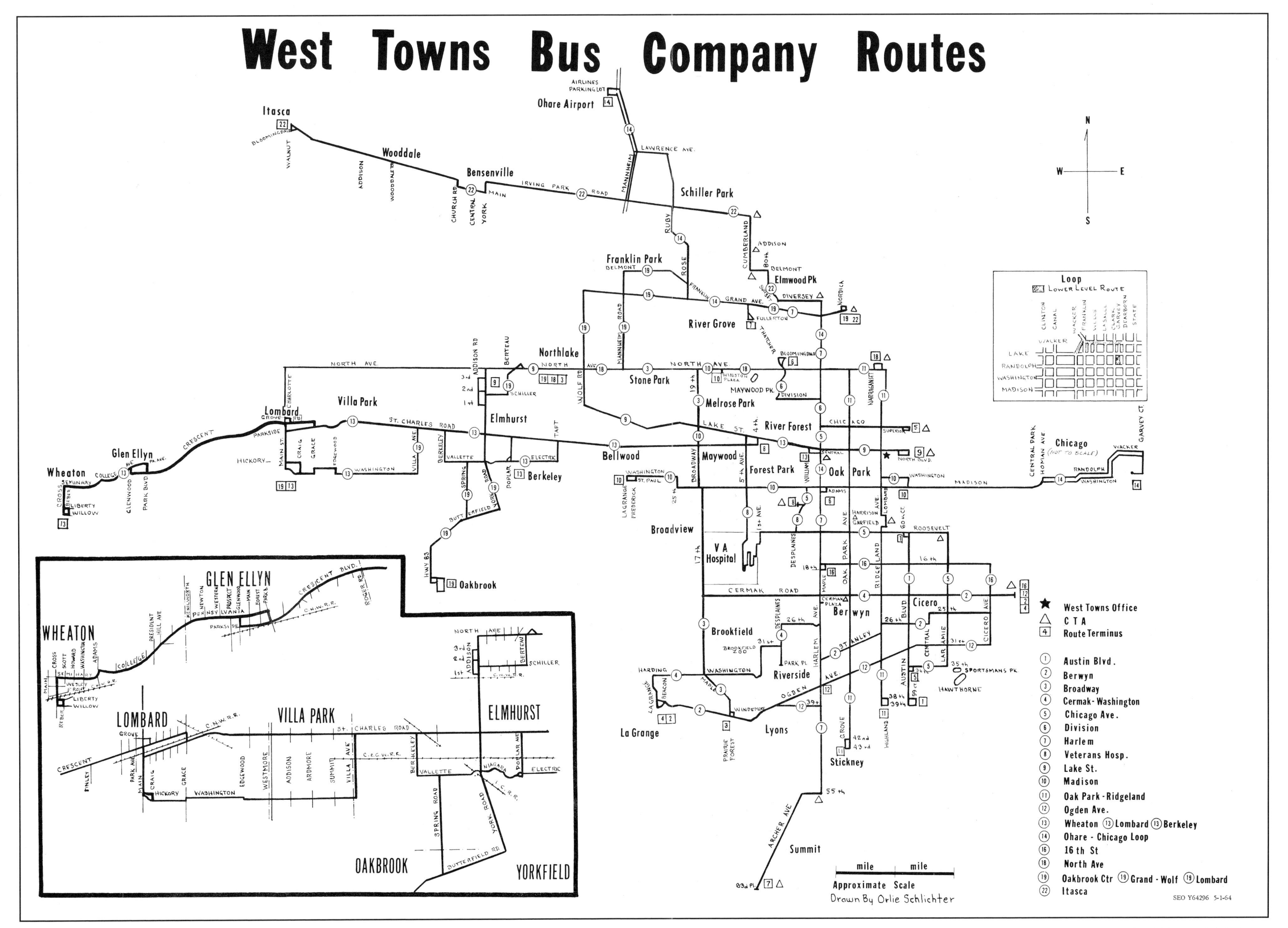

West Towns Bus Company Routes

144B

The Chicago & West Towns Railways

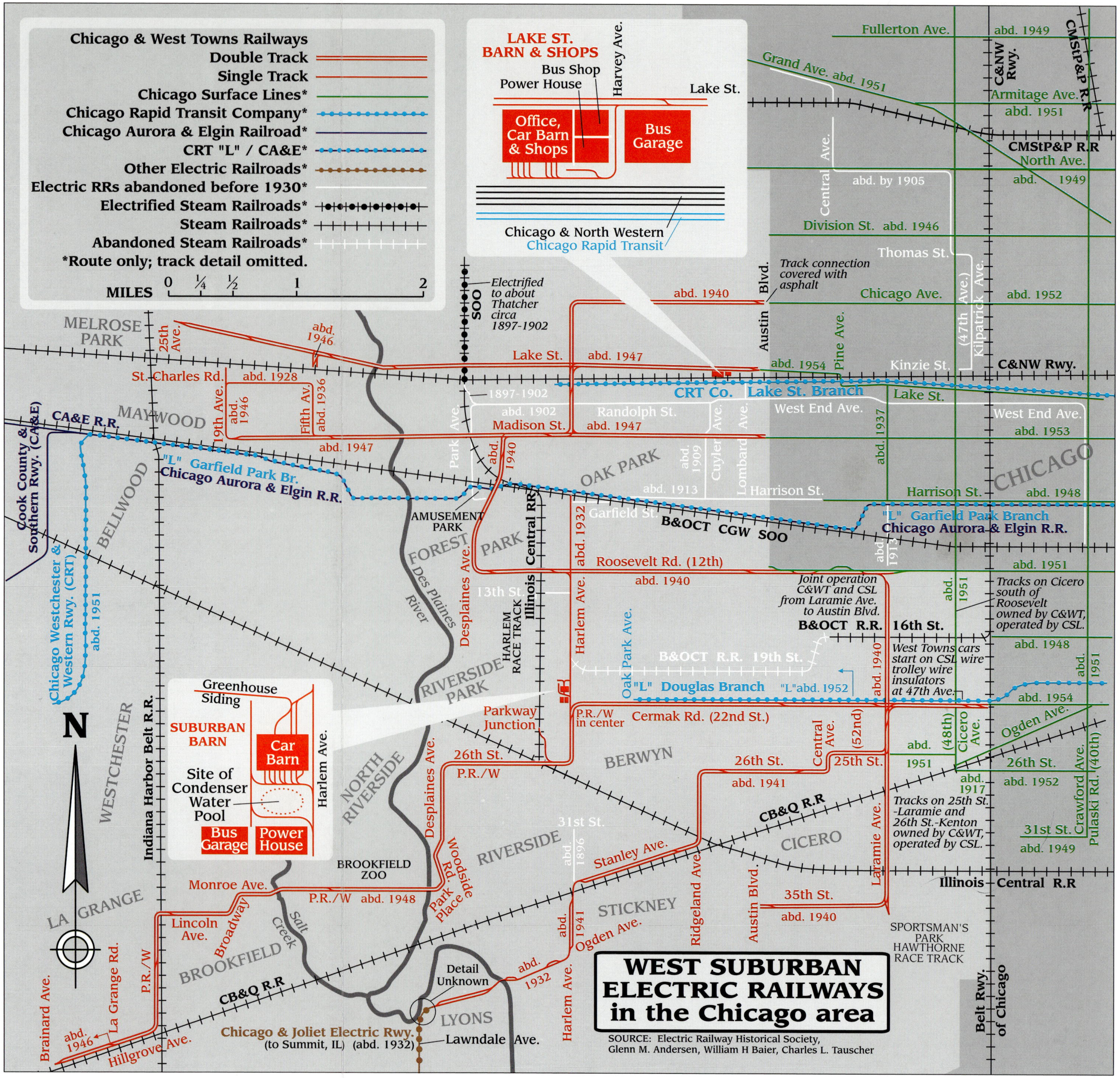

Chapter 13: Lake Street

144A

4 *By 2004, the terminal arrangements at Lake Street and Austin Boulevard had totally changed. The Chicago Transit Authority had stopped operating surface transportation on Lake Street so that transfer between the city and suburban bus operators was not needed. To serve the Lake Street "L" and to provide a loop for its buses, Pace rerouted its Lake Street buses via Mayfield Avenue, South Boulevard, and Humphrey Street. Pace bus 6055 had stopped for passengers at the "L" station and was crossing Austin Boulevard on September 12, 2004.*
Richard W. Aaron photo

5 *In its yellow livery, Chicago & West Towns car 142 waited at Lake Street and Austin Boulevard for its westbound departure. Circa 1938.*
Black and white photo hand colored by Verne Langdon/George E. Kanary Collection

6 *On a cold winter's day, Chicago & West Towns car 145 was operating eastbound on Lake Street at Cuyler Avenue. The Lake Street carbarn is behind the streetcar. February 15, 1947.*
Donald N. Idarius photo

Chapter 13: Lake Street

7 *The carbarn stood on the south side of Lake Street between Cuyler Avenue and Harvey Street. After the barn was sold, the property was redeveloped for use as a food store. Pace bus 6067 was eastbound on Lake at Harvey on April 25, 2003.*

Richard W. Aaron photo

8 *On February 16, 1947, the highest numbered sweepers in the fleet, sweepers 18 and 19 had returned to the Lake Street barn after completing their duties. The sweepers were painted in yellow with maroon window trim. In a little more than a month, buses would be substituted for streetcars on Lake Street and the carbarn would become a bus garage.*

Thomas H. Desnoyers photo/
Krambles-Peterson Archive

9 *Only a block west of the carbarn, the streetscape was totally different. West Towns car 164 stopped at Lake Street and Ridgeland Avenue on its trip west. The photograph was composed on March 29, 1947, the last full day of streetcar operation on Lake Street.*

Thomas H. Desnoyers photo/Krambles-Peterson Archive

10 Car 165 was westbound on Lake Street at Grove Avenue as it passed the First United Church of Oak Park. Although the magnificent church is still in use, the impressive building east of it was demolished in November 1962. This structure, known as the Scoville Institute, served for 75 years as the first Oak Park Public Library. Circa 1945.

Gordon E. Lloyd photo

11 A West Towns Bus Company bus 879, a GMC model TDH-4519 coach, purchased in 1965 with funding from the Illinois Regional Transportation Authority, traveled eastward on Lake Street at Grove Avenue. Circa 1970. The "second" Oak Park Public Library, as shown in the background of the photo, opened on May 31, 1964. This library, in turn was closed for demolition in November 2001 to permit construction of the "third" Oak Park Public Library to occupy this site.

Bruce G. Moffat Collection

Chapter 13: Lake Street

12 On September 12, 2004, Pace bus 6239 was eastbound on Lake Street at Grove Avenue. The "third" new Oak Park Public Library, as shown in the background of this photograph, opened on October 5, 2003.

Richard W. Aaron photo

13 Lake Street and Harlem Avenue in Oak Park was the major shopping area in Chicago's western suburbs. A streetcar plied westward near Marion in the early 1940s.
George E. Kanary Collection

148   *The Chicago & West Towns Railways*

14 *Car 142 was westbound on Lake Street at Harlem Avenue on March 15, 1946 when it stopped to pick up and discharge passengers. All three major merchants shown in this photo, Marshall Field & Company, Richman's and The Fair have either moved to other locations or gone out of business. The switches in the southeast quadrant of the intersection permitted cars on Harlem Avenue to reach the Lake Street carbarn.*
Robert W. Gibson photo

15 *Almost sixty years later, on September 12, 2004, Pace bus 6065 stopped for a traffic signal on Lake Street at Harlem Avenue. The former Marshall Field & Company store had been redeveloped with offices and shopping. The bus stop had been relocated to the northwest corner of the intersection.*
Richard W. Aaron photo

Chapter 13: Lake Street

16 *Snow sweeper 17 was eastbound on Lake Street, slightly west of Harlem Avenue on February 1, 1947. The side wing on the sweeper's right side had been extended to better clear the street.*
Robert W. Gibson photo

17 *In the last summer of operation of the Lake Street carline, car 151 was westbound at the Soo Line overpass. The Soo's tracks were elevated to cross both Lake Street and the Chicago & North Western Railway.*
James J. Buckley photo/
George E. Kanary Collection

18 *On September 9, 1946, West Towns streetcar 164 was operating westbound on Lake Street in River Forest as it approached Thatcher Avenue. The building in the background housed the River Forest United Methodist Church, a congregation formed by the merger of five churches over the last century and a half.*
Robert W. Gibson photo/
George E. Kanary Collection

20 *With the abandonment of streetcar operation on Lake Street approaching, many train buffs were recording their farewell photographs. Car 145 was westbound on Lake Street at Fifth Avenue on March 29, 1947. At this date, trackage to the right was out of service. Originally, all Lake Street cars turned south at this intersection to reach a terminal at the Chicago & North Western tracks. After the Lake Street car line was extended to 25th Avenue on November 29, 1930, tracks on Fifth Avenue were modified to permit short turns. The outbound and inbound tracks on Fifth Avenue merged as shown in the right of this photograph.*

Robert W. Gibson photo/George E. Kanary Collection

21 *On September 12, 2004, Pace bus 6218 was operating westbound on Lake Street at Fifth Avenue. The building behind the bus is the same building that stood behind streetcar 145 in the previous photo.*

Richard W. Aaron photo

Chapter 13: Lake Street

19 *On a cold Sunday, February 9, 1947, about two months before buses replaced streetcars, car 136 crossed the Des Plaines River on its westbound trip on Lake Street to Melrose Park.*
John F. Humiston photo

22 *On September 9, 1946, Chicago & West Towns car 164 was operating westbound on Lake Street at Eleventh Avenue, Melrose Park.*
Robert W. Gibson photo/George E. Kanary Collection

23 *On the final day of streetcar operation on Lake Street, March 29, 1947, West Towns car 134 was photographed westbound at 15th Avenue, Melrose Park*
Robert W. Gibson photo/George E. Kanary Collection

24 *On Sunday, September 12, 2004, Pace bus 6239 was operating westbound on Route 313, St. Charles Road, when it approached the stop at 15th Avenue and Lake Street. In the background, behind the trees, is Westlake Community Hospital. The pattern of reflective cracks in the street indicates that the streetcar tracks and ties were probably not removed when the trolley service was terminated. The street was simply paved over.*

Richard W. Aaron photo

Chapter 13: Lake Street

25 *The West Towns terminal at 25th Avenue on Lake Street in Melrose Park required only a switch to permit the streetcar to cross from the west-bound track to the east-bound track. Car 103 was about to change direction for its east-bound trip on February 9, 1947.*
John F. Humiston photo

26 *Fifty-Seven years later, in September 2004, Pace bus 6241 was eastbound on Lake Street at 24th Avenue.*
Richard W. Aaron photo

154 *The Chicago & West Towns Railways*

14 Madison Street

The Madison Street Line of the West Towns was the suburban extension of the Chicago Surface Lines' Madison Street route, beginning just west of Austin Boulevard and running 4-3/4 miles west to Maywood. Although the Chicago Surface lines operated an off-street terminal on the northeast corner of Madison Street and Austin Boulevard, the West Towns cars did not share this facility.

In its last major configuration, the cars operated west on Madison Street to 19th Avenue, where they turned north and terminated in the street at 19th Avenue, just south of the Chicago & North Western Railway's tracks. Streetcar service was discontinued on Madison Street in 1947. In 2001, four bus routes now provide this service.

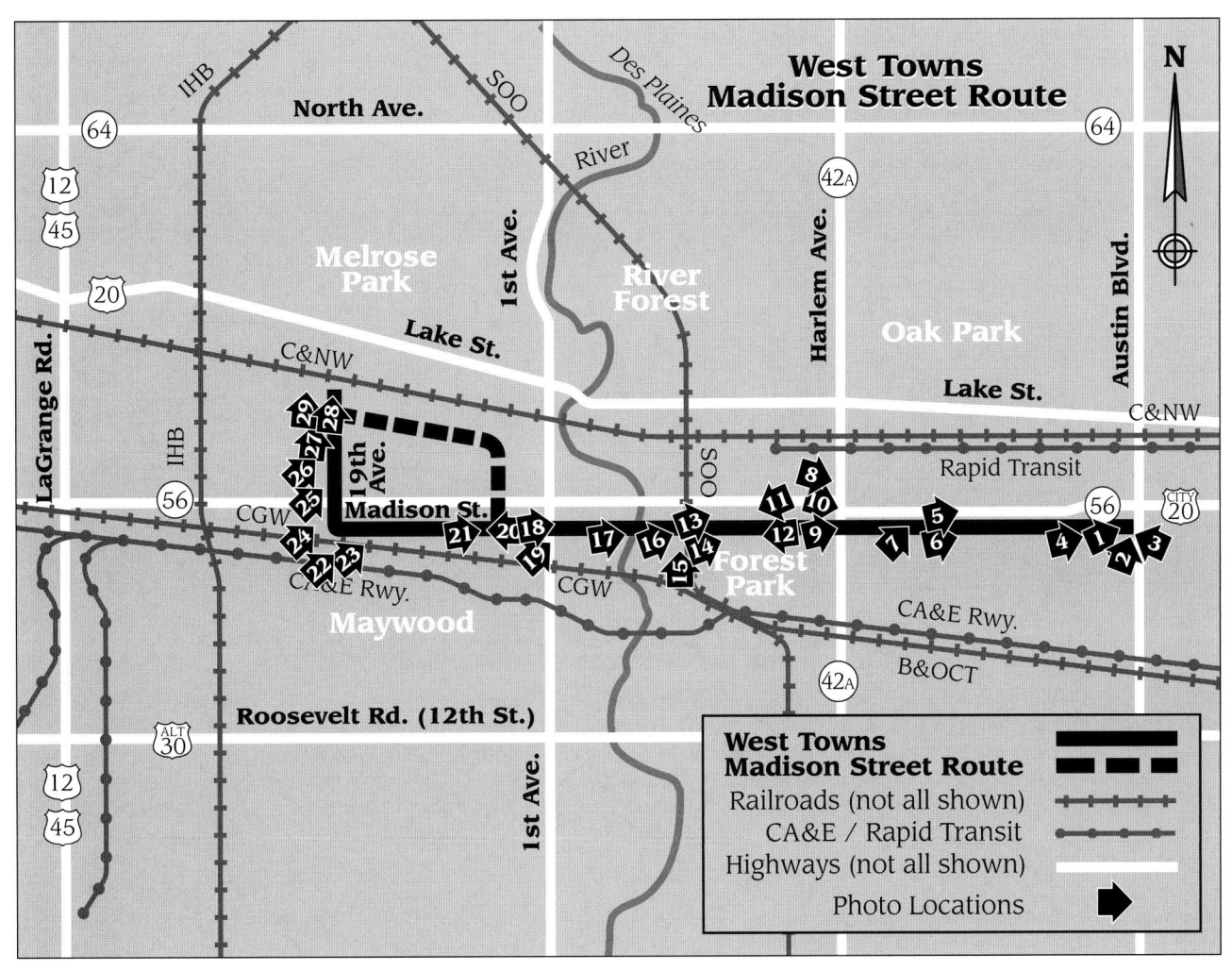

The dashed lines represent West Towns trackage on Fifth Avenue and St. Charles Road which was abandoned in 1929. When the single track "Maywood Loop" was in service, streetcars operated around the loop in either through or shuttle service.

1 *Car 101 stood at the Austin Boulevard terminal of the Madison Street line on November 2, 1946. West Towns passengers wishing to change to a streetcar on the Madison Street route of the Chicago Surface Lines had to walk across the street and pay an additional fare when boarding. A CSL PCC, in an experimental paint scheme, waited for its departure time while a second PCC waited in the pocket track in front of the loop and a third was about to enter the loop.*
William C. Hoffman photo/Michael M. McGowan Collection

2 *Public ownership of the transit agencies allowed for an easier transfer between carriers. At Madison Street and Austin Boulevard, Pace buses now use the same loop as do the buses of Chicago Transit Authority's Route 20, Madison Street. On March 12, 2004, Pace bus 6069 terminated its run on Route 315, Austin-Ridgeland, at the Madison and Austin loop. It then changed destination signs to Route 320, Madison Street, and began its journey west on Madison to Des Plaines Avenue and then southward to the Forest Park Transit Center.*
Richard W. Aaron photo

3 *Sweeper 18 had just completed its eastbound journey down Madison Street and waited for the in-service cars to reverse ends and head westward before it could do the same. The sweeper was photographed on Madison, slightly west of Austin Boulevard, on February 2, 1947. This was one of the sweeper's last trips on Madison Street because the route was converted to bus operation on February 16, 1947.*
Robert W. Gibson photo

156   *The Chicago & West Towns Railways*

4 West Towns car 127 was westbound on Madison Street, a block west of the Madison and Austin Boulevard terminal. The photograph was taken on February 16, 1947, the last day that the blue and white streetcars operated on Madison Street.

Thomas H. Desnoyers photo/Krambles-Peterson Archive

5 Car 136 was westbound on Madison Street on July 7, 1946, when it stopped at Ridgeland Avenue. On this portion of the street, the railway erected steel Bates poles to support the trolley wire.

James J. Buckley photo/Krambles-Peterson Archive

Chapter 14: Madison Street 157

6 Almost 60 years later, on January 12, 2006, Pace bus 6044 was operating westbound on Madison Street as it crossed Ridgeland Avenue. The vehicle was sporting an advertising livery promoting the Chicago Cubs baseball team. The building on the northeast corner of the intersection shown in the 1946 photo is still in use in 2006. The vacant lot east of it is occupied by a fast food restaurant. The building used by "Doc" Clayton Motors and other buildings to the east are also still used in 2006.

Richard W. Aaron photo

7 In the early 1940s, car 104 was operating westbound on Madison Street a few blocks east of Harlem Avenue at Grove Avenue.

James J. Buckley photo
Robert H. Hansen Collection

158   *The Chicago & West Towns Railways*

8 Cars 134 and 101 met on Madison Street at Harlem Avenue during 1946. The tracks to the left permitted access to and from Harlem.
Donald N. Idarius photo/
George E. Kanary Collection

9 Car 103 was operating westbound on Madison Street at Harlem Avenue on February 1, 1947. By the presence of the large crowd entering and exiting the car, the inclement weather must have caused the 103 to run late.
Donald N. Idarius photo

10 On April 2, 2004, Pace bus 6061 had turned off Harlem Avenue to continue its westward journey on Madison Street. The bus was in service on Pace route 305, Cicero-Forest Park, the present day replacement for the Chicago Avenue streetcar line. The Victorian building on the southwest corner of the intersection and several of the low rise structures on the southeast corner are all that remain from the 1946 view. Bus 6061 was manufactured by Orion in 2000. It is one of 88 identical units purchased for Pace's West and North Shore divisions.
Richard W. Aaron photo

Chapter 14: Madison Street

159

11 *Motor 12 was pulling two ash cars as it traveled between the Suburban and the Lake Street carbarns. It was photographed eastbound on Madison Street at Hannah Avenue in Forest Park on March 11, 1938.*

John F. Humiston photo

12 *Slightly more than 65 years later, Pace bus 6057 was operating eastbound on Route 320, Madison Street, at Hannah Avenue on March 12, 2004. Behind 6057 was Pace bus 2217 in service on Route 318, West North Avenue. Except for the fact that there are modern vehicles on a re-paved street and that some of the buildings have been repainted and have new tenants, the streetscape here has changed little since 1938.*

Richard W. Aaron photo

The Chicago & West Towns Railways

13 *Car 165 was westbound on Madison Street at Des Plaines Avenue in 1936. The car was resplendent in its "pennant" livery. This paint scheme proved unpopular with the company's management and a blue and white livery was adopted a few years later.*

Ed Frank, Jr. photo

14 *At the same intersection as the preceding photo, car 134 was westbound on Madison Street at Des Plaines Avenue on July 27, 1946. In the decade between the two photographs, three buildings on the northeast corner of the intersection had been demolished and a hamburger stand had been built.*
James J. Buckley photo

Chapter 14: Madison Street

15 *Car 102 was operating westbound on Madison Street as it crossed the tracks of the Soo Line on August 9, 1946. The photographer was standing on a platform of the Soo's station to frame this scene.*

Robert W. Gibson photo

16 *In 1946, car 128 crossed the Soo Line's tracks on Madison Street as it proceeded westward to its 19th Avenue terminal. The Soo's passenger station was out-of-sight to the right.*

Folger Smith photo/
George E. Kanary Collection

17 *Less than half a mile west of the Soo Line's crossing was the bridge which carried Madison Street over the Des Plaines River. Photographer Desnoyers recorded operation at this location on last day the streetcars ran: February 16, 1947. Car 130 was westbound.*

Thomas H. Desnoyers photo/
Krambles-Peterson Archive

162

The Chicago & West Towns Railways

18 *Proviso East High School was built on the northeast corner of Madison Street and First Avenue. Car 101 was westbound at this intersection on July 27, 1946. Portions of the school are visible behind the streetcar and the trees.*

James J. Buckley photo

19 *In April 2004, Pace bus 2258 was crossing First Avenue on Madison Street. The venerable high school still serves the community, although several new buildings have been built on the campus.*

Richard W. Aaron photo

20 *Car 102 was eastbound on Madison Street when it clattered its way through the crossover, just east of Fifth Avenue. Circa 1944.*

Thomas A. Lesh photo

Chapter 14: Madison Street

21 *Car 104 was operating westbound in Maywood at Eighth Avenue on February 16, 1947 when it passed an eastbound car.*

Thomas H. Desnoyers photo/ Krambles-Peterson Archive

22 *In the summer of 1946, Chicago & West Towns streetcar 135 turned off Madison Street for its northward trip on 19th Avenue to the Chicago & North Western Railway's tracks. Behind the car to the right, about 18th Avenue, the Madison Street operation became single track.*

Joe L. Diaz photo

23 *Streetcar 127 was photographed on February 16, 1947 at 19th Avenue and Madison Street in Maywood. This intersection served as the western terminal of the route effective December 23, 1946 when car service on 19th Avenue was abandoned.*

Thomas H. Desnoyers photo/ Krambles-Peterson Archive

24 In April 2004, Pace bus 2264 was operating westbound on Madison Street at 19th Avenue. At the time of this photo, Madison Street, between Des Plaines and 19th Avenues was being served by three bus routes: #303, Madison Street - 19th Avenue; #310, Madison Street - Hillside; #17/317, Westchester. The buses had a 20 minute base headway at this intersection, but had hourly headway on each individual route.

Richard W. Aaron photo

25 On the northeast corner of 19th Avenue and Washington Boulevard in Maywood stands an impressive church. Circa 1942, West Towns car 132 operated southward across this intersection. After the car proceeded one block further south to Madison Street, it turned eastward for its journey to Austin Boulevard.

Charles A. Brown photo/
Joe L. Diaz Collection

26 Over 60 years later, the Neighborhood United Methodist Church was still served by public transit. On April 2, 2004, Pace bus 6045 operated southbound past the intersection of 19th Avenue and Washington Boulevard in Maywood. The bus was in service on Pace route 303, Madison Street - 19th Avenue.

Richard W. Aaron photo

Chapter 14: Madison Street

27 *About a block from the end of the line, car 130 stopped to pick up passengers on 19th Avenue at St. Charles Road. The portion of the street railway from the terminal near the Chicago & North Western Railway's grade crossing of 19th Avenue to 18th Avenue and Madison Street was single track.*
James J. Buckley photo/Krambles-Peterson Archive

28 *On the morning of June 24, 1941, West Towns car 102 was waiting at the 19th Avenue terminal of the Madison Street line for the time to begin its journey back to Austin Boulevard. The Melrose Park station of the Chicago & North Western Railway was located out-of-sight to the right of the streetcar.*
James J. Buckley photo

29 *At the same place, almost 63 years later, Pace bus 2266 crossed the tracks of the former Chicago & North Western Railway on its way to the Yorktown Shopping Center. The bus was in service on route 313 - St. Charles Road and operated about a half mile on 19th Avenue as it transitioned from Lake Street to St. Charles Road.*
Richard W. Aaron photo

166   *The Chicago & West Towns Railways*

15 La Grange

The La Grange line of the Chicago & West Towns was considered the most beautiful streetcar ride in Chicagoland. No where else could one ride on a trolley through a forest preserve to sparsely developed suburbia. The La Grange line is also fondly remembered as the means a family would have used for a memorable Sunday excursion to Brookfield Zoo.

In the West Towns years, the eastern terminal of the route was at Kenton Avenue and Cermak Road. With the Hawthorne Works of Western Electric adjacent to this terminal, the line had a natural traffic generator. The line continued west in the center of Cermak Road to reach Harlem Avenue. From this point it meandered south and west on Harlem Avenue, 26th Street, and Des Plaines Avenue, and through the forest preserve on private right-of-way to reach Brookfield Zoo. From the zoo, the line continued to zigzag further south and west, finally reaching its western terminal in the northeast corner of La Grange.

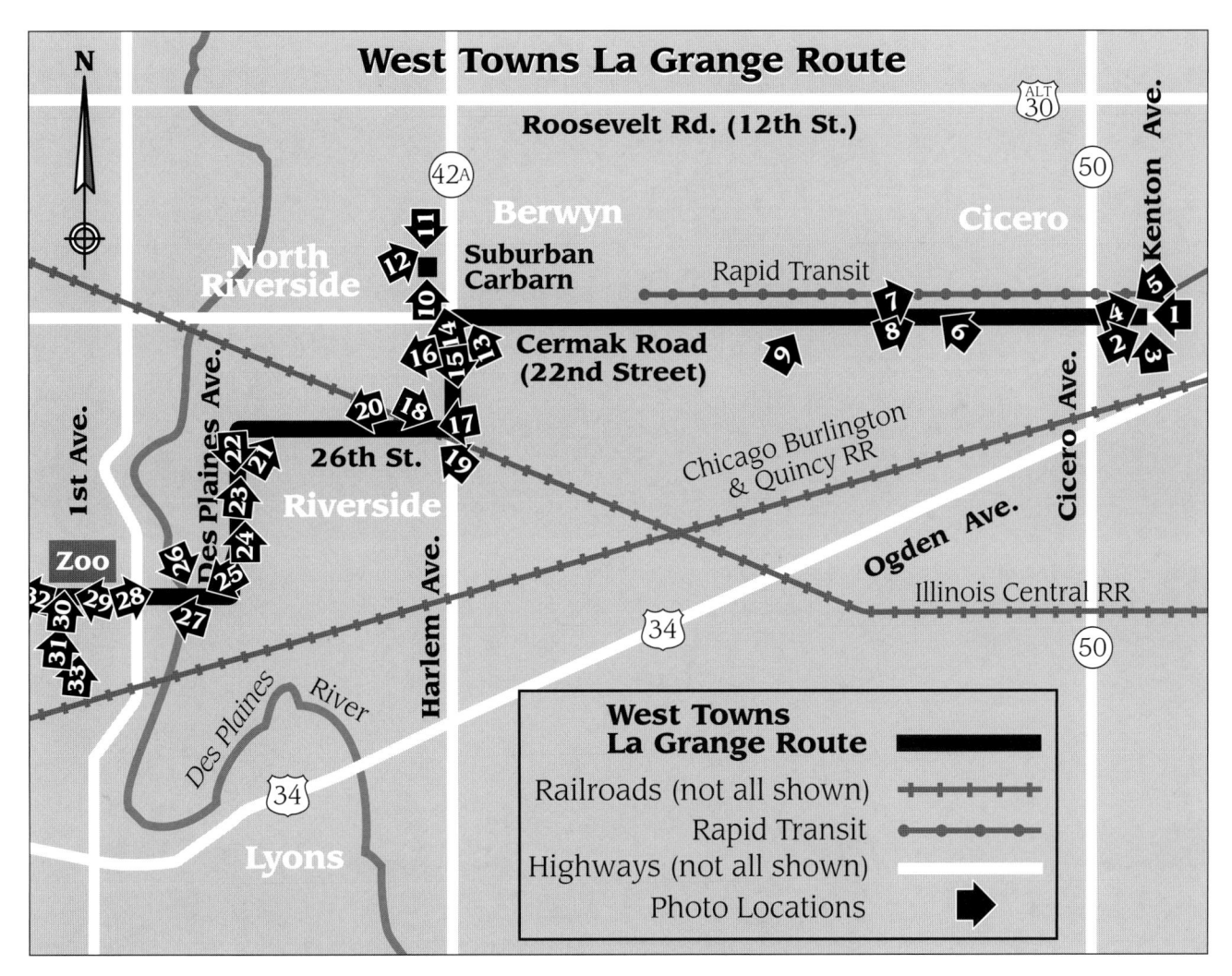

The east half of the route map is shown here, and the west half of the route map is shown on page 178.

Chapter 15: La Grange

1 *West Towns car 161 and Chicago Surface Lines Pullman 250 met at Cermak Road and Kenton Avenue on April 11, 1948. Because scheduled streetcar service on the La Grange line ended the previous day, this was the last day trolleys of the two companies would meet here. Car 161 was chartered by the Central Electric Railfans' Association for a ceremonial last ride.*

Richard H. Wiersema photo

2 *Three West Towns and two Chicago Surface Lines streetcars met at their joint terminal to discharge and receive passengers. Cermak Road and Kenton Avenue was a very busy place on the afternoon of June 22, 1947.*

Victor G. Wagner photo
Joseph M. Canfield Collection

3 *On September 18, 1939, a freshly repainted West Towns car 126 took spot time at the Cermak Road and Kenton Avenue terminal. The silver roof glistened in the noontime sun.*

Truman Heffner photo/
George E. Kanary Collection

4 Car 141 loaded passengers for its westbound journey at Cermak Road and Kenton Avenue on August 17, 1947. Although built for multiple unit operation, the car rarely saw service in this mode. Three Chicago Surface Lines "Big Pullmans" on the Cermak Road route waited for their time to return east. Streetcars on Cermak Road in Chicago were replaced by buses on May 30, 1954, almost six years after those of the West Towns had met that fate.

James J. Buckley photo/
George E. Kanary Collection

5 The Telephone Apparatus Building at Western Electric provided an imposing background for West Towns streetcar 111. The car was operating in charter service on April 11, 1948, the last day of operation of West Towns trolleys. Scheduled public streetcar service had ended a day earlier.

Thomas H. Desnoyers photo/Krambles-Peterson Archive

Chapter 14: Madison Street 169

6 On a quiet Saturday morning, August 17, 1947 car 119 was proceeding eastbound through an industrial section of Cicero, at Cermak Road and 54th Avenue.

Donald N. Idarius photo

7 Pace bus 2209 loaded passengers for its westbound journey on January 27, 1996. Signed for Route 322, the bus would travel on Cermak Road as far west as Butterfield Road. The bus was at its eastern terminal, the 54/Cermak station of the Cermak branch of CTA's Blue Line. The "L" station in the background was taken out of service for rebuilding on the weekend of February 23, 2002.

Richard W. Aaron photo

8 At the new 54/Cermak station, Pace bus 6222 stopped to pick up passengers on February 26, 2004. The new "L" station opened for public passenger use on August 18, 2003. During the construction period, a temporary station east of Laramie was provided.

Richard W. Aaron photo

170 *The Chicago & West Towns Railways*

9 Car 139 was westbound on Cermak Road at Ridgeland Avenue on September 14, 1947. The buildings behind the streetcar contained stores signed with some of the leading names in retailing, such as Walgreens and Spiegel.

R. V. Mehlenbeck photo/ Krambles-Peterson Archive

10 On a sunny day about a month before abandonment, West Towns cars 134, 119, 127, and 126 waited between runs on tracks 1-4 of the Suburban carbarn. Car 134 wore a hand painted sign on each side proclaiming: "Bus service starts April 11th."

Richard H. Wiersema photo

11 On the same day in March 1948 as the previous photo, sweepers 5 and 6 rested in the yard near the north end of the Suburban carbarn. In contrast to sweepers 17 and 18 which were painted in yellow, these sweepers were painted in the standard passenger car colors.

Richard H. Wiersema photo

Chapter 15: La Grange

171

12 *Motor 12 was operating at the north end of the Suburban carbarn. To illustrate why the train buff community held the West Towns in such high regard, railfan Wendell Dillinger was allowed to tend the trolley pole. Behind the work motor was acre after acre of undeveloped land on Harlem Avenue. March 1948.*

Richard H. Wiersema photo

13 *On August 17, 1947, Car 112 was southbound on Harlem Avenue at Cermak Road. The streetcar was entering the intersection from the carbarn. In the right of the photograph, behind the safety zone sign, was Don Idarius. Don's camera failed and he had borrowed one of the two that Jim Buckley carried that day. Jim would have preferred to use the camera with black and white film, but he loaned that one to Don. The one he kept was loaded with color slide film. The wonderful color photos credited to Jim Buckley, that appear on these pages, would not have been taken had Don Idarius' camera not failed.*

James J. Buckley photo/George E. Kanary Collection

172   *The Chicago & West Towns Railways*

14 As the streetcars had done before it since 1897, Pace bus 2249 negotiated the turn from Cermak Road to Harlem Avenue. Behind the bus, the site of the Suburban carbarn was redeveloped for use by an automobile dealership. Where the yellow balloon in the photo stands was the Suburban's power house. September 5, 2002.

Richard W. Aaron photo

15 In the middle 1940s, a West Towns streetcar ran north on Harlem Avenue and was approaching Cermak Road.

Bruce G. Moffat Collection

16 One of the advantages of operating a bus route vs. a streetcar line is that the bus can easily be re-routed as desired. On weekends and holidays, Pace short-turned its Cicero-La Grange bus, the replacement for the La Grange streetcar, at the North Riverside Mall. It did not operate the route section between the mall and 54/Cermak Transit Center via Cermak Road. On Saturday morning, June 26, 2004, the transit center was a beehive of activity. Pace bus 6043, assigned to the Cicero-La Grange route, and CTA bus 5510, in service on route X-21 Cermak, were waiting for their scheduled departure times. After Pace bus 6068 (on route 322, Cermak Road) transferred passengers, all three buses departed for their respective destinations.

Richard W. Aaron photo

Chapter 15: La Grange   *173*

17 Slightly west of the intersection of Harlem Avenue and 26th Street, the West Towns La Grange line crossed the Illinois Central Railroad. At this location, known as Parkway, car 141 was eastbound on August 17, 1947.
James J. Buckley photo/George E. Kanary Collection

18 The West Towns' one commercial freight customer was located adjacent to the Suburban barn. The firm, the Oechslin Florist Company, primarily received lumber and fuel oil by rail. In this case, Santa Fe Refrigerator Dispatch car 5134, brought in a shipment of palms. On the last day of scheduled streetcar service, April 10, 1948, motor 12 returned the empty refrigerator car to the Illinois Central interchange.
Richard H. Wiersema photo

19 The Illinois Central Railroad crossing with the West Towns at Parkway was always a place of action. In this view, a La Grange car had to wait for the IC's Chicago-bound Land O' Corn to pass. The two-car train, built by American Car & Foundry in 1940, made a daily round trip between Chicago and Waterloo, Iowa beginning on October 28, 1941. After being involved in a fatal grade crossing accident on February 18, 1942, it was subsequently withdrawn from service and returned to ACF. The units were repaired and sold to the New York, Susquehanna & Western Railroad in 1947.
Charles A. Brown photo/Joe L. Diaz Collection

20 *In this track segment, 26th Street crossed the streetcar private right-of-way and shifted from one side of the railway to the other. On August 17, 1947, streetcar 126 was photographed at the point where the street crossed the railway.*

James J. Buckley photo/
George E. Kanary collection

21 *In the last summer of streetcar service on the La Grange line, track work was necessary on Des Plaines Avenue. The company elected to install portable crossovers to provide single-track operation through the area needing repair. At the north end of single track, eastbound car 161 was slipping through the portable crossover to continue its journey to Cermak Road and Kenton Avenue. Westbound car 107 waited for its turn to enter the single-track segment. July 6, 1946.*

Donald N. Idarius photo/Roy G. Benedict Collection

22 *An eastbound car, its number obscured by the sign reading "Direct to Zoo," operated north on Des Plaines Avenue near 28th Street.*

James J. Buckley photo/
George E. Kanary Collection

Chapter 15: La Grange

23 *Car 128 was southbound on Des Plaines Avenue at 31st Street. The Tudor apartment on the northwest corner of the intersection was still in use in 2004.*
James J. Buckley photo/
George E. Kanary Collection

24 *Car 140 was westbound (running south) on Woodside Drive, the continuation of Des Plaines Avenue in Riverside, and was approaching the curve at Park Place. February 26, 1946.*
Victor G. Wagner photo/
Joseph N. Canfield Collection

25 *On December 29, 1946, West Towns car 152 was eastbound in Riverside on Park Place at Lincoln Avenue. A fresh blanket of snow had fallen the night before providing Don Idarius the opportunity to photograph the scene in unspoiled snow. After the abandonment of the trolley line, its right-of-way was converted into parking for use by the tenants of the apartment buildings on the left.*
Donald N. Idarius photo

176   The Chicago & West Towns Railways

26 On July 27, 1946, a westbound La Grange bound streetcar crossed the Des Plaines River bridge.
Donald N. Idarius photo

27 After the abandonment of the streetcar line, the bridge and its piers were removed. Almost 60 years later, the abutments at each end were still in place. On December 13, 2003, the west abutment was photographed among the trees at Zoo Woods.
Richard W. Aaron photo

28 On August 17, 1947, a westbound car had crossed the Des Plaines River bridge and was approaching First Avenue. The car was required to stop at the street as a safety measure because the very busy street crossing was not protected by gates or flashing lights. The zoo was a half-mile away.
James J. Buckley photo/George E. Kanary Collection

Chapter 15: La Grange

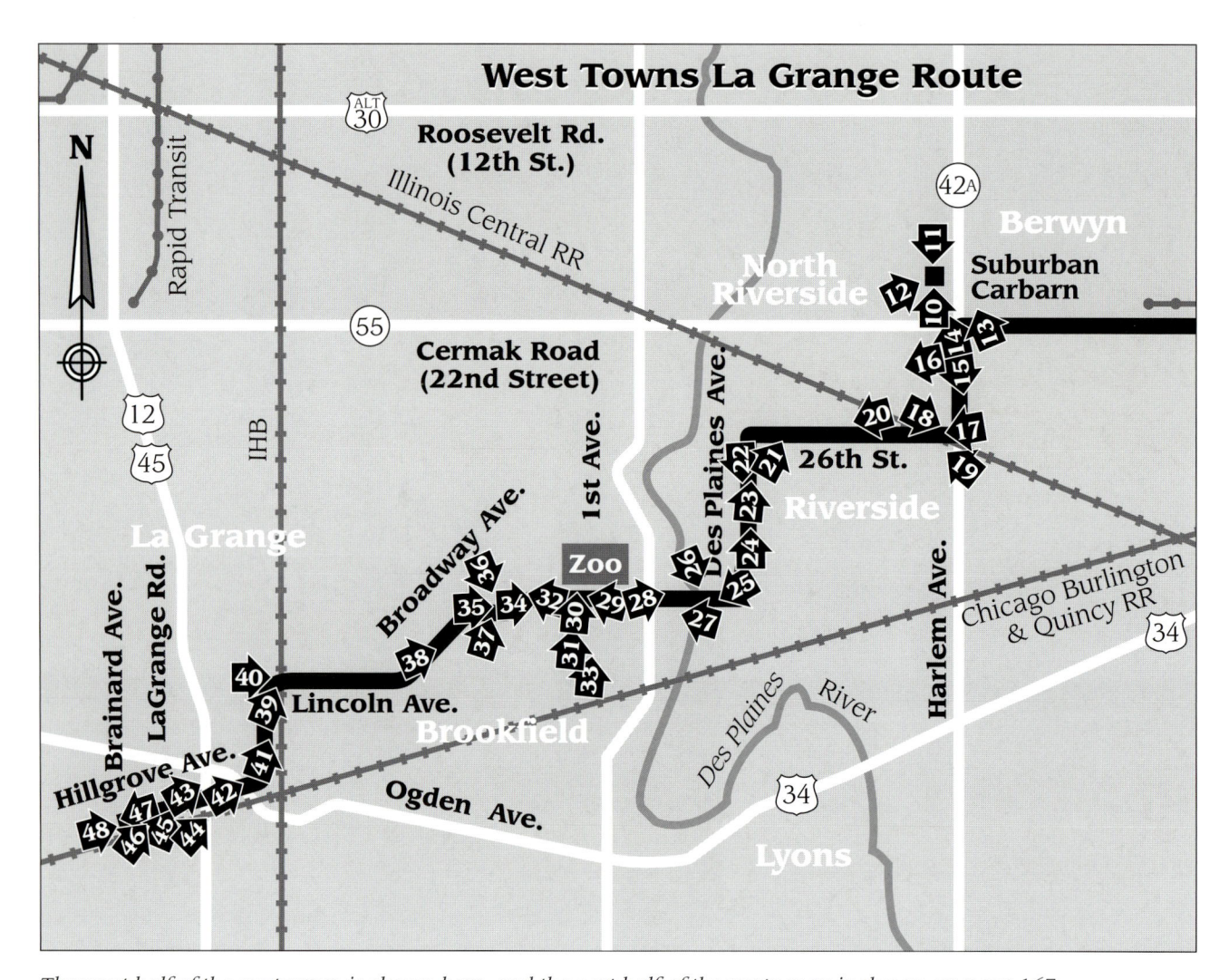

West Towns La Grange Route

The west half of the route map is shown here, and the east half of the route map is shown on page 167.

29 Car 159 was signed for Kenton Avenue as it traveled eastbound not far from the south gate of Brookfield Zoo. August 17, 1947.

James J. Buckley photo/
George E. Kanary Collection

178   *The Chicago & West Towns Railways*

30 On August 27, 1947, blue and white streetcar 159 had just arrived at Brookfield Zoo from Kenton Avenue and the passengers were waiting for the doors to open to alight. The streetcar stop was conveniently close to the zoo's entrance.

Richard H. Wiersema photo

31 Wood-sided car 105 was waiting at the Zoo for the scheduled departure time for its eastbound trip on September 19, 1937.

John F. Humiston photo

32 The 126 was in service on June 22, 1941, on a short-turn zoo tripper. After it had unloaded its passengers at the zoo, it pulled down the track to change ends. Next, it will switch from the westbound track to the eastbound track to begin its journey back to Cicero.

James J. Buckley photo

Chapter 15: La Grange

33 *The three arch south entrance to Brookfield Zoo was very much in use in 2004. The land occupied by the streetcar tracks had been incorporated into a large parking lot. December 12, 2003.*
Richard W. Aaron photo

34 *Just west of the zoo, near Forbes Road in Riverside, La Grange bound car 161 passed car 158. Since the trees in this scene had not yet begun to leaf out, the extent of the woods was revealed. The two trolleys were in service on April 4, 1948, the last Sunday of scheduled West Towns streetcar service.*
John F. Humiston photo

35 *The West Towns crossing of Salt Creek was unusual because it was on a section of curved track. Most railway bridges were built on straight track sections. La Grange bound car 141 was at the east edge of the span on August 17, 1947. The pedestrian walkway, on the south side of the viaduct, provided a vantage point for the photographer.*
James J. Buckley photo/George E. Kanary Collection

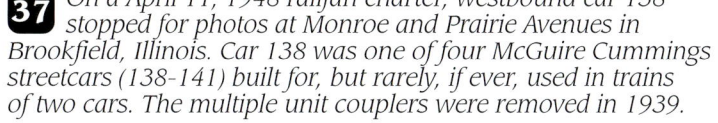

36 *Although the tracks and steelwork from the Salt Creek bridge were removed, the concrete bridge abutments and two of the piers remain. August 8, 2000.*
Richard W. Aaron photo

37 *On a April 11, 1948 railfan charter, westbound car 138 stopped for photos at Monroe and Prairie Avenues in Brookfield, Illinois. Car 138 was one of four McGuire Cummings streetcars (138-141) built for, but rarely, if ever, used in trains of two cars. The multiple unit couplers were removed in 1939.*
Bernard L. Stone photo/Krambles-Peterson Archive

Chapter 15: La Grange

38 *The center of downtown Brookfield is known as "Eight Points" because it is at the intersection of Maple Avenue, Washington Avenue, Grand Boulevard, and Broadway. On April 11, 1948, the day after the scheduled streetcars made their last run, line car 15 stopped there to allow some final photographs.*
Robert W. Gibson photo/George E. Kanary Collection

39 *An Indiana Harbor Belt freight train, powered by a steam locomotive, waited for car 141 to pass before it continued its journey south to Clearing Yard. After the West Towns stopped using conductors, a flagman was located at this rail junction to advise the motorman when it was safe to proceed. August 17, 1947.*
James J. Buckley photo/George E. Kanary Collection

40 Line car 15 and crew were dispatched to the Indiana Harbor Belt crossing to make repairs to the overhead wire on February 17, 1948. As the two men on the elevated platform spliced the wire, eastbound car 140 trundled by on its way to Kenton Avenue.

James J. Buckley photo

41 On the last day of scheduled streetcar service, April 10, 1948, West Towns car 152 traveled south along the west side the Indiana Harbor Belt tracks. As the trolley approached Ogden Avenue, there was evidence that civilization was beginning to reach this part of the metropolitan area.

Robert W. Gibson photo

42 Chicago & West Towns car 152 crossed over Ogden Avenue in La Grange on Sunday, October 18, 1936. The Chicago, Burlington & Quincy Railroad's tracks are to the right and much undeveloped land appears behind the car. The railway's electrical distribution was accomplished by the single feeder cable on the pole line opposite the eastbound track.

John F. Humiston photo

Chapter 15: La Grange

43 About a year and a half before abandonment, on July 13, 1946, car 158 was westbound on Hillgrove Avenue and was crossing La Grange Road. In December 1946, the trackage in Hillgrove west of this point was abandoned because of the construction of a sewer line. A new terminal was built by simply installing a switch to permit the cars to turn back.

Donald N. Idarius photo

44 By September 17, 2004, when this photo was made, the laundry plant that had stood on the northeast corner of Hillgrove Avenue and La Grange Road had been demolished and a block of stores had been erected. Pace bus 2202, in service on Route 304, Cicero-La Grange, waited on La Grange Road for its departure time. A double stack freight train ran eastbound on the busy triple-track main line of the Burlington Northern Santa Fe Railroad.

Richard W. Aaron photo

45 West Towns streetcar 155, resplendent in its "pennant" livery, stopped in front of the La Grange Post Office on May 1, 1937. The "pennant" livery was applied to cars 101, 114, 151, 155 and 165 in 1936. It is thought that car 155 was the first car to receive this paint scheme because the coloring of the side pennants was reversed from that on the other four units. By 1938, the cars were repainted. The "Farley Style" post office building, named for the man who was Postmaster General when Franklin D. Roosevelt was president, was still in use in 2004.

Ed Frank Jr. photo/ hand colored by Verne Langdon/George E. Kanary Collection

184 *The Chicago & West Towns Railways*

46 Car 111 was westbound on Hillgrove Avenue and was approaching its terminal at Brainard Avenue when it passed the Lord Lumber & Coal Company. A siding of the Chicago, Burlington & Quincy Railroad served the yard and therefore crossed the streetcar line. Circa 1942.
John Andresen photo/Robert H. Hansen Collection

47 Streetcar 161 had just arrived at its terminal on Hillgrove and Brainard Avenues on July 13, 1946. After the motorman "changed ends," the car would travel through the switch to reach the eastbound track, wait for its scheduled departure time, and then proceed to Kenton Avenue.
Donald N. Idarius photo

48 On another day in the 1940s, West Towns car 100 had reached the western terminal of the La Grange line at Hillgrove and Brainard Avenues. In this view looking southeast from Brainard, the Stone Avenue station of the Chicago, Burlington & Quincy Railroad dominates the background. In the process of preparing the car 100 for its return journey, the motorman would raise what would be the rear trolley pole before he lowered what would become the front trolley pole to provide the streetcar with a constant source of electricity.
Eugene Van Dusen photo/
George E. Kanary Collection

Chapter 15: La Grange

SECTION 4
Cars, Buses and Buildings

16 Cars and Buses

Cicero & Proviso Street Railway Company

In May 1890, the Pullman Palace Car Company of Chicago received an order for 12 double-truck closed motor cars. These cars seated 36 passengers on longitudinal seats, used McGuire 22 trucks and were equipped with two Edison 15-horsepower motors. The first four cars, numbers 1, 2, 3, and 10, were delivered in February 1891. When put into service, it was immediately apparent that these cars were significantly underpowered. The purchase order for these streetcars was then amended to provide cars with larger motors and cross seats. After the remaining eight cars were delivered in April 1891, the first four cars were sent back to Pullman for remodeling and increased power.

In April 1891, an additional twelve double-truck closed motor cars were ordered from Pullman. Carrying road numbers 13-24, these new cars were similar to the first cars except that they were one window longer and had improved vestibules. The original 12 cars had open vestibules.

These 24 cars were retired by the late 1890s. In 1896, one was sold to the North Chicago Street Railroad Company and another to the West Chicago Street Railroad Company. The cars were rebuilt into party cars named *Sunbeam* and *Arcturus*. In 1898, cars 1-16, were sold to the Suburban Railroad for use as trailers. In 1899, two more cars, numbers 17 and 18, were sold to the Suburban. These trailers were retired in 1923.

Although the company continued to obtain new cars, fragmentary data exist about these purchases. At the end of 1895, the roster of the Cicero & Proviso included 61 motor cars and 45 trailers. When the Cicero & Proviso was purchased by the Chicago Consolidated Traction Company on February 27, 1899, the company owned 76 motor cars and 11 trailers. Unfortunately, we know about only 47 of these vehicles.

Suburban Railroad Car 504 carried a standing room only crowd when it departed on its trip west, circa 1905. The photograph was taken at the railroad's Cermak and Pulaski Road terminal. To the left of car 504 was a Chicago Union Traction streetcar at the west end of the Ogden Avenue line.

James J. Buckley Collection

Cicero & Proviso Street Railway Company
Known Roster Information

Car Numbers	Builder (order)	Year	Notes
1-12	Pullman (683)	1890	Double-truck closed motor cars.
13-24	Pullman (711)	1891	Double-truck closed motor cars.
25-34	St. Charles	1891	Open cars.
35-41	St. Charles	1892	Open cars.
42-47	American	1892	Single-truck closed motor cars.

Car 5 from the Cicero & Proviso's first order of cars posed for a builder's photograph at the Pullman plant in 1890. The 32' 6" long car had eight side windows.

Krambles-Peterson Archive

A car from the Cicero & Proviso's second car order, cars 13-24, was photographed late in the car's life on Cicero Avenue at the Garfield Park "L" station. At the time of the photo, it had been sold to the Suburban Railroad, converted to a trailer, and renumbered car 7. The car had nine side windows.

Fred Borchert photo

Ogden Street Railway Company

The Ogden Street Railway owned no cars. Its vehicle fleet was leased from the Cicero & Proviso Street Railway and the Chicago Consolidated Traction Company.

County Traction

County Traction leased the equipment necessary to operate its lines from the Chicago Railways. In the first lease agreement between the two companies, dated December 27, 1910, rental of 55 passenger cars, 5 snow sweepers, 5 snow plows, one coal motor, 3 coal trailers, one wrecker and one line wagon was specified. The double-truck passenger cars were leased for $1.45 per day, the single-truck cars and wrecker were leased at 60¢ per day and the line wagon was leased at a mere 23¢ per day.

The lease agreement for cars from the Chicago Railways was modified and renewed on September 1, 1911. The type of car leased and the per-diem rental rate are specified in the following table.

The number and type of cars leased from Chicago Railways changed as frequently as County Traction's needs changed. On November 9, 1911, 15 ex-Buffalo, New York cars were leased at the rate of 90¢ per day. On November 16, 1911, 6 single-truck cars and the sprinkler car were returned. In January and February 1912, 10 additional double-truck cars, built by the St. Louis Car Company, and one Chicago Union Traction rebuilt double-truck car were leased at the $1.04 daily rental rate. On May 24, 1912, 10 more single-truck cars were leased at 50¢ per day. The Chicago Railways also agreed to rent to County Traction double-truck cars, to handle the Sunday and holiday traffic, not to exceed 20 in number on any one day. Chicago Railways would supply equipment out of the Kedzie Avenue car house. This contract was renewed on January 31, 1913 and terminated on July 18, 1913.

County Traction used the equipment in groups on a given line. The double-truck ex-Buffalo, New York cars were confined to service on the Madison Street and Berwyn-Lyons lines. The rental of the one-of-a-kind rebuilt Chicago Union Traction car number 4474 was used only on the Berwyn-Lyons route.

The only new equipment purchased by County Traction were utility cars. In November 1911, 3 steel-underframe, single-truck, long-broom sweepers (cars 1-3) and a single-truck snow plow (car number 4) were ordered from the McGuire-Cummings Car Manufacturing Company. In 1912, another sweeper (car number 5), a double-truck sprinkler (car number 9), a double-truck work motor (car number 12), 3 single-truck dump cars (car numbers X1-X3), and a 36-foot double-truck flat car (car number 0001)

Cars Leased from Chicago Railways
Effective September 1, 1911

Quantity	Type of Car	Daily Rental Rate
18	Single-truck	50 ¢
1	Double-truck Ex-Buffalo, N.Y. Car	90 ¢
10	Double-truck St. Louis Car Co. Cars	$1.04
1	Single-truck Wreck Car	57¢
1	Line Wagon	23 ¢
1	Sprinkler	50 ¢

The Chicago & West Towns Railways

Cars 107-120 were delivered from the McGuire-Cummings Manufacturing Company to County Traction in 1912. These cars were similar in appearance to the "turtleback" cars being built at the same time by the Chicago Railways. Car 111 was photographed on the Chicago Avenue line at Roosevelt Road and Austin Avenue in 1940. An interior view of car 108 shows the rattan seats, coal stove, and controller.

James J. Buckley photos

were obtained from the same builder. A 24-foot work motor was built in County Traction's Lake Street shop in 1913. In 1912 and 1913, two single-truck flat cars (car numbers 02 and 03) were also constructed at the Lake Street shop. The two double-truck ex-Buffalo, New York cars, numbered 3819 and 3828, which were destroyed in accidents, were converted into double-truck flat cars (car numbers 0002 and 0003) in 1913. Finally, two single-truck sand cars, (car numbers 001 and 002) were built at the Lake Street shops in 1912 and 1913. County Traction had obtained an impressive array of utility cars.

Just before the strike that resulted in County Traction going out of business, on the night on July 3, 1913 and in the early morning of July 4, 1913, the Chicago Railways sent out a group of trainmen to

The leased 3800-series "Buffalo Cars" were the best known cars used to operate on the County Traction Lines. They were built for the International Railway Company of Buffalo, New York by the American Car Company. Car 3838 was photographed in service on Madison Street.

LeRoy Blommaert Collection

Chapter 16: Cars and Buses

County Traction Company Equipment Roster
Cars Leased From Chicago Railways

Numbers	Builder	Date	Length	Width	Height	Seats	Weight	Motors	Trucks	Control	Comments
201, 202, 207-209, 221, 228-231	Brownell	1895	28' 9"	7' 7"	11' 0"	24	17,000	2-GE800	Brownell	GE-K2	Returned 11/16/1911
404-409	CWDRwy	1884	31' 4"	7' 6"	11' 0"	24	17,000	2-GE800	Brill 21C	GE-K2	Returned 11/16/1911
410-411	WCStRRCo.	1892	32' 6"	7' 6"	11' 0"	24	18,450	2-GE800	Brill 21C	GE-K2	
3819, 3821-3830, 3836, 3837	Gilbert	1891	36' 6"	8' 2"	11' 10"	36	29,000	2-GE57	Bemis	GE-K11	Acq. 1906 from Int'l Rwy. Co. Buffalo N.Y.
3839-3841, 3843, 3845, 3846-3852, 3855, 3860, 3862-3866, 3868	American	1895	38' 0"	8' 7'	11' 10"	35	34,200	2-GE57	McGuire 3	GE-K11	Acq. 1906 from United Rwys of St. Louis, MO
3975	Brownell	1895	30' 6"	-	-	28	17,000	2-GE800	Brill 21C	GE-K2	Motorized 1896
4051	Wells & French	1895	30' 0"	7' 6"	10' 9"	24	17,000	2-GE800	Brill 21C	GE-K2	Ex-No. Chicago Street RR Co #951
4096	Stephenson	1886	29' 10"	7' 7'	10' 6"	30	17,000	2-GE800	Brill 21C	GE-K2	Motorized 1895
4287	American	1892	31' 2"	7' 6"	10' 10"	28	17,500	2-GE800	Brill 21E	GE-K	Motorized 1895
4302, 4388	American	1895	30' 0"	-	-	28	17,000	2-GE800	Brill 21C	GE-K2	Motorized 1896
4378	Brill	1900	31' 0"	-	-	-	-	2-GE800	Brill 21C	GE-K2	Compressed air car, motorized 1906
4403, 4422, 4427	American	1895	31' 2"	7' 6"	10' 10"	28	17,500	2-GE800	Brill 21C	GE-K2	Motorized 1906
4474	Chgo. Union Traction	1907	38' 5"	7' 4"	11' 10"	36	33,600	2-GE57	McGuire 3	GE-K11	Ex-Grip car rebuilt 1907

Cars 3840, 3841, 3845, 3846, 3848, 3850, 3852, 3855, 3865, and 3868 were used on the Evanston line.

Cars 3843, 3849, 3851, 3860, 3862-64, and 3866 were leased January 3, 1912 and used on the Madison Street line.

retrieve most of the cars that it had leased to County Traction. Four single-truck cars that were standing on Madison Street, west of the Des Plaines River, were not brought back. Also, one single-truck wrecker was left at the Lake Street car house. Apparently, the Chicago Railways felt that these five cars were not worth the effort to reclaim.

County Traction Company Equipment Roster

Cars Leased From Chicago City Railway

Numbers	Builder	Date	Length	Width	Height	Seats	Weight	Motors	Trucks	Control
2143, 2147, 2188, 2118,	Wells & French	1896	31' 1"	7' 8'	10' 4"	30	18,030	2-WH12B	McGuire A1	GE-K
2260	Pullman	1896	30' 0"	7' 7"	10' 6"	30	18,020	2-WH12B	McGuire	GE-K

Leased 2/23/1912 for 6 months.

Cars Owned by County Traction

Numbers	Builder	Date	Length	Width	Height	Seats	Weight	Motors	Trucks	Control
107-120	McGuire-Cummings	1912	45' 0"	8' 8"	11' 10"	44	44,000	4-GE226	McGuire-Cummings 10B	GE-K35G2

Ex-Suburban Railroad 107-120.

Cars of the Suburban Railroad

In 1896, the Suburban Construction Company ordered 24 cars from the Pullman Company for service on the Suburban Electric Railway Company. This order was for 12 motor cars, numbered 100–111 and 12 trailers, numbered 500–511. The motor cars were 42 feet 6 inches long with vestibules at the ends. Twenty-four Hale and Kilburn "walkover" spring edged pattern, rattan covered, double seats were provided. Push buttons were furnished at each seat enabling a passenger to signal the motorman to stop. The trailers were of the same dimensions but, were open-ended and seated only 36. The cars were mounted on McGuire 26 trucks. Upon each powered truck was mounted a Walker 2000 50-horsepower motor. Controls were of the Walker series-parallel type. Christensen air brakes were used, the compressor being driven from the car axle. The motor cars weighed 40,000 pounds and the trailers 26,000 pounds. These cars were considered suitable for year around use.

Even before the cars were delivered, it was realized that more motor cars would be needed. Trailers 504 and 505 were rebuilt into motor cars at the Pullman Works and the open-ends were replaced with vestibules. The cars were renumbered 112 and 113.

When the Chicago, Harlem & Batavia lines were electrified, six trailers, numbers 513, 516-517, and 519-521 were sent back to Pullman in 1898 and rebuilt into motor cars like the 504 and 505. The cars were equipped with General Electric motors and controls. For heating, cars were initially furnished with Gould hot water heaters

The Suburban Railroad's first car order included twelve motor cars, numbered 100-111 and twelve trailers numbered 500-511. Car 111, photographed at the Pullman plant, was the highest numbered motor car in this order.

Krambles-Peterson Archive

Chapter 16: Cars and Buses

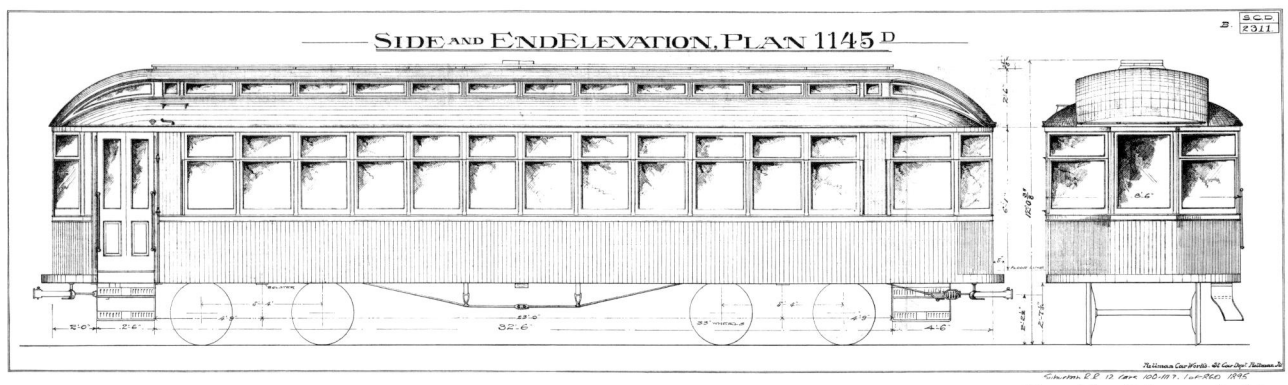

The company photographer recorded an interior view of car 111 before it was shipped from the Pullman plant. The car had seating for 48 passengers provided on 24 double seats.
Krambles-Peterson Archive

which were later replaced with Peter Smith stoves. The cars were equipped with Christensen brakes. These were replaced with Allis-Chalmers equipment

For operation on the Chicago & Southwestern, which was not electrified, one steam engine and 4 coaches were used. The locomotive, number 7, was purchased second hand from the Wisconsin Central. It was a 4-4-0 built by Baldwin. In 1888, it was rebuilt for suburban service and converted to a 4-4-4 and sold to the Chicago & Northern Pacific. The locomotive retained its original number on each railway that owned it. The coaches were disposed of during 1902, but the steam locomotive was retained for hauling coal from the Chicago Terminal Transfer interchange at Harlem Avenue to the powerhouse.

Trailers were still needed for the summer picnic and cemetery business. Sixteen car bodies were purchased in 1898 from the Cicero & Proviso Street Railway Company. These cars were built by the Pullman Company in 1891 as motor cars. They were mounted on Jackson & Sharp trucks. These trucks were originally used on the

192

The Chicago & West Towns Railways

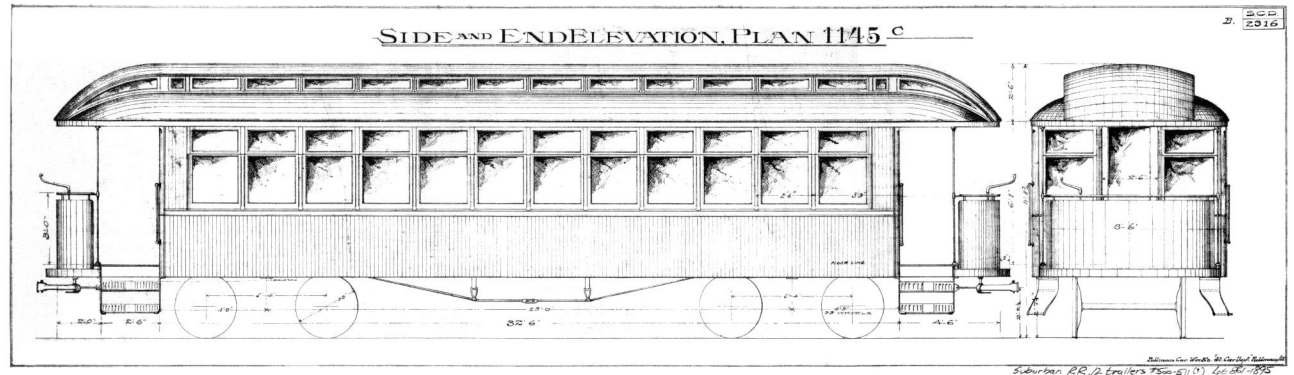

Car 507's distinctive open-ends are prominent in this side view. The trailers were the same length as the powered cars, but provided seating for 36 passengers.

Krambles-Peterson Archive

The interior photograph of Suburban Railroad car 500 reveals that the interiors of the trailers were very similar, except for the number of seats, to those of the powered cars.

Krambles-Peterson Archive

Intramural Railway cars at the World's Columbian Exposition held in Chicago in 1893. In 1900, two more of these cars were purchased. As the windows were removed, they became open cars. These cars were numbered 1–18.

The ownership of the Suburban also had an interest in the Chicago, Harvard & Geneva Lake Railway Company. This 11-mile line connected Harvard, Illinois and Fontana, Wisconsin on the southern shore of Lake Geneva. Every summer from 1898 until 1912, two of the four remaining Suburban trailers were shipped to Harvard for service on this line. When the County Traction Company gained control of the Suburban in 1912, this arrangement was terminated. Instead, two cars, 504 and 505, were sold to the Chicago, Harvard & Geneva Lake becoming numbers 5 and 7 on this road. The cars were rebuilt with a baggage compartment.

Further changes in car numbering took place at the time County Traction

Chapter 16: Cars and Buses

Car 113 began its career as trailer 511. When the Suburban realized it needed more motor cars than it had originally ordered, trailers 510 and 511 were returned to Pullman for rebuilding. Emerging from this process as an enclosed motor car, the 113 was photographed at the Pullman plant in Chicago prior to being shipped back to the railroad. The cars were renumbered again in 1912, with 510 becoming 504 and 511 becoming 505.
Krambles-Peterson Archive

purchased the Suburban. Cars 112 and 113 were renumbered 504 and 505. In addition, cars 100–111 were renumbered 510–521. Thus, all Suburban cars were numbered in the 500-series.

In March 1912, 20 arch-roof semi-steel cars, numbered 101-120, were ordered from the McGuire-Cummings Car Manufacturing Company. These cars were 45 feet, 6 inches long and seated 40 people They were equipped with McGuire-Cummings model number 10B4 trucks, four General Electric model number GE-226A 40-horsepower motors, and General Electric type K35G2 controls. They weighed 47,000 pounds. These cars were patterned after the "turtleback" cars 1506-1720, that were being built at this time by the Chicago Railways Company.

The order for 20 cars was canceled after construction of the cars was completed. Cars 101-106 were never delivered. They were sold to the Seattle, Renton & Southern Railway and were re-numbered 201–206. The cars were used between Seattle and Rainier Beach. Cars 107–120 were delivered to the County Traction Company.

In 1912, the 500 series cars were rebuilt with front exits and converted for pay-as-you-enter loading. General Electric 203L motors were also installed. Until this time, the cars had only a single rear door for entrance and exit. In 1914, all 21 cars were further rebuilt. Seventeen were kept as motor cars each getting four General Electric 203 50-horsepower motors and McGuire Cummings 10B4 trucks with General Electric K35A controls. Four cars, 505 and 507–509, received C97A multiple unit controllers. Four other cars, numbers 500, 501, 503 and 512 became control trailers with the installation of C97A controls. However, these four cars retained their McGuire model number 26 trucks. The paint scheme was changed from orange to deep green with gold striping.

Seven of the old Cicero & Proviso Street Railway Company trailers were also rebuilt in 1914 and renumbered 20–26. One of these cars was rebuilt into a utility motor car and renumbered 14. The remaining cars were not rebuilt. None of these trailers had controls. Therefore, when these cars were in use, they could not be at the head end of the train. These trailers saw peak load service, on Sundays during the summer months, in two and three car trains.

The Suburban had very few service cars. In 1896, a 5000-gallon sprinkler was acquired second-hand from the West Chicago Street Railroad Company. A McGuire sweeper was purchased in 1897. In 1900, a single-truck Taunton snow plow was purchased.

When cars 107–120 were transferred to the County Traction Company, some utility cars were transferred to the Suburban. These included snow sweepers 2 and 3, snow plow number 4, and a double-truck cab-on-flat utility motor number 12. All were built by McGuire-Cummings in 1912. Also single-truck flat cars 01–04 and double-truck flat cars 0001–0003 were transferred.

Chicago & West Towns Railway Company

The Chicago & West Towns Railway Company acquired 51 passenger cars, 12 utility motor cars, and 12 utility trailers when it began operating the lines in 1913. All of the passenger cars and most of the utility cars were owned by the Suburban Railroad Company. In addition to these cars, 10 streetcars were leased from the Chicago Railways Company.

In January 1914, 10 cars were ordered from the McGuire-Cummings Manufacturing Company. They were delivered in May 1914. These cars, numbered 121 through 130, were standard arch-roof, semi-steel cars. They were similar in appearance to Suburban Railroad cars 107 through 120, although their body construction was a little different. The cars had rattan seats for 44 passengers and were equipped with 2 General Electric 203L motors and General Electric K51A controls. The streetcars replaced cars, dubbed by the trainmen as "antiquated bicycle" cars, that the West Towns had leased from the Chicago Railways Company. The term "antiquated bicycle" was derived from the design of the car's truck. The design, also known as a maximum traction truck, featured one large wheel and one smaller wheel as one would see in an early model bicycle. These new McGuire-Cummings cars, powered with only 2 motors, were considered by the operating personnel to be "slow." They operated satisfactorily when traffic was light and when there weren't too many cars on the line. However, on sunny summer days when large crowds needed to be carried, their lack of adequate horsepower became evident.

Two wooden double-truck streetcars, numbered 105 and 106, were purchased from McGuire-Cummings in May 1915. The two cars were built in 1912 for the Midlothian & Blue Island Railroad Company. This line, owned by the Midlothian Country Club, provided shuttle service on 1-1/4 miles of track between the club and the Chicago, Rock Island & Pacific Railroad's main line station at Midlothian, Illinois, a suburb about 18 miles southwest of Chicago. The Midlothian canceled its order with McGuire-Cummings when its plan to extend the railway to Blue Island did not materialize. As delivered cars 105 and 106 had rattan seating for 40 passengers, McGuire-Cummings 10B4 MCB trucks, 4 General Electric 80 motors, and General Electric K35G2 controls. As opposed to cars 121-130, the West Towns crews considered these four-motor cars to be "fast."

The Chicago & West Towns acquired an additional 12 cars from McGuire-Cummings over a two year period. Cars 100-104 arrived in March 1917; Cars 131-132 arrived in July 1918; Cars 133-137 in April 1919. These arch roof cars were of steel construction with rattan seats for 44 passengers. These 12 cars were equipped with McGuire-Cummings 10B4 trucks, 4 General Electric 247D 35- horsepower motors, and General Electric K35G2 controls. The 1918 order appears to have

The first 10 cars purchased by the newly formed Chicago & West Towns, numbered 121-130, were ordered in January 1914. Car 123, representative of this group of cars, was photographed in front of the Suburban barn in April 1939.
James J. Buckley photo

Chapter 16: Cars and Buses 195

Two wooden streetcars, numbered 105 and 106, were purchased in 1915. Car 105 posed at the Harlem Avenue carbarn on April 23, 1939. An interior photo of car 106 was taken on July 4, 1941. In 1928, the West Towns converted its fleet of cars from two-man operation to one-man. This conversion necessitated removal of the car's bulkheads. Car 106 was an exception and the bulkhead had not been removed; the vestibule remained intact. The car continued to require two men for operation.

James J. Buckley photos

been placed for 7 cars (5 delivered in 1917 and 2 in 1918) because 5 identical cars were offered for sale by the manufacturer at this time and 7 Suburban Railroad cars (504, 513, 516, 517, 519, 520 and 521) were traded in for them. Car 506 was scrapped after being involved in an accident with an Indiana Harbor Belt train on April 14, 1918.

McGuire-Cummings did a brisk business in reselling the cars it accepted in trade with the West Towns. Three of the cars were sold to the Washington & Virginia Railway and became numbered 32, 33, and 120 on this railway. Two of these cars, numbers 32 and 33, were later re-

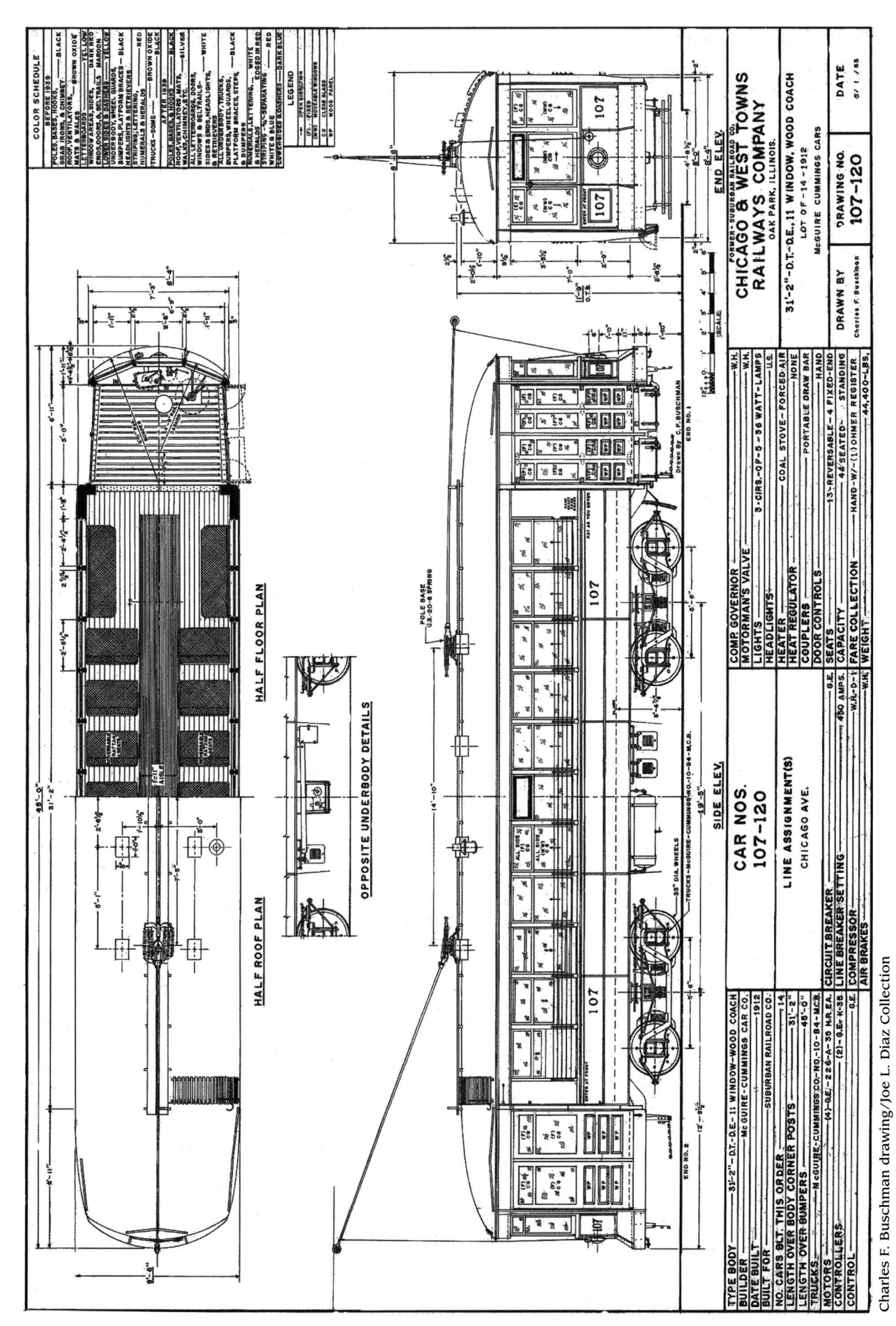

Charles F. Buschman drawing/Joe L. Diaz Collection

The Chicago & West Towns purchased an additional 12 identical arched roof cars in 1917, 1918, and 1919. The five that arrived in March 1917 were numbered 100-104. The car numbers were selected to complete gaps in the 100-series numbering sequence. The two cars that arrived in July 1918 were numbered 131 and 132 while the five delivered in 1919 were numbered 133-137. Car 135 was photographed at the 19th Avenue terminal of the Madison Street line on July 20, 1941.

James J. Buckley photo

sold to the Mesaba Electric Railway in Minnesota. In 1920, two additional cars were sold to the Escanaba Traction Company in Michigan and were assigned numbers 120 and 121 on this property. Another sale of two Suburban Railroad cars was completed with the Washington & Virginia Railway and carried car numbers 237 and 238 on this carrier. Three cars were also sold to the Cincinnati, Lawrenceburg & Aurora Electric Street Railroad Company. One of these cars was former Suburban Railroad 516. In 1921, two of these cars were rebuilt into container cars. Finally, several other cars were sold to an unknown railroad in the Buffalo-Niagara Falls, New York area.

All of the West Towns cars 100-137 were arranged for pay-as-you-enter operation with two-man crews. The cars were equipped with Ohmer fare registers. As delivered, the streetcars were painted yellow with maroon striping and lettering. The interior finish of cars 107-120 was cherry while the remaining cars had an oak finish.

In 1923, 14 medium-weight steel cars were ordered from McGuire-Cummings. The cars were of the straight-side girder-type of construction with an arch roof. The streetcars were equipped with folding doors and steps at both front and rear. Ten of these cars, numbers 142 through 151, were built for service on the Lake Street route while the remaining four, numbers 138-141, were designed to operate on the La Grange line. Cars 138-141 were provided with Van Dorn tightlock drawbars as part of the equipment needed for multiple-unit operation. All 14 cars were placed into service in May 1924.

Cars 142-151 were built with platforms flush with the car body floor. A 3½ inch ramp from the bolsters to the end sills served to reduce the height of the steps. The side posts were spaced on 29-inch centers and with a 46-foot overall length, providing seating for 44 passengers. The streetcar body was mounted on McGuire-Cummings 62 low-level trucks. These trucks were especially designed to maintain a minimum four-inch clearance above the rail. The cars were powered with four General Electric 247T 35-horsepower motors. Twenty-six inch rolled steel wheels were used. Six cars were equipped with General Electric K35HH controls while the remaining four streetcars used General Electric K35G2 controls. The seats were upholstered in leather.

The other four cars in this order, numbers 138 through 141, were built for service on the Suburban's La Grange route. The streetcars were obviously of similar construction to their sisters numbers 142-151. However, they were one foot longer, three inches taller, and 8,700 pounds

Of the 14 streetcars purchased in 1923, four were designed for use on the La Grange line. Cars 138-141 had different technical specifications including drop platforms, high-level trucks equipped with 34-inch wheels, and couplers to permit multiple-unit operation. Car 141 waited at the Cermak Road and Kenton Avenue terminal of the La Grange line to begin its westbound run in 1947.

Robert W. Gibson photo

The interior of car 139 is illustrated in this photograph. The four cars of this type, numbered 138-141, were delivered with rattan seats. Over the years, the railway upgraded the seats in some cars to leather, but not those in cars 138-141.

James J. Buckley photo

Chapter 16: Cars and Buses 199

Cars 142-151 were ordered along with cars 138-141 in 1923 and were placed in service during May 1924. Designed for service needs primarily on Lake Street, the cars featured low level trucks equipped with 26-inch wheels. The car was operating on Lake Street at 25th Avenue in 1936 when this photograph was composed.

Ed Frank, Jr. photo

The leather seats shown in the interior view of car 151 were installed by the manufacturer prior to delivery.

Robert W. Gibson photo

heavier than their sister cars. These streetcars were equipped with McGuire-Cummings 77 MCB trucks with 34-inch wheels. With the selection of these wheels and trucks, the cars were built with drop platforms. The four cars were built for multiple-unit operation. The cars had Van Dorn tightlock couplers, four General Electric 247D motors and General Electric PC5 controls.

In 1927, 14 additional streetcars were purchased from Cummings Car & Coach Company. Ten of these cars were built for the La Grange line to replace a like number of 500-series streetcars while the other 4 cars on the order were for service on the Madison Street and Lake Street routes.

The cars for the La Grange line were

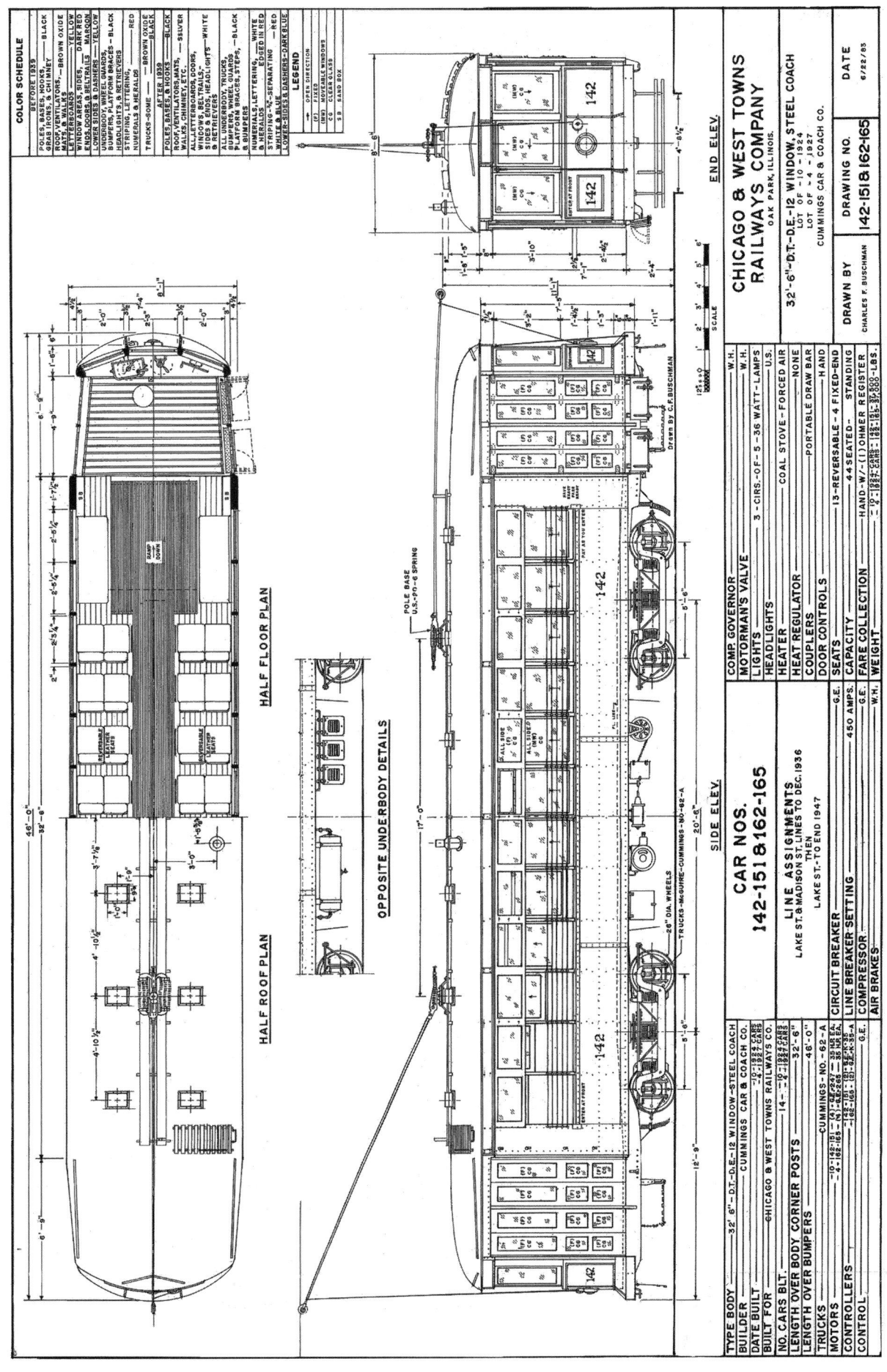

Chapter 16: Cars and Buses

Charles F. Buschman drawing/Joe L. Diaz Collection

The West Towns' last order of streetcars included 10 units for the La Grange line, numbered 152-161. The highest numbered unit of this group, car 161, was westbound on the La Grange line as it turned off Cermak Road to continue it journey south on Harlem Avenue. Robert W. Gibson photo

The interior view of car 157 showed its leather seats and coal stove. James J. Buckley photo

similar in appearance and design to the cars ordered in 1923. The bodies were of steel construction. However, certain equipment was salvaged from the retired 500-series cars. For the salvage operation, the cars were shipped to the Cummings plant at Paris, Illinois. The new cars were equipped with the big MCB trucks. This design feature necessitated building the cars with drop platforms. All ten cars received four General Electric 203L 50-horsepower motors each, salvaged from the old cars. A variety of General Electric control apparatus was used

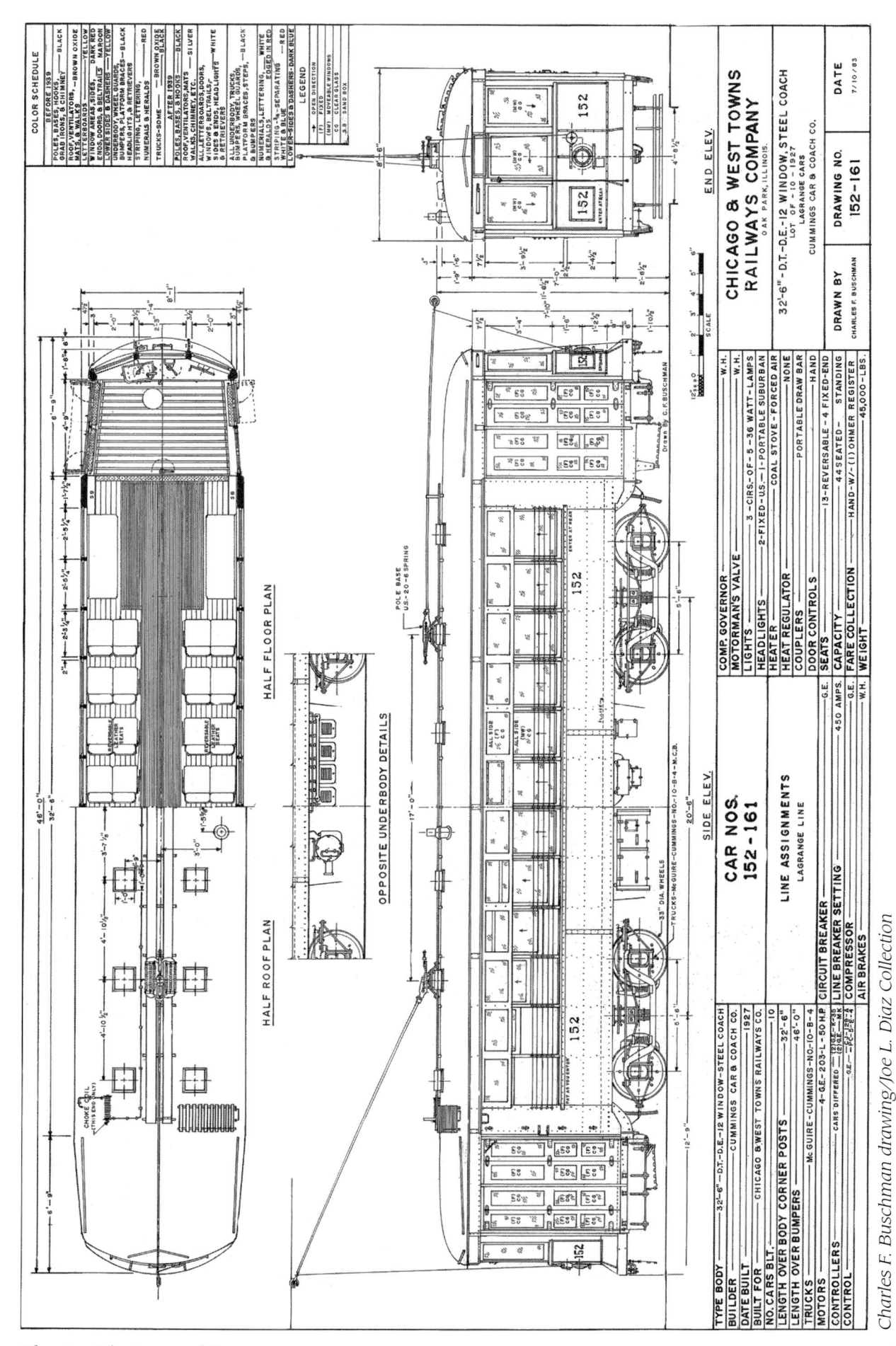

Chapter 16: Cars and Buses

Charles F. Buschman drawing/Joe L. Diaz Collection

Cars 162-165 were manufactured by the Cummings Car & Coach Company in 1927. Car 163, representative of the last group of four streetcars received by the Chicago & West Towns, was proceeding eastbound on Lake Street near the Des Plaines River in River Forest. Circa 1945.   Robert W. Gibson photo

By the time this photograph was taken, the electrical propulsion equipment had been removed from car 503 and it was used as a trailer. The unit was photographed at the Suburban carbarn circa 1940.

Donald N. Idarius photo

on these cars. The ten cars had rattan seats accommodating 44 passengers. The cars were placed into service in March 1927.

The four cars, numbered 162 through 165, were built for service on the Lake Street route. These cars were built low level like the cars 142-151. The cars were equipped with Cummings 62A trucks with 26-inch wheels. The cars were powered with 4 General Electric 265D 35 horsepower motors and General Electric K75A controls. These four streetcars were built with rattan seats.

In 1928, the West Towns chose to convert 26 cars in its fleet from two-man operation to one-man. Cars 100-102, 107-120, 121, 125, 129, 142-147 were selected for conversion. The Cummings Car & Coach Company sent a crew up to the Lake Street car house in Oak Park from the plant at Paris, Illinois to do the work. The largest part of the task was to remove

204   *The Chicago & West Towns Railways*

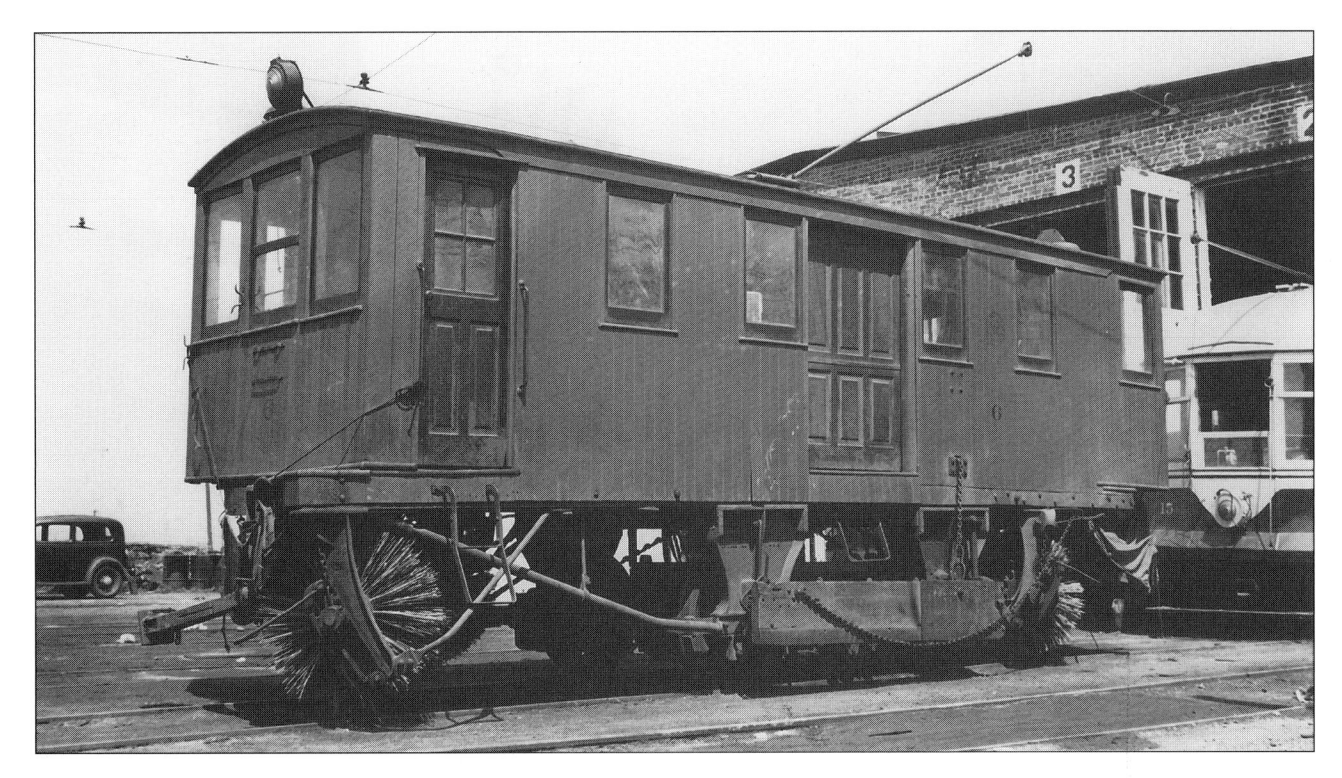

Sweeper 6 was also brought out of the barn in the middle of summer for photographs. Sweeper 6 was built by the McGuire Manufacturing Company in 1897. This unit was the earliest built of all West Towns sweepers and was identifiable from the others by its flat front. June 22, 1941.

James J. Buckley photo

the bulkheads from the cars constructed from wood. Steel cars, numbers 138-165, did not have bulkheads. Other work consisted of changing the door opening mechanism from the center of the platform to the corner so that the motorman could work the doors. The rear doors were sealed off.

Seventeen cars were converted to "one-man, two-man" operation in 1928. These cars were numbered 103-105, 122-124, 126-128 and 130-137. With this scheme, the rear doors could be used. Two sets of door controls were installed so that either the motorman or the conductor could operate the doors. For one-man service, a device locked the rear doors. Later, 15 of these cars were converted to one-man operation. In 1940, cars 103-104 and 132-137 were made one-man while the remaining seven cars, 122-124, 126-128 and 130 were converted to one man operation in 1942.

Not all streetcars were converted to one-man operation in 1928. For some reason, wooden car 106 was retained for strictly two-man operation and, therefore, was the only wooden car in which bulkheads were not removed. The regular La Grange cars, numbered 152 through 161, remained two-man until 1942. The multiple-unit cars 138-141, which were not

In addition, on June 22, 1941, plow 7 was brought out from the dark reaches of the Suburban barn. The unit was built by the Taunton Locomotive Works of Taunton, Massachusetts in 1900 for the Suburban Railroad.

James J. Buckley photo

Chapter 16: Cars and Buses

An interior view of car 502. Ed Frank, Jr. photo

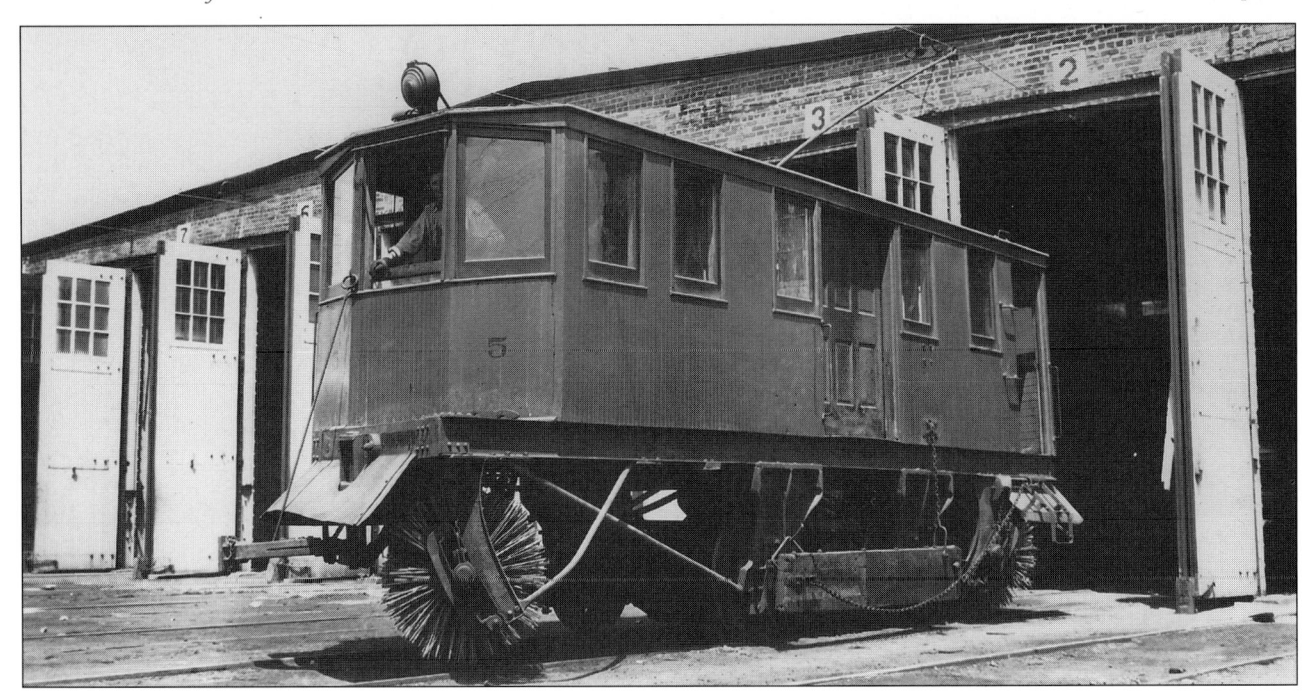

Sweeper 5 was pulled out of the Suburban carbarn for photographs on June 22, 1941. Since the West Towns was controlled by the Cummings family, rolling stock was purchased from a Cummings-owned company. Over the years, the firm had several names. It began manufacturing in the late 1880s as the McGuire Manufacturing Company. Later, the firm was renamed the McGuire-Cummings Manufacturing Company. Finally, the name became the Cummings Car & Coach Company. It produced its last cars in 1930, but produced spare parts until 1943 when the firm went out of business. James J. Buckley photo

used that often, remained two-man until 1947.

A small number of other modifications were also performed. Quite a bit of motor switching was done after the Oak Park car house fire in December 1936. Cars 122, 123, 127, 128, and 130 were delivered with two GE-203L motors and K51A controls. Cars 122, 123 and 127 had four GE-226A motors and K35G2 controls installed after the fire. Similarly, cars 128 and 130 were re-equipped with four GE-247D motors and K35G2 controls after the fire. The best equipment remaining after the conflagration was salvaged and re-used. Over a period of years, leather seats were installed in cars 112, 115, 119 and 152-165. The multiple-unit cars kept their rattan seats.

The utility cars had a varied history.

206   The Chicago & West Towns Railways

Plow 8 was designed to clear the tracks from a heavy snow storm. To the basic flat workcar design, Cummings Car & Coach added air operated shear plows, side wings to direct the snow away from the tracks, and ice diggers. Among the railway's motormen, the car was affectionately known as a "double truck nightmare" because, while bucking snow, the car would tend to derail. The plow was photographed in the rear yard of the Suburban carbarn on March 1, 1947. The greenhouses of the Oechslin Florist Company, the railway's only commercial freight customer, appear behind the car.
Donald N. Idarius photo

Snow sweeper 9 was simply doing its job on February 19, 1938 as it operated north on Harlem Avenue at 36th Street.
John F. Humiston photo

In December 1910, when County Traction began operating the lines, the only vehicle remaining in the Lake Street car house was an old single-truck pull car. It was apparently left there because the Chicago Railways did not want it. In 1912, the Suburban Railroad owned 3 utility cars: A single-truck sweeper, a single-truck snow plow, and a double-truck sprinkler. These vehicles were numbered 6, 7, and 8 respectively. A joint County Traction-Suburban Railroad order was placed with McGuire-Cummings in 1912 for 9 utility cars. This order included one double-truck sprinkler (numbered 9), three snow sweepers (numbered 1-3), a single-truck snow plow (numbered 4), a double-truck cab-on-flat work motor (numbered 12), and three single-truck dump cars (numbered X1-X3). In addition, in 1913, a

Chapter 16: Cars and Buses

The "first" car 10 on the West Towns' roster was the shop dinky. It was used to pull streetcar trucks around the shop, but was not allowed on the street. It had a long history as it was built in 1895 to haul trailers to the cable cars of the West Chicago Street Railroad. After the cable cars were retired, the large center door was cut in and the car was used in work service. Car 10 carried its 1895 yellow paint job and hole in the side until its demise in the 1936 carbarn fire.
Electric Railway Historical Society Collection

The "second" motor 10 was used as a wrecker. With shop foreman Ben Gosse, Sr. at the controller, car 10 was dispatched to all accidents and derailments on the former Cicero & Proviso lines. Unfortunately, it was destroyed in the Lake Street carbarn fire on December 2, 1936.
Ed Frank, Jr. photo

single-truck work car was built in the Lake Street shop. Also in 1913, another snow sweeper, numbered 5, was added to the fleet. Even though County Traction operated the Suburban Railroad, for legal reasons it was not purchased until 1918. Utility cars on the Suburban's roster included snow sweepers numbered 2 and 6, snow plows numbered 4 and 7, sprinkler car number 8, and work motor number 12. In 1914, one of the former Cicero & Proviso Street Railway trailers was motorized, numbered as car 14, and used in utility service. Miscellaneous utility equipment included double-truck flat car 0001 (McGuire-Cummings, 1912) and double-

Chicago & West Towns Railway Company Equipment Roster
Passenger Cars

Numbers	Builder	Date	Length	Width	Height	Seats	Weight	Motors	Trucks	Control	Notes
1, 5, 6, 8, 9, 10, 15, 16, 20-26	Pullman	1891	32" 6"	7' 10"	11' 0"	36	-	None	Pullman 22	None	Ex-Suburban RR. Cars 2-4, 7, 11-13 rebuilt in 1914 and renumbered 20-26. Car 14 rebuilt into work motor in 1914. All cars scrapped in 1923.
100-104	McGuire-Cummings	1917	45' 0"	8' 8"	11' 10"	44	43,500	4-GE247D	McGuire-Cummings 10B4	K35G2	Car 102 scrapped 1947; 100-1 and 103-4 scrapped 1948.
105	McGuire-Cummings	1912	44' 1"	8' 8"	12' 1"	40	45,000	4-GE80	McGuire-Cummings 10B4	K35G2	Built for Midlothian & Blue Island. Out-of-service by July 1940; scrapped 1943.
106	McGuire-Cummings	1912	44" 1"	8' 8"	12' 1"	40	45,000	4-GE226A	McGuire-Cummings 10B4	K35G2	Built for Midlothian & Blue Island. Delivered with GE80 motors; motors changed before May 1, 1936.
107-120	McGuire-Cummings	1912	45' 0"	8' 8"	11' 10"	44	44,400	4-GE226A	McGuire-Cummings 10B4	K35G2	Ex-Suburban RR 107-120. Cars 109-10, 113, 117, and 120 burned 12/2/36. Car 115 scrapped 1944; cars 108, 114, and 116 scrapped 1947; cars 107,111-12, and 119 scrapped 1948.
121, 125, 129	McGuire Cummings	1914	45' 0"	8' 8"	11' 10"	44	44,400	2-GE203L	McGuire-Cummings 10B4	K51A	Lost in 12/2/1936 carbarn fire.
122, 123, 127	McGuire-Cummings	1914	45' 0"	8' 8"	11' 10"	44	44,400	4-GE226A	McGuire-Cummings 10B4	K35G2	Car 123 scrapped 1943; cars 122 and 127 scrapped 1948.
124, 126	McGuire-Cummings	1914	45' 0"	8' 8"	11' 10"	44	44,400	2-GE203L	McGuire-Cummings10B4	K51A	Scrapped in 1948.
128, 130	McGuire-Cummings	1914	45' 0"	8' 8"	11' 10"	44	44,400	4-GE247D	McGuire-Cummings 10B4	K35G2	Scrapped 1948.
131-132	McGuire-Cummings	1918	45' 0"	8' 8"	11' 10"	44	43,500	4-GE247D	McGuire-Cummings 10B4	K35G2	Car 131 lost in 12/2/1936 carbarn fire. Car 132 scrapped in 1947.
133-137	McGuire-Cummings	1919	45' 0"	8' 8"	11' 10"	44	43,500	4-GE247D	McGuire-Cummings 10B4	K35G2	Car 137 lost in 12/2/1936 carbarn fire. Car 135 scrapped 1947; 133-4, and 136 scrapped 1948.
138-141	McGuire-Cummings	1924	47' 0"	8' 4"	11' 6"	44	46,200	4-GE203L	McGuire-Cummings 77	PC5	Cars 138-140 scrapped 1948. Car 141 at Illinois Railway Museum. Motors changed from GE247D in 1947. Master control: 129A.
142-147	McGuire-Cummings	1924	46' 0"	8' 1"	11' 1"	44	37,500	4-GE247T	McGuire-Cummings 62A	K35HH	Cars 143, 146-7 lost in 12/2/1936 carbarn fire. Cars 142 and 144-5 scrapped in 1947.
148-150	McGuire-Cummings	1924	46' 0"	8' 1"	11' 1"	44	37,500	4-GE247T	McGuire-Cummings 62A	K35JJ	Cars 148-150 lost in 12/2/1936 carbarn fire.
151	McGuire-Cummings	1924	46' 0"	8' 1"	11' 1"	44	37,500	4-GE265D	McGuire-Cummings 62A	K35G2	Scrapped 1947.
152	Cummings Car &Coach	1927	46' 0"	8' 1"	11' 6"	44	45,000	4-GE203L	McGuire-Cummings 10B4	K35JJ	Scrapped 1948. Used trucks, motors and controls from scrapped 500-series cars.
153, 155	Cummings Car & Coach	1927	46' 0"	8' 1"	11' 6"	44	45,000	4-GE203L	McGuire-Cummings 10B4	C97A	Scrapped 1947. Used trucks and motors from scrapped 500-series cars. Built with C97A control.
154	Cummings Car & Coach	1927	46' 0"	8' 1"	11' 6"	44	45,000	4-GE203L	McGuire-Cummings 10B4	K35G2	Scrapped 1947. Used trucks, motors and controls from scrapped 500-series cars.

Chicago & West Towns Railway Company Equipment Roster
Passenger Cars

Numbers	Builder	Date	Length	Width	Height	Seats	Weight	Motors	Trucks	Control	Notes
156-159	Cummings Car & Coach	1927	46' 0"	8' 1"	11' 6"	44	45,000	4-GE203L	McGuire-Cummings 10B4	PC5	Scrapped 1948. Used trucks, motors and controls from scrapped 500-series cars. Master control: 129A.
160-161	Cummings Car & Coach	1927	46' 0"	8' 1"	11' 6"	44	45,000	4-GE203L	McGuire-Cummings 10B4	K35G2	Scrapped 1948.
162	Cummings Car & Coach	1927	46' 0"	8' 1"	11' 1"	44	37,500	4-GE265D	Cummings Car & Coach 62A	K75A	Lost in 12/2/1936 carbarn fire.
163-165	Cummings Car & Coach	1927	46' 0"	8' 1"	11' 1"	44	37,500	4-GE265D	Cummings Car & Coach 62A	K75A	Scrapped 1947.
500, 501, 503	Pullman	1897	42' 6"	8' 8"	12' 1"	48	40,000	none	McGuire 26	C97A	Ex-Suburban RR. Pullman order 861.
502	Pullman	1897	42' 6"	8' 8"	12' 1"	48	50,000	none	McGuire Cummings 10B4	C97A	Ex-Suburban RR 102, 512. Pullman order 860. Renumbered from 512 after 1920. Out-of-service 1927; scrapped 1936.
504	Pullman	1897	42' 6"	8' 8"	12' 1"	48	50,000	4-GE203L	McGuire-Cummings 10B4	K35G2	Ex-Suburban RR trailer 510; rebuilt 1898 as motor car 112; renumbered 1912. Pullman order 861.
505	Pullman	1897	42' 6"	8' 8"	12' 1"	48	50,000	4-GE203L	McGuire-Cummings 10B4	C97A	Ex-Suburban RR trailer 511; rebuilt as motor car 113; renumbered 1912. Pullman order 861.
506	Pullman	1897	42' 6"	8' 8"	12' 1"	48	50,000	4-GE203L	McGuire-Cummings 10B4	K35G2	Ex-Suburban RR 506. Pullman order 861.
507, 508, 509	Pullman	1897	42' 6"	8' 8"	12' 1"	48	50,500	4-GE203L	McGuire-Cummings 10B4	C97A	Ex-Suburban RR 507-9. Pullman order 861.
510, 511	Pullman	1897	42' 6"	8' 8"	12' 1"	48	50,000	4-GE203L	McGuire-Cummings 10B4	K35G2	Ex-Suburban RR 112,113; 510, 511. Pullman order 860.
512	Pullman	1897	42' 6"	8' 8"	12' 1"	48	50,000	4-GE-203L	McGuire-Cummings 10B4	K35G2	Ex-Suburban RR 105, 515. Pullman order 860. Rebuilt into line car 15 in 1927; scrapped 1948.
513, 514	Pullman	1897	42' 6"	8' 8"	12' 1"	48	50,000	4-GE203L	McGuire Cummings 10B4	K35G2	Ex-Suburban RR 103, 104; 513, 514. Pullman 860.
516-521	Pullman	1897	42' 6"	8' 8"	12' 1"	48	50,000	4-GE203L	McGuire-Cummings 10B4	K35G2	Ex-Suburban RR 106-111; 516-521, Pullman 860.

Cars Leased from Chicago Railways Company
July 1913 to May 1914

Numbers	Builder	Date	Length	Width	Height	Seats	Weight	Motors	Trucks	Control	Notes
9 Cars	American	1895	38' 0"	8' 7"	11' 10"	35	34,200	2-GE57	Brill	K11	Cars 3840, 3841, 3846, 3847, 3849, 3851, 3860, 3862, and 3863. American 95.
4474	CUT	1907	38"5"	7' 4"	11' 0"	36	33,600	2-GE57	Brill	K11	Built by Chicago Union Traction.

Cars Leased from Chicago Surface Lines
January 3, 1936 to March 14, 1937

Numbers	Builder	Date	Length	Width	Height	Seats	Weight	Motors	Trucks	Control	Notes
6 cars	St. Louis	1907	41' 0"	8' 4"	11' 3"	40	46,640	4-GE80A	St. Louis 47B	K28A	Cars 1357, 1361, 1380, 1381, 1389, and 1397. St. Louis Car Company Lot 715.

Chicago & West Towns Railway Company Equipment Roster
Utility Cars

Numbers	Builder	Date	Length	Width	Height	Seats	Weight	Motors	Trucks	Control	Notes
1, 3	McGuire-Cummings	1912	28' 3"	8' 11"	10' 9"	n/a	30,000	2-GE57A	McGuire-Cummings	K10A	Single-Truck Sweeper. Cars 2 & 3 Ex-County Traction.
2	McGuire-Cummings	1912	28' 3"	8' 11"	10' 9"	n/a	30,000	2-GE80	McGuire-Cummings	K10A	All lost in Dec 2, 1936 carbarn fire.
4	McGuire-Cummings	1912	29' 6"	8' 6"	10' 6"	n/a	34,000	2-GE80	McGuire-Cummings	K10A	Single-Truck Plow. Ex-County Traction 4. Lost in Dec 12, 1936 carbarn fire.
5	McGuire-Cummings	1913	28' 3"	8' 11'	10' 9"	n/a	30,000	2-GE57A	McGuire-Cummings	K10A	Single-Truck Sweeper. Ex-County Traction 5.
6	McGuire	1897	29' 0"	9' 0"	10' 9"	n/a	30,000	2-W2000	McGuire	K11	Single-Truck Sweeper. Ex-Suburban RR 6.
7	Taunton	1900	27' 6"	8' 6"	11' 0"	n/a	25,000	2-W2000	Taunton	K10A	Single-Truck Snow Plow. Ex-Suburban RR 7.
8	West Chgo Street RR	1896	19' 3"	7' 2"	11' 0"	n/a	17,400	2-GE52	Brill 21E	K2	Double-Truck Sprinkler. Ex-Suburban RR 1. Scrapped 1923.
8	Cummings Car & Coach	1928	58' 6"	9' 2"	11' 7"	n/a	57,120	4-GE203L	McGuire-Cummings 10B4	K35G2	Double-Truck Snow Plow. Scrapped 1947.
9	McGuire-Cummings	1912	29' 6"	7' 6"	11' 1'	n/a	50,000	4-GE203L	McGuire-Cummings 10B4	K35G2	Ex-County Traction double-truck sprinkler. Sold in 1928 to Quebec Rwy, L&P. Renumbered 200.
9	Cummings Car & Coach	1928	28' 3"	8' 11"	10' 9"	n/a	30,000	2-GE80A	Cummings Car & Coach	K68	Single-Truck Snow Sweeper. Sold in 1948 to Sand Springs Rwy. Renumbered A-11.
10	Company Shops	1913	24' 0"	7' 4"	11' 1"	n/a	15,000	2-GE800	Brill	K10	Single-Truck Wrecker. Ex-County Traction. Lost in 12/2/1936 carbarn fire
10	Cummings Car & Coach	1930	28' 3"	8' 11'	10' 9"	n/a	30,000	2-GE57A	Cummings Car & Coach	K36	Single-Truck Sweeper. Lost in 12/2/1936 carbarn fire.
11	Wells & French	1895	13' 0"	7' 2"	11' 0"	n/a		2-GE800	Brill	K10A	Single-Truck Work Car. West Chgo St RR and Chgo Consolidated Traction 996. Purchased in 1916. Lost in 12/2/1936 carbarn fire.
12	McGuire-Cummings	1912	45' 0"	8' 6"	12' 3"			4-GE203L	McGuire-Cummings 10B4	K35G2	Double-Truck Work Car. Ex-County Traction 12. Built with 4-GE 226 motors; replaced with 4- 203L motors before 1920.
14	Pullman	1891	32' 6"	7' 11"	11' 4"			2-GE57A	McGuire 26	K10	Double-Truck Work Car. Ex-Suburban RR 14.
15	Pullman	1897	44' 6"	8' 6"	12' 0"		44,000	2-GE203L	McGuire-Cummings 10B4	K35G2	Double-Truck Line Car.
16	McGuire-Cummings	1914	28' 3"	8' 11"	10' 9"		30,000	2-GE88	McGuire-Cummings	K36	Ex-Evanston Rwy single-truck sweeper #1. Acquired 1936.
17	McGuire-Cummings		28' 3"	8' 11"	10' 9"		30,000	2-GE88	McGuire-Cummings	K36	Ex-Evanston Rwy single-truck sweeper #2. Acquired 1936.
18-19	McGuire-Cummings	1913	28' 3"	8' 11"	10' 9"		30,000	2-WH514	McGuire-Cummings	K51	Ex-Tri-City Rwy & Light Co single-truck sweepers 2 and 3. Acquired 12/1936.

Chapter 16: Cars and Buses

Chicago & West Towns Railway Company Equipment Roster
Utility Cars

Numbers	Builder	Date	Length	Width	Height	Seats	Weight	Motors	Trucks	Control	Notes
01	Company Shops	1912	22' 6"	7' 0"	4' 8"			none	Brill 21C	none	Single-Truck Flat Car.
02-03	Company Shops	1913	15' 0"	6' 0"	4' 6"			none	Stephenson	none	Single-Truck Flat Cars.
04	Company Shops		19' 6"	6' 4"	5' 0"			none	Brill 21C	none	Single-Truck Flat Car.
001	Company Shops	1912	12' 0"	8' 0"				none	Jackson & Sharp 22	none	Single-Truck Sand Car.
002	Company Shops	1913	12' 0"	8' 0"				none	Jackson & Sharp 22	none	Single-Truck Sand Car.
0001	McGuire-Cummings	1912	36' 4"	8' 5"	4' 0"			none	McGuire Cummings	none	Double-Truck Flat Car.
0002-0003	Company Shops	1913	36' 0"	8' 0"	4' 0"			none	Jackson & Sharp 22	none	Double-Truck Flat Cars.
X1-X3	McGuire-Cummings	1912	16' 0"	7' 0"	8' 1"			none	McGuire-Cummings	none	Single-Truck Cinder Cars.

There is some confusion regarding the cars of the Cicero & Proviso Street Railway Company that were purchased by the Suburban Railroad in 1899. Trade journals of the time said that sixteen cars were purchased. The Cicero & Proviso purchased the cars in two lots. Pullman lot number 683 was for twelve cars which the Cicero & Proviso had numbered 1-12. These cars were delivered with open ends. Pullman lot 711 was also for twelve cars which were numbered Cicero & Proviso 13-24. The cars from lot 711 were one window longer than the cars in lot 683. In addition, the cars in lot 711 had a semi-enclosed end. This was actually a windbreak because the cars did not have any doors.

Suburban Railroad inventory, dated December 31, 1915, states that cars 2, 3, 11, 12, 14, 17, and 18 had open ends and Ohmer fare registers. Cars 19-26 were built to the same specifications, but had closed ends and Meaker fare registers. One car was motorized for utility car service and was renumbered car 14.

The Chicago & West Towns Railway Company inventory, dated July 26, 1920, states that cars 1, 5, 6, 8, 9, 10, 15 and 16 had open ends with no fare registers. Cars 20-26, rebuilt in 1914, now are listed as having open ends and Ohmer fare registers. The utility motor 14 also had open ends.

Both of these two groups of cars were also described as open-end cars. Both inventories give the same dimensions for both lots of cars. This can not be correct since some cars were one window shorter than others.

Motor 12 hauled freight cars regularly from the Illinois Central interchange at Parkway to the Suburban barn and also moved ash cars between the two carbarns. It was photographed at the Suburban carbarn on Sunday, August 1, 1937.

John F. Humiston photo

Work motor 14 had a varied career starting as a Cicero & Proviso passenger car and was converted to a Suburban Railroad trailer in 1898. In 1914, the car was rebuilt into a work motor, the configuration shown in the photo, before being scrapped in 1923. The car was photographed on track 1 at the Suburban barn, circa 1920.

Evelyn Wilson Collection

truck flat cars 0002-0003 (Company Shops, 1913), and single-truck flat cars numbered 01 through 04 (Company Shops). The single-truck flat cars were built using trucks, frames, and other parts from several ex-Chicago Railways single-truck passenger cars.

There were several other utility car additions and dispositions. The old wooden sprinkler car (number 8) was scrapped at the Suburban barn in 1923. The steel sprinkler car, number 9, was sold in 1928 to the Quebec Railway, Light & Power Company and became car 200 on the Canadian property. By 1928, the steel sprinkler had been equipped with a snow plow and was used as such. A large double-truck snow plow was purchased from the Cummings Car & Coach Company in 1928. A single-truck sweeper, numbered 9, was also delivered from Cummings in November 1928. In Decem-

Chapter 16: Cars and Buses

Although the front dash sign claims the vehicle to be a work car, it actually was a line car, designed to service the overhead electrical supply. Car 15 started its career as Suburban Railroad passenger car 105. In 1912, it was renumbered car 515 and in the 1920s, it was renumbered again as car 512. In 1927, the car was converted into a line car and numbered 15. In this 1936 photograph at the Suburban carbarn, the line car wears its original livery.
Ed Frank, Jr. photo

Line car 15 was rebuilt and repainted in the blue and white livery during 1940. The rebuilding included changing the car's two motors (from GE-57 to GE 203L), changing the cars's trucks (from McGuire 26 trucks to McGuire-Cummings 10B4 trucks), and changing the car's electrical controller (from GE K-10 to GE K35G2).
James J. Buckley photo

210   *The Chicago & West Towns Railways*

The West Towns replaced the four sweepers that were lost in the Lake Street carbarn fire by immediately purchasing a like number of second-hand sweepers. The railway subsequently renumbered these 16-19. Sweeper 16, a McGuire-Cummings product, was acquired from the Evanston Railway in 1936 (where it was Sweeper 1). The unit had been pulled out of the Lake Street carbarn onto North Boulevard for photographs on a hot June 29, 1941.

James J. Buckley photo

Sweeper 17 had returned to the Lake Street carbarn after sweeping snow. Sweeper 17 was also acquired by the West Towns in 1936 from the Evanston Railway. In Evanston, the vehicle wore number two. Circa 1942.

Charles A. Brown photo/
Joe L. Diaz Collection

ber 1930, another sweeper, numbered 10, was acquired. Oddly enough, for some unknown reason, there were now two utility cars on the property both numbered 10.

During the 1930s, the Chicago & West Towns management was bombarded with criticism from area municipalities about the quality of streetcar service. In 1936, as a means to thwart the criticism, the West Towns repainted five streetcars in an experimental and flamboyant yellow and silver color scheme. The five cars repainted were 101, 114, 151, 155, and 165. The change in appearance of the trolleys did not appease the village officials and no other cars were painted in this manner.

On December 2, 1936, a fire at the Lake Street car house destroyed 18 passenger cars and 7 utility cars. The passenger cars destroyed were 109, 110, 113, 117, 118, 120, 121, 125, 129, 131, 137, 143, 146, 147, 148, 149, 150, and 162. The seven utility cars destroyed were both cars numbered 10 and cars 1, 2, 3, 4, and 11. The loss of these cars had a minimal effect on the operation of the railway.

To eliminate the passenger equipment shortage caused by the fire, the West Towns leased 6 streetcars from the Chicago Surface Lines. These cars, numbered 1358, 1361, 1380, 1381, 1389, and 1397 were built by the St. Louis Car Company in 1906 and had been in storage at the Kedzie Avenue and Lawndale Avenue depots. The cars were leased on December 2, 1936, the date of the fire and were delivered to the West Towns at Cermak Road and Kenton Avenue. Since the Surface

Chapter 16: Cars and Buses 211

Sweeper 18 was waiting on Madison Street at Austin Avenue to begin its westbound run. Sweepers 18 was acquired from the Tri-City Railway & Light Company of Rock Island, Illinois in December 1936, the same month as the Lake Street carbarn fire. West Towns sweeper 18 had been numbered in the Tri-City fleet as sweeper 2. Circa 1945.

William H. Baier photo/ Joe L. Diaz Collection

Lines cars had wheels with a very small flange, these cars had to be nursed over CSL and C&WT Cermak Road trackage. When the trolleys operated on Laramie Avenue and other streets, the cars stayed on the tracks a lot better. The six cars, designed for two-man operation, were placed into service on the Madison Street route. The streetcars were returned to the Chicago Surface Lines on Sunday morning, March 14, 1937 at Roosevelt Road and Austin Boulevard. The Surface Lines charged a very reasonable daily rental of $7.00 for each car. The 6 St. Louis built streetcars were in use on the West Towns for a little more than 3 months.

To replace the utility cars lost in the fire, the West Towns purchased 4 second-hand McGuire-Cummings snow sweepers in December 1936. Two sweepers came from the Evanston Railway Company. They were numbered 1 and 2 in Evanston; the West Towns renumbered them 16 and 17, respectively. The other 2 sweepers were purchased from the Tri-City Railway & Light Company of Rock Island, Illinois. These cars were numbered 2 and 3 in Rock Island and became numbers 18 and 19 on the West Towns. These snow sweepers were reconditioned, painted, and renumbered in 1937. These 4 cars were the last rail equipment acquired by the Chicago & West Towns.

Although much was lost in the fire, most of the electric motors survived unscathed. There was so much rubble and debris piled on top of the car frames and trucks that the motors were protected from the fire and heat. These motors were salvaged and used on other cars. Car 106 had General Electric 226A motors installed to replace the original GE-80 motors in 1937. Cars 122, 123, and 127 were rewired to operate with four General Electric 226A motors. Cars 124 and 126 kept their two General Electric 203L motors, while four General Electric 247D motors were installed in cars 128 and 130. Multiple-unit cars 138-141 also had their GE-247D motors replaced with GE-203L motors. The four General Electric 265D motors from burned car 162 were transferred to car 151. All the rewiring and motor changing was completed at the Company's Lake Street shops. It took about two weeks to rewire a car.

During the World War II period, the West Towns made a number of improvements to its streetcar system. By the Summer of 1940, the fleet of trolleys had been repainted in the new blue and white paint scheme. Also, car interiors were renovated. Cars 105 and 106 were not repainted, however, but were retired in July 1940 and junked in May 1943. The body of car 106 was sold and was used as a diner on Division Street in Chicago for about a decade.

In 1942, cars 152-161 were converted to one-man operation to permit all service on the La Grange line to be furnished by one-man cars. The door controls were moved so that the operator could open and close the front doors. Previously, in the two-man design, the door controls were not accessible to the motorman. The rear doors were also sealed and the rear steps were removed. Also, the fare register rods were rebuilt so that the opera-

Sweeper 19 was the highest numbered snow sweeper in the West Towns' fleet. Like its sister car, sweeper 18, the unit was purchased in December 1936 from the Tri-City Railway & Light Company of Rock Island, Illinois. In Rock Island, the sweeper was number 3. In this photo, the sweeper was on its death bed. It would be turned over on its side and burned about an hour after the photograph was exposed. May 24, 1947.

James J. Buckley photo

The interior of sweeper 19 was recorded in this photograph by Bob Gibson on the night the Lake Street car line was abandoned. The West Towns allowed non-employees to ride the sweeper as part of the transfer of surplus vehicles from the Lake Street barn to the Suburban barn. In the photograph, Jim Buckley, our author, was standing on the left and Dick Race, his face partially obscured by a pole, was on the right. March 30, 1947.

Robert W. Gibson photo/George E. Kanary Collection

Chapter 16: Cars and Buses

Flat car 04 was assisting in the rebuilding of Cermak Road at Ridgeland Avenue on August 13, 1944. It carried four streetcar-type air compressors ganged together to provide power for the air operated jack hammers and other tools used in the construction. The car was built by County Traction incorporating a surplus streetcar truck.

Robert W. Gibson photo/ George E. Kanary Collection

The West Towns owned three double-truck flat cars. This one was being stored in the back reaches of the yard behind the Suburban barn on June 9, 1946.

Robert W. Gibson photo/ George E. Kanary Collection

tor could ring up his fares.

The remaining cars designed for one-man or two-man operation were then used in the one-man configuration. Cars 122, 123, 124, and 126 had been assigned to runs on the La Grange line. Seven other "one-man, two-man" cars were in service on the Berwyn-Lyons route. These cars were numbered 103-105, and 133-136. When the Berwyn-Lyons streetcar line was replaced with buses in 1941, these cars joined the pool of cars for further service on the La Grange line.

Two cars were retired in 1943. Car 115 was so badly damaged in a rear end collision that it was retired and scrapped. Car 123 was in owl service on the La Grange line when it collided with an Indiana Harbor Belt train. It was cut up at the site of the accident.

After the War, management of the West Towns intended to renovate enough streetcars to continue to operate the La Grange streetcar line. As part of this program, car 142 was selected to be the prototype for this modernization program. When the car was in the shop and stripped, it was found to be very badly rusted. In-

As an aid to the passenger, it has been customary for a transit vehicle to provide a means to identify its route or destination. For a major portion of the twentieth century, signs have been used. These were painted on long, narrow linen rolls. The rolls were mounted in a mechanical device which allowed a person to crank through the roll to select an appropriate sign for the journey. In transit vehicles of the twenty-first century, technology has advanced whereby electronic signs are common. The data for this presentation was gathered by Barney Neuberger.

Front Sill Roll on Car 510

RIVERSIDE
BROOKFIELD
LA GRANGE
46TH AVE. & 22ND ST.
HARLEM AVE.
BERWYN-LYONS
52ND AVE.
ROOSEVELT RD
MADISON ST
CHICAGO AVE.
SPECIAL
CAR BARNS

Front and Side Rolls on Car 164

CHARTERED
CAR BARN
CHICAGO AVE.
AUSTIN AVE. & 35TH ST.
CHICAGO & AUSTIN AVE.
LAKE STREET
AUSTIN AVE. & LAKE ST.
MELROSE PARK
25TH AVE.
MADISON STREET
AUSTIN AVE. & MADISON ST.
MAYWOOD
9TH & ST. CHARLES AV.
HARLEM & STANLEY AVE.
HARLEM & OGDEN
BERWYN & LYONS
RIVERSIDE
BROOKFIELD
BROOKFIELD ZOO
LA GRANGE
KENTON & CERMAK RD.
52ND & CERMAK RD.

Front and Side Rolls on Car 126

CHARTERED
CAR BARN
CHICAGO AVE.
LAKE ST.
MADISON ST.
ROOSEVELT & 60TH
HARLEM AVE.
BERWYN & LYONS
RIVERSIDE
BROOKFIELD
LA GRANGE
DESP. AV. & MADISON
MAYWOOD
BERWYN TO RIVER
STANLEY & HARLEM AVE.
CICERO AVE.
52ND & 22ND
52ND & 25TH
52ND & 36TH
MELROSE PARK
AUSTIN & 35TH

Front and Side Rolls on Car 127

LAKE ST
CHICAGO AVE
ROOSEVELT RD
52ND AVE
MADISON ST
HARLEM AVE
BERWYN-LYONS
SPECIAL
CAR BARNS

Front and Side Rolls on Car 164

Front

CHARTERED
MELROSE PK.
AUSTIN BL.
MAYWOOD
LAKE ST.
MADISON ST.
CAR BARN

Side

CHARTERED
MELROSE PARK
AUSTIN BL.
MAYWOOD
LAKE ST.

Chapter 16: Cars and Buses

Chicago & West Towns Roster of Buses

Vehicle Numbers	Builder	Type	Seats	Date Acquired	Comments
1	Mack	AB	25	1923	Cummings Body.
2	Reo	W	22	1924	
3-12	Mack	AB	25	1924	Cummings Body.
13-22 (1st)	Reo		21	1925	Cummings Body. Sold/retired by 1929.
13-22 (2nd)	Available	T25	22	1929	
23	Cummings		26	1927	Gas/Electric bus retired in 1941.
24-29	Mack	AB	25	1927	Cummings Body. Acquired used.
30	Cummings		29	1928	
31-35	Mack	AB	29	1928	Cummings Body.
36-41	Mack	AB	29	1929	Cummings Body.
42	Pierce-Arrow	33	29	1930	Ex-Speedway "Zephyr Sedan". Built in 1921; retired in 1941
43	Yellow	X	21	1930	Ex-Speedway. Retired before 1936.
44	Pierce-Arrow		25	1930	Ex-Speedway. Built in 1927 and retired before 1936.
45-46	White	50	21	1930	Ex-Speedway. Retired before 1936.
47	International	54WC	29	1931	Acquired used.
48-55	ACF	H12S	30	1934	
56-58	Mack	AB	25	1935	Acquired used; Cummings bodies
59	Ford	A	27	1935	Acquired used; sold in 1946.
60	Yellow	Z	21	1935	Ex-CA&E # 1; ex-Marigold #40
61-64	Yellow	Z	21	1935	Ex-Northwestern; ex- Marigold 41-44. 61-63 retired 1941; 64 sold.
65-67	Yellow	Z	21	1935	Ex-Marigold 45-47.
68	ACF		29	1935	Ex-Marigold Parlor Coach 507.
69-70	Yellow	Y	29	1935	Ex-Marigold Parlor Coach 511-12
71-73	Yellow	Y	31	1935	Ex-Marigold Parlor Coaches 513-15.
74-77	ACF		29	1935	
200-209	ACF	H13	30	1937	Sold in 1951.
210-227	Available	WS175P	25	1937	Sold in 1948-1949.
228-237	ACF	26S	27	1940	Sold in 1951.
238-252	ACF	31S	31	1940	Sold in 1956-1957.
253-292	Ford	19B	27	1941	Sold in 1949.
293-302	Ford	19B	27	1942	Sold in 1950.
303-313	Ford	29B	27	1943	Sold in 1950.
314-332	Ford	29B	27	1944	Sold in 1950.
333-336	Ford	69B	27	1945	Sold in 1951.
337-342	Ford	69B	27	1946	Sold in 1951.
415-419	Available		25	1936	Ex-315-319; to Sioux Falls in 1946.
435-447	ACF-Brill	C36	36	1947	All sold or scrapped 1959-1960.
500-509	GMC	TGM-3609	36	1944	
510-529	GMC	TGM-3609	36	1945	
530-569	GMC	TGH-3207	32	1947	

Chicago & West Towns Roster of Buses

Vehicle Numbers	Builder	Type	Seats	Date Acquired	Comments
600-619	Mack	C45	38	1948	#600 to diesel; others sold 1960-61.
620-621	Mack	C45GT	45	1957	Built 1955; bought used from Oklahoma City; sold 1960.
622-631	Mack	C45DT	45	1959	Built 1951; bought used from Jacksonville, Fl; sold 1960.
700-719	GMC	TDH-4509	38	1949	
720-744	GMC	TDH-4509	38	1950	
745-748	GMC	TDH-4509	45	1952	
10 buses	ACF-Brill	C36	36	1957-8	Built 1946. Ex CTA 2310, 2312, 2322, 2323, 23272336, 2346, 2348, 2352 and 2354.
751-762	GMC	TDH-4509	45	1961	Built 1952; from Indianapolis, IN.
100	Ford			1962	School Bus.
7 buses	Twin Coach	44S	44	1963	Built 1948. Ex Waukegan-North Chicago 1718, 1720, 1725, 1749, 1785, 1795 and 1796.
763-767	GMC	TDH-4509	45	1963	Built 1949; from San Diego.
768-782	GMC	TDH-4509	45	1964	From San Diego
801-810	GMC	TDH-4517	45	1959	
101-110	ACF-Brill	C36	36	1960	Ex-CTA; Built 1947.
811-820	GMC	TDH-4517	45	1960	
821-830	GMC	TDH-4517	45	1961	
831-850	GMC	TDH-4517	45	1962	
851-860	GMC	TDH-4519	45	1963	
861-870	GMC	TDH-4517	45	1964	
871-880	GMC	TDH-4519	45	1965	
881-890	GMC	TDH-4519	45	1967	
8018-8073	GMC	TDH-4523A	45	1976	
3702-3	Flxible	111CD-05		1977	Built 1967. Ex-CTA 3702-3.
166	GMC	TDH-5304	53	1979	Built 1965. Ex-North Suburban Mass Transit Dist.
8361-8370	Grumman	53096-B-1		1979	
8396-8399	Grumman	53096-B-1		1979	
3700	Flxible	111CD-05		1980	Built 1967. Ex-CTA 3700
603	GMC	TDH-5303	53	1980	Built 1967. Ex-South Suburban Safeway

The West Towns converted a number of GMC buses in the 500-569 roster group, delivered with gasoline engines and manual transmissions, to diesel engine propulsion with hydraulic transmissions. These included vehicles 502, 504, 508, 510-521, 526-527, 529, 530, 532, 548, 555, and 565. Bus 562 was retired in 1949 while bus 541 was scrapped in 1954. All other buses that were not converted to diesel/hydraulic were sold in 1960-63.

stead of becoming the jewel of the fleet, car 142 was scrapped at the Lake Street shop on February 23, 1947.

By this time, permission had been obtained to discontinue streetcar service on both the Lake Street and Madison Street routes. About a week after the abandonment of the Madison Street line, on Sunday February 23, 1947 at 3:00 a.m., 9 streetcars and 2 sweepers were moved to the Suburban car barn via Chicago Surface Lines trackage. Later, after enough buses had been delivered for replacement of trolleys on the Lake Street line, the balance of equipment at the Oak Park carbarn was moved to the Suburban barn.

Chapter 16: Cars and Buses

Bus 5 was parked on North Boulevard in Oak Park at the Lake Street carbarn on February 19, 1946. The bus, with Mack mechanicals and a Cummings body, was acquired in 1924.

Robert W. Gibson photo/George E. Kanary Collection

Bus 25 was also a Mack with a Cummings body. In 1946, it was photographed equipped with a snow plow.

Donald N. Idarius photo/George E. Kanary Collection

In May and June 1947, the most of the streetcars that had operated the Lake Street and Madison Street routes were scrapped. Seventeen cars were junked: Cars 102, 108, 114, 116, 132, 135, 136, 144, 145, 151, 153, 154, 155, 160, 163, 164, and 165. Many of the car bodies were sold. Also burned at this time were snow plow number 8 and the four Lake Street snow sweepers, 16-19.

In the Spring of 1947, the four multiple-unit cars, numbers 138-141, were overhauled and converted to one-man operation. At this time, the cars received four General Electric 203L motors from scrapped Lake Street cars to replace the original GE 247D motors. After the higher horsepower motors were installed, the cars were used regularly in service.

After the abandonment of the La Grange line in 1948, the remaining 25 cars were junked at the Suburban car house.

Bus 56 was representative of the last group of 3 Mack buses acquired by the West Towns. Buses 56-58 were purchased used in 1935. It was parked at the Lake Street carhouse in 1947.
Bruce G. Moffat Collection

In the late 1930s, the West Towns' management purchased several lots of ACF buses. Buses 48-55 were purchased in 1934, 200-209 were acquired in 1937, and 228-252 were added to the fleet in 1940. The photo shows bus 246, an ACF 31-seat model in 1944.
Bruce G. Moffat Collection

These cars were numbered: 100, 101, 103, 104, 107, 111, 119, 122, 124, 126-128, 130, 133, 134, 138-141, 152, 156-159 and 161. As was the case a year earlier, many of the car bodies were sold. Car 130 had just received a new roof and other modernization, but never turned a wheel in regular service. It was transported to Marion, Illinois for use as a diner. The body of car 141 was sold to a farmer in Lisle. In 1959, this body was purchased by the train buff community for eventual restoration. It now resides at the Illinois Railway Museum at Union, Illinois.

Representatives from the Sand Springs Railway inspected the surviving equipment. The Sand Springs Railway operated between Tulsa and Sand Springs, Oklahoma. They selected six passenger cars to replace their fleet of lightweight cars which were acquired second-hand from the Cincinnati, Lawrenceburg & Au-

Chapter 16: Cars and Buses

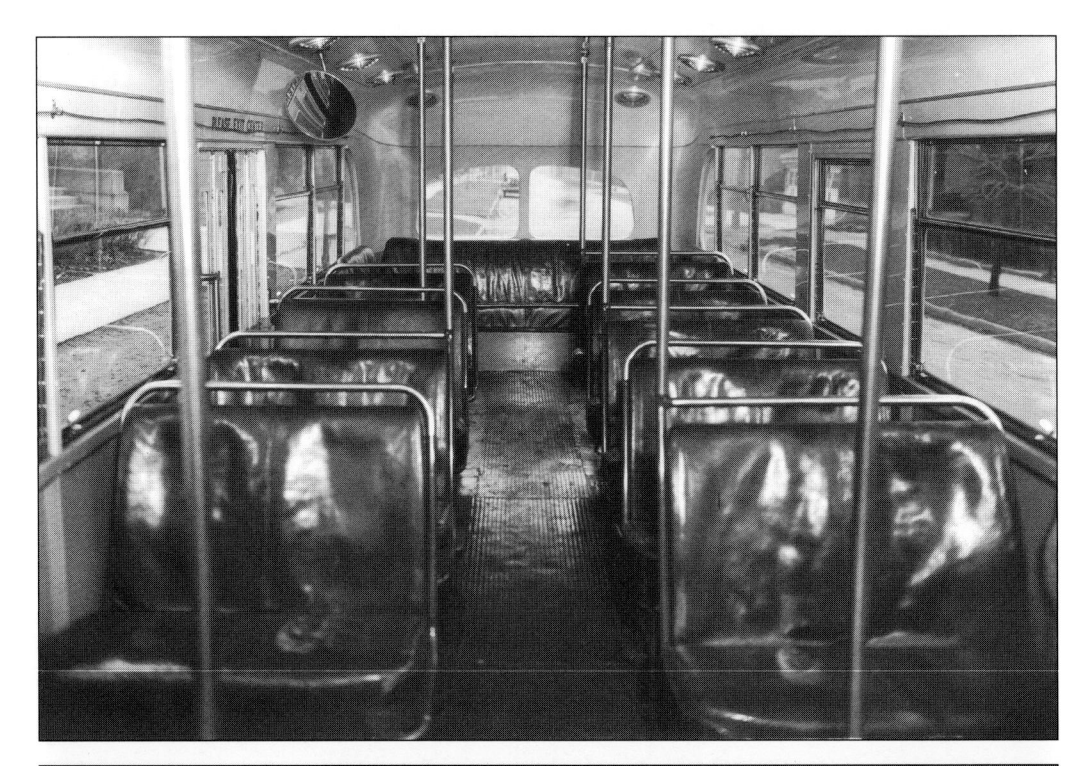

An interior view of bus 246, an ACF model 31S unit. Purchased in 1940, the 15 buses of this model were sold in 1956-57.
Bruce G. Moffat Collection

A photo of the front interior of bus 235 (ACF, model 26S) showed the driver's area, steering wheel, and Ohmer fare register. June 1940.
Motor Bus Society Collection

rora Electric Street Railroad. However, when interurban cars much closer to home became available from the Union Electric Railway, Sand Springs chose these instead. The Union Electric Railway operated between Parsons, Kansas and Nowata, Oklahoma. The Sand Springs Railway did purchase West Towns snow sweeper number 9 and a large lot of spare parts. The sweeper was renumbered A-11 at Sand Springs. No other West Towns street railway equipment was purchased by an electric railway.

The balance of the utility car fleet was also scrapped. Work car number 12 was used by the company scrapping the railway for about six weeks to pull up the rails on the La Grange line. This car and the four other utility cars, numbered 5, 6, 7 and 15, were scrapped at the Suburban car house. The body of car 15 was moved to the scrapping company's yard in Clearing where it was used for storage.

Between 1940 and 1946, the West Towns acquired 92 Ford buses. The largest lot of these buses were the 40 vehicles acquired during 1941. Bus 260, representative of the first lot of Ford vehicles was parked at the Lake Street carbarn in 1947. These 27 passenger Ford buses were sold between 1949 and 1951 as larger capacity units arrived.
Bruce G. Moffat Collection

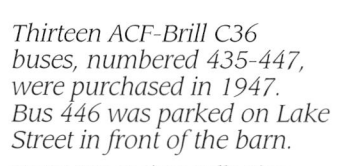

Thirteen ACF-Brill C36 buses, numbered 435-447, were purchased in 1947. Bus 446 was parked on Lake Street in front of the barn.
Motor Bus Society Collection

The West Towns purchased its first General Motors buses in 1944 when it acquired 10 model TGM-3609 buses, numbered 500-509. An additional 20 model TGM-3609 vehicles, numbered 510-529, were added to the fleet the following year. As the model number indicates, these buses had a seating capacity for 36 passengers and were equipped with gasoline engines and manual transmissions. Bus 521 was parked in front of the Lake Street carbarn, circa 1947.
Bruce G. Moffat Collection

Chapter 16: Cars and Buses

Parked on Lake Street at the carbarn between runs, Mack bus 618 was one of 20 units purchased in 1948.
Motor Bus Society Collection

The West Towns purchased 82 General Motors Coach model TDH-4509 buses in 6 lots between 1949 and 1964. Coach 702 was one unit in the first order for 20 GMC "old-look" buses placed in 1949. As the "DH" in the model designation indicates, these units were equipped with diesel engines and hydraulic transmissions. Bus 702 was parked in front of the Lake Street carbarn.
Bruce G. Moffat Collection

The West Towns began purchasing General Motors "new look" or "fish bowl" coaches, model TDH-4515 in 1959 and the company placed an additional orders for these buses in 1960, 1961, 1962 and 1964. In 1963, 1965, and 1967, the company purchased similar style vehicles, model TDH-4517. This GMC coach, seating 45 passengers and equipped with a diesel engine and hydraulic transmission, was widely used in the transit industry throughout the country. By the end of 1967, the company's fleet of "fish bowl" design buses reached 90 units. Bus 870, a model TDH-4517 unit, purchased in 1964 as part of an order totaling 10 vehicles, was parked in front of the Lake Street carbarn.
Bruce G. Moffat photo

17 Facilities

Car Houses and Garages

The West Towns' two-story office, shops, and car house were located at Lake Street and Cuyler Avenue in Oak Park, and were constructed by the Cicero & Proviso Street Railway Company. This pressed brick and steel structure, measuring 192-feet by 227-feet, occupied the entire block bounded by Lake Street, Harvey Avenue, North Boulevard, and Cuyler Avenue.

The entrance to the offices was on Lake Street while access to the car house and repair shops were on North Boulevard. Cars entered the barn via a ladder track, with three tracks available in the repair shop area of the facility. Two of these tracks were equipped with concrete inspection pits extending nearly the full length of the shop. The remainder of the building was equipped with the typical repair shop machinery.

Above the arch, at the main entrance to the company office's, was carved the name of the company that built the structure, "Cicero & Proviso St Ry Co."
Bruce G. Moffat photo

Connected to shops was a one-story brick car house. A brick partition wall with fire doors separated the repair shop from the car house, and the bays in the car barn were also protected by brick walls and fire doors. As described earlier, the center bay was destroyed by fire on December 2, 1936. It was rebuilt with fire walls and other precautions so that a fire would not devastate the barn again. The 1936 blaze was the second conflagration at this site,

One of the concessions to the motor bus era was the renaming of the company as West Towns Bus Company in 1956. In the early 1960s, a "new look" GMC bus was parked in front of the company office on Lake Street near Cuyler Avenue. The sign on the building was a low cost affair with red raised lettering on a light blue brick background.
Richard Kunz photo/David S. Stanley Collection

Chapter 17: Facilities 223

In the last winter of streetcar service on Lake Street in Oak Park, car 144 was operating eastbound at Harvey. The lead into the barn was a single track on both Harvey and North Boulevard.

Robert W. Gibson photo/
George E. Kanary Collection

On a winter's day, March 25, 1947, a company truck, buses and a snow sweeper were parked on North Boulevard at Cuyler Avenue.

Robert W. Gibson photo

as earlier fire, on July 15, 1902, nearly destroyed not only the building, but also about 100 cars.

The West Towns performed all of its heavy maintenance at the Lake Street barn. Interestingly enough, the Available Truck Company of Chicago leased space at the Lake Street site to build bodies for the buses that they supplied to the West Towns.

A new garage building was constructed in 1924 on the southwest corner of Lake Street and Harvey Avenue, adjacent to the West Towns' existing facilities at this location. During 1929, an additional bus storage garage was built on the east side of Harvey Avenue between Lake Street and North Boulevard.

The company's other car house, located on the west side of Harlem Avenue, just north of Cermak Road, was known as the Suburban barn because it was built by the Suburban Railroad. (The building was described in detail in the chapter on the Suburban Railroad.) Cars for the La

The Chicago & West Towns Railways

In the 1940s, washing a streetcar was a manual task. West Towns crews erected a scaffold and used brushes to scrub the roof of car 134.
Thomas A. Lesh photo

Grange and Berwyn-Lyons routes were based here, as well as a few for the Chicago Avenue line. A large yard was available for open storage at the north and west sides of the property.

When the Lake Street car barn was closed in March 1947 and became a bus-only facility, space was made available at the Suburban barn to overhaul cars. The office and shop was heated but the car storage area was unheated. In the winter, the barn was affectionately known among the employees as "Little Siberia."

All buses were operated out of the Lake Street facilities until the start of World War II. In order to reduce tire mileage and to house the ever expanding bus fleet, a new garage was constructed to the south of the Suburban barn facing Cermak Road, just west of the former powerhouse. When the last blue and white streetcars were removed from the grounds, the car house was converted into a garage. Beginning in April 1948, the servicing of buses was performed in the garage while the former barn was used for bus storage.

The former Suburban depot site was used for bus storage until 1959, when West Towns' management decided to sell this property in order to raise cash. An alternative storage site was found when the company reached an agreement with the Village of Oak Park to purchase the segment of North Boulevard between Cuyler and Harvey Avenues, directly south of the Lake Street bus garage. The purchase enabled the company to store buses on the vacated street in the village.

Power Plants

The Chicago & West Towns Railway Company acquired two power plants when it assumed control of the County Traction routes. One was at the Lake Street car barn and was built by the Cicero & Proviso Street Railway, the other was at the Suburban car barn and was built by the Suburban Railroad. (The Suburban's power station is described in detail in the chapter devoted to the Suburban.) This narrative will document the Lake Street power plant.

Located adjacent to the car house in

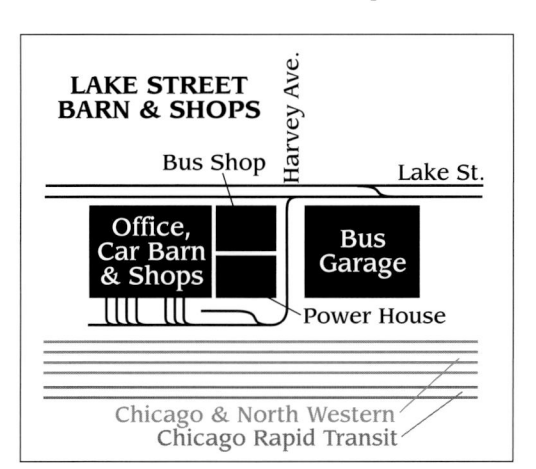

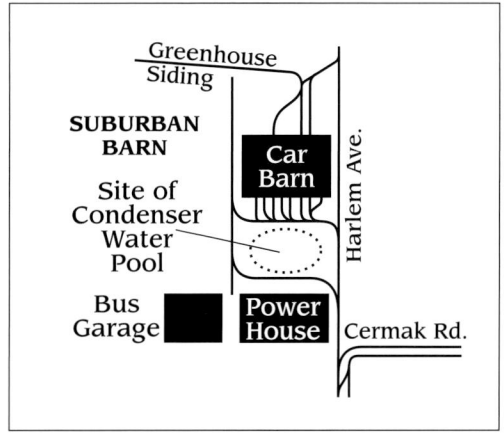

Chapter 17: Facilities

The most impressive structure on the Suburban carbarn property was the power house located on the northwest corner of Harlem Avenue and Cermak Road.

Bruce G. Moffat Collection

Oak Park at the southwest corner of Harvey Avenue and North Boulevard, the original plant was first modified in 1895 when new power generation equipment was purchased. The equipment installed consisted of eight 300-horsepower Campbell & Zell water tube boilers with Murphy automatic stokers and smokeless furnaces. Two 26 by 40 by 48 cross-compound Allis Chalmers engines were directly connected to 750-kilowatt Siemens & Halske railway generators. A third machine, a 24 by 36 by 60 tandem-compound Corliss engine, was installed in 1903. The engine was originally built by the Allis-Chalmers Company and installed in the Van Buren Street powerhouse of the West Chicago Street Railroad Company in 1893. However, it was never used because the demand for power from this facility was very light. It was directly connected to two Siemens and Halske 465 kilowatt generators, and was compounded by the Fulton Iron Works and equipped with new 7 by 10 stroke valve gears with double admission valves on high and low pressure. The detailed cost of all this work was approximately $34,000.

After the plant was closed in 1917, power was purchased from several sources. The first power contract was signed on December 6, 1917, with the Sanitary District of the City of Chicago. Between 1928 and 1930, power was also obtained from the Lombard Avenue substation of the Lake Street "L". In 1930, supplementary power was obtained from the Public Service Company of Northern Illinois. During the following year the contract with the Sanitary District was canceled and power was purchased solely from the Public Service Company.

On April 3, 1948, one week before the end of West Towns streetcar service, five streetcars were visible at the front of the Suburban carhouse. They were numbered 107, 119, 161, 127, and 126.

Robert W. Gibson photo

226 *The Chicago & West Towns Railways*

Behind the carbarn was a large yard. On May 24, 1947, a crew was preparing to tip over sweeper 19 before burning it.

Donald N. Idarius photo

At the suburban site, directly west of the power house, the West Towns constructed a bus garage. This photograph shows the Cermak Road facade of the structure.

Bruce G. Moffat Collection

After the carbarn was vacated, a company photographer recorded a final photo of the structure before demolition.

Bruce G. Moffat photo

Chapter 17: Facilities

SECTION 5
After the Streetcars Quit

18 The Road to Pace

Car 128 was operating southbound, circa 1940, on the Chicago Avenue line as it traversed the Laramie Avenue viaduct. The bridge carried Laramie over Ogden Avenue and Clyde Yard of the Chicago, Burlington & Quincy Railroad. The photo shows the car at the south end of the bridge.
Ed Frank, Jr. photo/ Joe L. Diaz Collection.

During the period of time from 1948 to 1984, when this history ends, the West Towns performed a complete renewal of its equipment, facilities, routes and corporate form. As with any business, the West Towns needed to continually keep its operations contemporary with the times. But of all the challenges that the company faced, it was the increases in wage rates and the preference of passengers to use the automobile that proved to be the most challenging — and ultimately near fatal. The economic environment in the 1970's necessitated public funding to permit continued operation of bus service. Initially, the Regional Transportation Authority was founded with taxing powers to generate subsidies for the private carriers, but this arrangement did not prove successful. Eventually, the RTA would purchase the service providers and operate the bus service itself.

Facilities

As referred to earlier, the Village of Oak Park sold the section of North Boulevard between Cuyler and Harvey to the West Towns in 1959 so the company could store buses behind its Lake Street garage. This transaction permitted the West Towns to sell the Suburban Barn and to consolidate operations at one site. The Suburban site, on the northwest corner of Cermak Road and Harlem Avenue, was redeveloped as an automobile dealership. Twenty-five years later, on October 24, 1986, a new bus garage and maintenance facility at 3500 West Lake Street in Melrose Park was dedicated. The Oak Park bus garage was closed on the same date, and the site was sold and redeveloped for shopping.

With the substitution of buses for streetcars, the eastern terminal of the Lake Street line was made more convenient for passengers to transfer to both bus and "L" by routing the coaches south of Lake. In December 1968, bus 816, a General Motors model TDH-4517, was waiting for passengers to load on Austin Boulevard at North Boulevard. A home-made, roof-mounted sign featured paid advertising about the ABCO Job Center.
Motor Bus Society Collection

Built in 1949, General Motors Coach 717 was southward on Oak Park Avenue at 43rd Street on March 21, 1962. With the introduction of a new GMC design in 1960, these buses became known as "old look" units.

Michael M. McGowan photo

West Towns Bus Company "new look" GMC 816 was traveling southbound on Oak Park Avenue near 26th Street through a block composed of typical Berwyn bungalows. November 24, 1963.

Michael M. McGowan photo

Equipment

Throughout the years, new equipment was introduced to the fleet on an irregular basis. The early buses were of small capacity and were powered with gasoline engines. As bus design evolved, the West Towns eventually opted for 45-passenger diesel buses.

In the 1940's, new buses were purchased frequently, with major purchases made during 1941, 1947 and 1948. During 1941, 40 Ford buses were purchased, while in 1947, 40 GMC Model TGH-3207 buses were obtained. Twenty Mack Model C45 coaches were bought in 1948 to replace streetcars on the La Grange line.

During the early 1950's, 25 GMC Model TDH-4509 buses were purchased and two years later, in 1952, another 3 GMCs of the same model were obtained. The buses bought in 1952 seated 45 passengers each vs. 38 for those bought in 1950.

During the 1959-1967 period, new buses were purchased in all years except for 1966. In all years that buses were purchased except for 1962, ten buses per year were the norm. In 1962, 20 were bought. By this time, all buses purchased were GMC 45-passenger diesel buses. The 1962 purchase permitted the retirement of the remaining 32 passenger coaches.

In 1976, the Illinois Regional Transportation Authority provided the West Towns funding to revitalize its bus fleet. The money paid for the one-for-one replacement of 51 vehicles in the fleet that were in the poorest condition, as well as the renovation another 51 buses in repairable condition.(The cash-starved company had not been able to buy replacement buses since 1967.)

On April 21, 1962, West Towns "fish bowl" design or "new look" bus 821 was operating southbound when it crossed the Douglas "L" on Laramie Avenue near Cermak Road. The vehicle, purchased in a lot of 10 during 1961, was about a year old.

Michael M. McGowan photo

Chapter 18: The Road to Pace

Routes

The West Towns bus system was shortened when service on two unprofitable routes was discontinued. On August 1, 1949, the La Grange-La Grange Park Transit Company began operating the West Towns La Grange Road bus route. This route ran on Mannheim Road between Harding Avenue and the General Motors Corporation's Electromotive Division plant at 55th Street. Also on August 1, 1949, the Safety Transportation Company began operating the West Towns Hillside bus route. The Hillside route ran between the Hillside Shopping Center at York Road via Roosevelt Road and Des Plaines Avenue to the Forest Park terminal of the Garfield Park "L." In 1946, Safety began to acquire permits to operate a number of widely scattered intercity bus routes in the western and northwestern suburbs. In 1955, Safety sold this route to the Leyden Motor Coach Company. When the shopping center eliminated its subsidy for the route, Leyden cut the service back to two trips a day before discontinuing service altogether.

As the west suburban population grew during the post-war years, routes were integrated, combined or otherwise rearranged as customer demand, or cash-flow dictated. Following are a few of the more notable changes:

1957 - St. Charles Road (Route #13) was extended to Wheaton in response to the abandonment of the Chicago, Aurora, & Elgin Railway on July 3, 1957.

1960 - West Towns begins aggressive advertising to develop charter bus business.

1965 - West Towns reroutes Grand Avenue-Lombard line (Route #19) on eastern end from Grand and Nordica to North and Narragansett,

1968 - St. Charles Road (Route #13) service extended to Yorktown Mall.

1969 - Harlem Avenue(Route #7) extended to O'Hare Airport.
Lake Street (Route #9) extended to Oak Brook Center.
Division Street (Route #6) combined with Chicago-Division (Route #5) via Roosevelt Road to 35th Street and Austin.

1970 - North Avenue (Route #18) and Austin Avenue (Route #1) lines were extended to the Lake Street "L".

1976 - Two new routes were added: La Grange-Mannheim (Route #330) and Cumberland-Fifth Avenue (Route #331).

1977 - Bus service was expanded on several routes: 22nd Street (Route #322) , Chicago (Route #305), Harlem (Route #307), Oak Park (Route #311), Ridgeland(Route #315) and Lake (Route #309).

1978 - Service was expanded on Roosevelt (Route #305). Lake Street (Route #309), St., Charles Road (Route #313), 22nd Street (Route #322), and York Road (Route #332) were restructured.

1980 - RTA routes #307 - Harlem and #325 joined. Owl service provided on York Road line (Route #332). Peak, mid-day or Saturday service expanded on Roosevelt Road (Route #301), Austin-Ridgeland North (Route #315), Chicago Avenue (Route #305), Oak Park Avenue (Route #311), and Berwyn (Route #302).

1981 - Harlem Avenue (Route #307) increased Sunday service.

1982 - On several West Towns routes, including Chicago Avenue (Route #305), 25th Street (Route #325), and 22nd Street (Route#322), service was reduced by discontinuing evening or Saturday service and lengthening headways.

1983 - With the opening of rapid transit service to River Road on CTA's O'Hare line, the Cumberland/Fifth Avenue bus (Route 331) was rerouted to terminate at the Cumberland Avenue "L" station. Also, The Mannheim/La Grange (Route #330) was rerouted to terminate at the River Road "L" station.

In 1983, a small number of other changes took place as well. With the extension of CTA bus lines on North Avenue (Route #72) to Harlem Avenue and the Narragansett/Ridgeland line (Route #86) to Lake Street and Ridgeland Avenue, the West Towns Ridgeland Avenue - North Avenue (Route #315), was realigned. The various services using Cermak Road were realigned and consolidated under RTA auspices. Included are CTA West Cermak Road line (Route #25) and West Towns routes Cermak (Route #304) and 22nd Street (Route #322).

Uniform patches were redesigned to reflect the new corporate name.
Dorothy Anderson Collection

Corporate Form

Of all the changes brought about after the cessation of streetcar service in 1948, changing economic conditions were the largest. In response to a decline in the profitability of the bus transportation business, public monies were first used to provide operating subsidies to existing transit operators. This approach worked for about five years, but as business economics further deteriorated the individual suburban transportation carriers were purchased by the Regional Transportation Authority and operations combined.

The balance of the 1940s and all of the 1950s were fairly uneventful years. To better reflect that fact the company did not operate any streetcars, the corporate name was changed from the Chicago & West Towns Railways, Inc. to the West Towns Bus Company on November 29, 1956.

In August 1963, the West Towns Bus Company acquired the Leyden Motor Coach Lines as the result of an emergency order of the Illinois Commerce Commission. Financially struggling Leyden Motor Coach Lines operated a service territory adjacent to that of the West Towns. Fares on the ex-Leyden routes were increased 5¢ to 10¢ per ride to correspond to those charged on the West Towns' routes.

Also in the 1960's, Minneapolis investor and president of the Marquette National Bank, Carl Pohlad, began acquiring a financial stake in the bus company. By 1964, Pohlad's equity position in the company earned him a seat on the Board of Directors and the title of Vice-Chairman. By January 1966, one of Pohlad's companies, Minnesota Enterprises, Incorporated, had acquired in excess of 90% of the common stock.

During the late 1960's and early 1970's, the economics of operating a transit business deteriorated. As use of the automobile increased, the use of transit correspondingly decreased. To make matters even worse, the urban sprawl which the automobile facilitated moved a large number of potential riders away from any resonable access to public transit. As ridership dropped fares were increased which resulted in further loss of patronage. The 30¢ base fare established in 1959 was increased to 35¢ in 1968 and to 40¢ in 1970. In 1971, the base fare was increased again to 45¢ as the result of a labor agreement which increased bus driver's wages a whopping 93¢ per hour. At this time, with the company's future very much in doubt, the management began to issue public statements about its poor financial condition

After much political discussion, bickering, and posturing, it became evident that the only way for transit to survive was with public funding. The key event in providing public monies to subsidize private transportation carriers was the adoption of the 1970 Illinois Constitution. After the new constitution became effective on July 1, 1971, legislation was drafted to create the Regional Transportation Act. This legislation, signed by Illinois Governor Dan Walker on December 13, 1973, also required approval by referendum, which was affirmed on March 19, 1974. Several subsequent legal challenges to the RTA Act were successfully defended. On June 28, 1974, the last hurdle was cleared when the Illinois Supreme Court ruled in favor of the RTA.

Substantial funding began to flow to the West Towns Bus Company, which in turn fueled greater and greater deficits. On December 19, 1974, the company received its first grant: $149,100. Funding increased in each of the following years: $847,000 in 1975, $1.6 million in 1976, $2.8 million in 1977, and $3.7 million in 1978.

Chapter 18: The Road to Pace

During the early 1960s, the West Towns Bus Company conducted an advertising campaign to build a charter bus business. Advertisements appeared regularly in many of the local town newspapers. Normally, the ads included a photograph of a bus. One memorable ad, however, featuring a streetcar, was placed in the August 9, 1963 issue of Oak Leaves.

Historical Society of Oak Park and River Forest Collection

MEMORIES — MEMORIES

Pot Belly Stove

—Clang
Clang
Clang

WEST SUBURBAN TRANSPORTATION

PROVED & IMPROVED SINCE 1895

Charter a bus for August Special Events

Chicagoland Music Festival Sat., August 18

Clyde Beatty & Ringling Bros. Circus

Soldier Field August 24

Bus schedules available from your bus driver

WEST TOWNS BUS COMPANY

FOR SCHEDULE INFORMATION & LOST & FOUND PHONE EU 3-6668

259 Lake Street, Oak Park   Phone: EUclid 3-0100

The escalating deficits were not an isolated situation, as all of the carriers under the RTA umbrella were experiencing balooning costs. Excluding the Chicago Transit Authority, RTA financial assistance to commuter rail and suburban bus operators increased from $31.4 million in fiscal year 1976, to $52.8 million in fiscal year 1977 to $65.5 million in fiscal year 1978. The RTA raised fares in 1976 and again in 1979. In 1977, it imposed a 5% tax on the purchase of gasoline in the metropolitan Chicago area. When all these measures failed to generate enough funds, the RTA appealed to the state for authority to levy a sales tax. The legislature balked, realizing that more and more money in the past had not cured the problem. Ultimately, the legislators repealed the gasoline tax and the operating subsidy provided from general state funds and authorized a sales tax of 1% in Cook County and one-quarter of 1% in Lake, DuPage, McHenry, Will and Kane counties. The transit reporter for the *Chicago Tribune* estimated that the change in legislation reduced the RTA's revenue by $60 million annually, and by 1981 the RTA was virtually insolvent.

Service on the West Towns was stopped on May 30, 1981 due to the RTA funding crises. At this time, the company had a $9 million operating budget with the

To announce the expected delivery of ten new buses, the West Towns placed ads in the local newspapers.

The 10 GMC "new look" buses, model TDH-4519, were numbered 861-870.

This ad appeared in the January 9, 1964 issue of Oak Leaves.

Historical Society of Oak Park and River Forest Collection

WE KNOW YOU LIKE THEM

...SO WE HAVE ORDERED MORE

LUXURY COACHES FOR YOU

Your response to West Towns first 50 air-ride Luxury Coaches has been overwhelming—and we are most appreciative. We have ordered 10 more just like them to go into service throughout our area about Feb. 1.

GET THE LUXURY HABIT!

Go the Safe, Easy, Economical Way

WEST TOWNS BUS COMPANY

259 Lake Street, Oak Park   **Phone: EUclid 3-0100**

FOR SCHEDULE INFORMATION & LOST & FOUND PHONE EU 3-6668

RTA providing two-thirds of this total. In June 1981, the West Towns received $248,562 from the RTA as a partial payment of its deficit, but the company needed a sum twice that. By the middle of July, when the buses had not operated for six weeks, the Illinois General Assembly granted the RTA more than $20 million in additional state sales tax revenue.

On August 5, 1981, the company resumed skeletal service on 11 of its 19 bus routes, using only 48 of the company's 170 drivers. The company hoped that all routes would be fully operational by the end of the year, but that would not come to pass.

In November 1981, the RTA purchased the West Towns Bus Company. After 80 years of discussion and debate, the transit provider was now owned by the public it served. Included in the purchase agreement was the transfer of 106 buses, assorted service vehicles and equipment,

Chapter 18: The Road to Pace

Leyden Motor Coach bus 151 was photographed on York Road at Dubuque Avenue in Elmhurst, Illinois on November 25, 1961. The unit was a GMC model 4509.
Michael M. McGowan photo

and a three year leasing arrangement for the venerable old garage at 259 Lake Street. The RTA hired ATE Management to operate the bus system.

The long-term funding issue took more time to resolve. In 1983, a compromise was reached by the state legislature, governor, and mayor of Chicago to cure the problems at the RTA. The entire RTA board was dismissed and the Authority lost its right to operate suburban transit systems. As a means to force financial discipline in the future, the fares that would be collected for transit services must amount to at least half of total operating costs. Finally, to provide political payback to the suburbs, two new agencies were created: one for commuter rail and the other for the suburban bus system. The board members of a metropolitan commuter rail authority, known as Metra, would be appointed by the six metropolitan area county boards. Similarly, the directors of the bus system, known as Pace, would be controlled by the suburban mayors. The function of the RTA would be to disburse funds and audit results. What was the old West Towns Bus Company became the Pace West Division in 1984.

Leyden buses 86 and 95 were parked at Itasca, Illinois terminal of route 42 on June 17, 1961. The vehicles, model C-31, were manufactured by ACF Brill.
Michael M. McGowan photo

On October 24, 1986, Pace put into service a new garage constructed at 3500 Lake Street in Melrose Park to house and repair buses assigned to all routes in the western suburbs. On September 17, 2004, bus 2239 pulled out of the garage to go into service.
Richard W. Aaron photo

236   The Chicago & West Towns Railways

19 Epilogue

The last streetcars of the Chicago & West Towns Railways, Inc. were replaced with buses in 1948 and the company itself was absorbed into the Regional Transportation Authority in 1981. However, after all these years, two waiting shelters that the railways built still exist and a small number of vehicles have been preserved. A West Towns streetcar is in the final phases of a multi-year restoration at the Illinois Railway Museum in Union, Illinois. Pace has preserved one West Towns bus and another three are known to be held in private collections.

When the Chicago & West Towns ended street railway service, most of the streetcars were scrapped. A small number of cars, however, were stripped of salvageable parts and the remaining car bodies sold for use as sheds. The body of car 141 ended up on a farm in Lisle, Illinois. In 1959, it was purchased by the Electric Railway Historical Society from the farmer and moved to a storage facility not far away in Downers Grove. While in storage, the society's members began the lengthy process of collecting the parts necessary for the car's restoration. When the vehicles owned by Electric Railway Historical Society were transferred to the Illinois Railway Museum, the collection of components continued. By 1997, the time was right for the process of restoration and re-assembly to begin. At the time of this writing in late 2004, the restoration was nearing completion.

On a sunny day in October 2004, the staff of the Illinois Railway Museum pulled Chicago & West Towns car 141 out of Barn 4 for photos ostensibly for this bulletin. The nearly completed car body sits on shop trucks. When restoration of the operating trucks is completed and they are installed under the car, the body will ride about a foot lower. West Towns car 141 glistened in the late afternoon northern Illinois sun.

David H. Mewhinney photo

Pace owns and maintains former West Towns Bus Company 771 for use at special events. On September 12, 1992, it was operating eastbound on Madison Street at the Soo Line crossing in River Forest. A typical "old-look" General Motors Coach bus, the West Towns acquired the unit used in 1964 from the San Diego Transit System.
Bruce G. Moffat photo

West Towns sold bus 776 to a private party. A sister unit to the 771, it was in excursion service on October 13, 1985 when the vehicle stopped for photographs on Ridgeland Avenue at Fillmore Street in Oak Park. The destination curtain on the bus provides the best photo caption, "Antique 1950 Bus."
Bruce G. Moffat photo

The former West Towns streetcar waiting shelter on Des Plaines Avenue at 27th Street has been preserved by Pace for use by its bus patrons. A second shelter, on 26th Street at Harlem Avenue, has also been preserved. During a private trip on June 1, 1996, West Towns replica bus 343 made an obligatory stop at the shelter on Des Plaines Avenue. The Ford bus, owned by the Illinois Railway Museum, represents over 90 buses of this type operated by the West Towns. This specific unit, however, never served on the West Towns. The museum purchased the bus from another transit agency, accurately restored it to a West Towns configuration, and assigned it number 343, one roster number greater than that carried by the highest numbered Ford bus in the West Towns fleet.

Bruce G. Moffat photo

In 2004, the Now Serving Café & Catering, 725 Hillgrove Avenue, La Grange, Illinois, expanded into adjacent space. The owner, Paul Link, wishing to have distinctive decor, commissioned two local artists to create a wall rendering showing the scene outside the restaurant in the late 1940s. The 5-foot by 16-foot mural shows a West Towns streetcar at the Brainard Avenue terminal of the La Grange line, the Stone Avenue station of the Chicago, Burlington & Quincy Railroad, and the building which houses the restaurant. The photo was taken in September 2005.

Richard W. Aaron photo

Chapter 19: Epilogue

SECTION 6
Bibliography, Appendices and Index

Bibliography

Periodicals:

The Economist
The Electrical Engineer
First & Fastest
The La Grange Citizen
Moody's Industrial and
    Transportation Manuals
Oak Leaves
Street Railway Journal
Western Electrician

Books, Pamphlets and Web Sites:

Annual Program and Budget; Five-Year Transit Program Regional Transportation Authority. Chicago: A separate report was issued and referenced for each of the following fiscal years: 1978, 1979, 1980, 1981, 1982, 1983, and 1985.

Appraisal: Chicago & West Towns Railways Inc. as of May 1, 1936
Byron T. Gifford, Consulting Engineers, Chicago: 1936.

Chicago & West Towns Railways, Inc. Report on Operations, Property, and Earnings
W. C. Gilman & Company, New York: 1956.

Hilton, George W. *Cable Railways of Chicago*
Electric Railway Historical Society, Bulletin #10. Chicago: 1954.

Johnson, James D. *A Century of Chicago Streetcars*
Wheaton, Illinois: The Traction Orange Company, 1964.

Krambles, George and Arthur H. Peterson. *The CTA at 45*
Chicago: George Krambles Transit Scholarship Foundation, 1993.

Lind, Alan R. *Chicago Surface Lines, An Illustrated History*
Park Forest, Illinois: Transport History Press, 1974.

Moffat, Bruce G. *The "L" - The Development of Chicago's Rapid Transit System*
Central Electric Railfans' Association, Bulletin 131. Chicago: 1955.

RTA Transit Information Suburban Bus and Rail
Regional Transportation Authority. Chicago: April 1979.

Reinschmidt, Andrew J. *Bus Rosters on the WEB*
Web site: www.geocities.com/~buslist.

Sieroslawski, Jennifer. *Suburban Transit History*
Arlington Heights, Illinois: Pace Division of the Regional Transportation Authority, 1996.

Shore Line Interurban Historical Society
(P.O. Box 425, Lake Forest, Illinois 60045-0425). Web Site: www.shore-line.org.

Stats, Charles. *"Wisconsin Central Lines, Suburban Service at Chicago, Part I"*
The Soo, Vol. VI, No. 1 (January 1984), pp. 10-31.

Stats, Charles. *"Wisconsin Central Lines, Suburban Service at Chicago, Part II"*
The Soo, Vol. VI, No. 2 (April 1984), pp. 8-33.

Tecson, Joseph A. *The Regional Transportation Authority in Northern Illinois*
Chicago: Regional Transportation Authority, 1975.

Vandervoort, William. *West Towns Suburban Transit*
Web site: http://members.aol.com/chictafan/histcwtr.html.

Young, David M. *Chicago Transit, An Illustrated History*
DeKalb, Illinois: Northern Illinois University Press, 1998.

After discharging his passengers at the zoo, motorman Ben Goss, Jr., found time to pose for a photo. Goss looked most dapper in his uniform, which featured a three-piece suit with a double-breasted jacket, shirt and tie, and hat. April 23, 1939.
John F. Humiston photo

Appendix 1

Chicago & West Towns Key Financial & Operating Statistics

Year	Gross Earnings	Operating Expenses and Taxes	Net Operating Earnings	Interest	Net Earnings	Passenger Motors
1915	$505,061	$346,430	$158,631	$37,976	$120,654	26
1916	566,675	377,078	189,597	38,511	151,086	26
1917	587,292	413,597	173,695	39,799	133,896	26
1918	594,773	475,953	118,820	50,487	68,332	45
1919	792,221	626,805	165,416	59,886	105,530	48
1920	1,000,096	816,829	183,267	73,702	109,565	48
1921	1,108,617	879,687	228,930	91,545	137,385	48
1922	1,132,426	888,825	243,601	85,497	158,104	48
1923	1,202,218	934,186	274,032	91,689	182,343	48
1924	1,273,701	985,524	288,177	105,287	182,890	62
1925	1,348,901	1,031,338	317,563	119,201	198,362	62
1926	1,441,083	1,091,814	349,269	119,201	230,068	62
1927	1,472,099	1,109,099	277,388	130,217	147,217	66
1928	1,515,529	1,124,544	303,502	153,051	150,451	66
1929	1,567,333	1,160,976	315,449	177,369	138,080	66
1930	1,445,692	1,098,857	177,369	79,046	79,046	66
1931	1,225,305	1,027,730	139,390	177,372	-37,982	66
1932	1,020,847	927,023	93,824	20,933	72,891	66
1933	943,513	871,673	71,840	117,946	-46,106	66
1934	995,217	939,607	55,610	114,388	-59,778	66
1935	1,022,870	994,445	28,425	112,041	-83,616	66
1936	1,129,991	1,091,918	38,073	121,398	-73,325	48
1937	1,170,174	1,137,664	32,510	111,269	-78,760	48
1938	1,081,426	1,118,146	-36,720	112,400	-149,120	48
1939	1,087,087	1,078,975	8,112	111,422	-103,310	48
1940	1,142,520	1,081,590	60,929	110,823	-49,894	48
1941	1,287,832	1,205,594	18,361	110,630	-87,843	48
1942	1,713,315	1,454,217	185,105	110,631	74,474	48
1943	2,321,195	1,735,164	488,577	111,144	377,433	45
1944	2,639,166	2,124,573	514,593	110,607	403,987	45
1945	2,794,888	2,527,097	267,790	110,511	157,280	45
1946	3,096,828	2,923,969	172,864	110,615	62,249	45
1947	3,129,742	3,240,024	-114,281	121,152	-235,433	25
1948	3,378,469	3,511,509	-133,039	132,682	-265,721	0
1949	3,312,808	2,799,650			-15,717	0
1950	2,945,767	2,616,847			9,067	0
1951	2,807,236	2,585,519			-121,344	0
1952	2,824,006	2,563,193			-78,127	0
1953	2,965,348	2,645,595			-14,381	0
1954	1,423,458	1,281,623			-10,236	0

Passenger Trailers	Utility Motors	Utility Trailers	Buses	Passenger Cash Fares	Miles of Track	Employees Trainmen	Employees Total
0	6	3	None		38.82		
0	6	3	None	13,510,195	38.82		
0	6	3	None	11,193,557	38.82	160	243
19	12	13	None	11,111,783	38.82	160	261
19	12	13	None	11,209,361	70.77	172	280
19	12	13	None	11,415,194	70.77	180	288
19	12	13	None	11,099,959	70.77	180	288
19	12	13	None	11,380,857	70.77	180	293
4	11	12	2	12,115,838	70.77	180	293
4	11	12	12	12,792,893	70.77	180	293
4	11	12	22	13,553,341	70.77	240	353
4	11	12	22	14,499,650	79.65	240	353
4	12	12	29	14,818,246	79.65	260	378
4	13	12	35	15,313,242	79.65	282	400
4	13	12	41	15,890,745	79.65	313	478
4	14	12	46	14,659,874	79.65	324	495
4	14	12	46	12,823,019	79.65	324	495
4	14	12	46	—	79.65	310	478
4	14	12	46	9,639,243	79.65	216	351
4	14	12	47	10,139,557	79.65	219	355
4	14	12	74	10,430,194	73.10	229	365
0	10	12	74	11,466,940	73.10	238	380
0	10	12	79	11,896,093	73.10	239	383
0	10	12	78	11,375,759	73.10	247	397
0	10	12	78	11,148,129	73.10	238	391
0	10	12	103	11,804,232	69.94	227	382
0	10	12		13,230,593	69.94	205	358
0	10	12	139	17,713,477	46.78	224	373
0	10	12	151	24,033,133	46.78	266	438
0	10	12	194	27,307,937	46.78	297	473
0	10	12	167	28,839,106	46.78	321	523
0	10	12	171	31,744,962	44.91	365	677
0	4	3	226	32,061,206	25.01	418	676
0	0	0	229	28,939,268	None		
0	0	0	207	24,045,630	None	345	521
0	0	0	192	20,714,395		319	470
0	0	0	162	19,619,066		291	425
0	0	0	166	18,121,004		299	430
0	0	0	166	16,336,550		299	425
0	0	0	165	14,561,883		262	387

Appendices

Appendix 2

Suburban Railroad Company   Key Financial & Operating Statistics

Year Ending	Gross Earnings	Operating Expenses	Net Earnings	Passenger Paid Fares
12-31-1898	$53,880	$ 89,838	$ - 35,958	
12-31-1899	54,734	67,863	-13,182	
12-31-1900	41,622	64,963	-23,341	
06-30-1901	52,732	64,443	-99,390	715,082
06-30-1902	40,185	47,313	-98,576	803,694
06-30-1903	45,904	57,214	-86,384	918,076
06-30-1904	49,467	69,482	-70,372	983,344
06-30-1905	54,934	59,544	-75,922	1,034,349
06-30-1906	61,072	78,381	-76,318	1,204,963
06-30-1907	65,664	84,038	-78,550	1,293,668
06-30-1908	65,918	64,743	1,255	1,299,211
06-30-1909	68,946	84,555	-81,874	1,359,799
06-30-1910	73,649	84,459	-81,484	1,432,537
06-30-1911	96,424	83,554	-68,682	1,909,351
06-30-1912	121,394	128,834	-108,448	2,400,113
06-30-1913	117,512	96,071	-50,128	2,118,665
06-30-1914	103,138	78,727	18,867	1,880,806
06-30-1915	112,603	81,058	5,500	1,974,053
12-31-1916	113,105	84,660	28,445	

Motor Cars	Trailer Cars	Other Cars	Suburban RR Track Miles	Chicago, Harlem & Batavia Track Miles	Chicago Consolidated Traction Track Miles	Employees Trainmen	Total
20	20	2	29.80	7.04	1.00		
20	20	2	29.80	7.04	1.00		
20	21	2	29.80	7.04	1.00		
20	21	2	29.80	7.04	1.00	21	32
20	21	2	29.80	7.04	1.00	21	33
20	21	3	30.80	0	1.00	21	33
20	21	3	31.30	0	1.00	23	46
20	21	3	31.30	0	1.50	24	46
20	21	3	32.30	0	1.50	24	40
20	21	3	32.30	0		26	51
20	21	3	32.30	0		26	52
20	21	3	32.30	0		32	52
20	21	3	32.30	0		34	56
20	21	3	32.30	0		36	61
20	21	3	32.30	0		40	66
35	18	8	32.30	0		36	89
17	22	6	22.49	0		66	78
17	22	6	24.82	0			
17	22	6					

Appendices

Index

A

Aluminum Company of America 105
Amalgamated Association of
　Street Railway Employes of America ... 58, 64, 67
American Can Company 51, 78
American Transit Association 110
Apelt, C. P. 83, 86
ATE Management 236
Available Truck Company 96, 103, 224

B

Baltimore & Ohio
　Chicago Terminal Railroad 26, 68, 75, 139
Baltimore & Ohio Railroad 26
Barclay, Philander W. 19, 29, 36
Berwyn, City of 51, 54, 66, 73, 74, 99-102, 117
Blanchard, George 43, 51-53
Bluebird Coach System, Inc. 107, 108, 115, 117
Bollard, Frank 11
Brookfield Zoo 91, 92, 104, 106, 108, 110,
　　　　　　　　　　　　114-116, 167, 178-180
Buehler, John 23
Butler, Frank L. 61

C

Carey, Thomas S. 69
Chase, Charles W. 110
Chicago & Joliet Electric Railway 91, 103
Chicago & Joliet Transportation Company 107
Chicago & North Western Railway 9, 11, 13, 14,
　　　　　　　　　　　20, 21, 23, 41, 47, 51, 56, 62,
　　　　　　　　　　　65, 68, 69, 71, 72, 76, 77, 83,
　　　　　　　　　　　84, 86, 89, 108, 118, 119, 134,
　　　　　　　　　　　135, 150, 151, 155, 164, 166
Chicago & Northern Pacific 23, 26, 27, 30,
　　　　　　　　　　　　　　　　31, 33, 37, 192
Chicago & Southwestern Railway 26, 33, 36,
　　　　　　　　　　　　　　　　40, 75, 139, 192
Chicago & Western
　Dummy Railway Company 23
Chicago City Council 21, 40, 49, 58, 63, 65
Chicago City Railway 37, 40, 45, 191
Chicago Consolidated Traction 14, 20-22, 41, 43,
　　　　　　　　　　　　　　　　47-49, 51, 52, 64,
　　　　　　　　　　　　　　　　121, 130, 131, 187, 188
Chicago Great Western 36, 37, 41, 57
Chicago Motor Coach Company 70, 108, 117
Chicago Motor Speedway 141
Chicago Railways 20, 21, 43, 45-53, 55,
　　　　　　　　　　　　57-59, 62, 64-66, 119, 121,
　　　　　　　　　　　　188-191, 194, 195, 207, 209
Chicago Rapid Transit Company 74, 92, 93, 107,
　　　　　　　　　　　　　　108, 111, 122, 136

Chicago Surface Lines 45, 63, 64, 66, 68, 73,
　　　　　　　　　　　　79, 91, 92, 94, 95, 97,
　　　　　　　　　　　　100, 106, 110, 111, 114,
　　　　　　　　　　　　122, 124, 132, 138, 144, 155,
　　　　　　　　　　　　156, 168, 169, 211, 212, 216
Chicago Terminal Transfer 26, 27, 36, 37, 192
Chicago Title & Trust Company 29, 40
Chicago Transit Authority 14, 101, 111, 116,
　　　　　　　　　　　　117, 122, 136, 144,
　　　　　　　　　　　　156, 170, 233, 234
Chicago Union Traction 14, 20, 47-50, 188
Chicago, Alton & St. Louis 9
Chicago, Aurora & Elgin Railroad 84-86, 108,
　　　　　　　　　　　　　　　　　　136, 232
Chicago, Burlington &
　Quincy Railroad 9, 16, 17, 23, 29, 41, 42, 45,
　　　　　　　　　　　54, 65, 67, 81, 86, 95, 96, 104,
　　　　　　　　　　　107, 126-129, 139, 140, 183, 185
Chicago, City of 13, 35, 40, 43, 51,
　　　　　　　　　　　　　　　52, 57, 63, 65, 70
Chicago, Harlem & Batavia 23-26, 191
Chicago, Harvard & Geneva 1 93
Chicago, Riverside, & La Grange 40, 42, 55
Chicago, Rock Island & Pacific 195
Cicero & Proviso
　Street Railway 9-16, 18, 20, 22, 26,
　　　　　　　　　　　　45, 187, 188, 192, 194,
　　　　　　　　　　　　208, 209, 223, 226
Cicero & Southwestern Railway 52
Ciccro Association of Commerce 95
Cicero Centennial Bridge 140
Cicero Town Board 16, 30, 35, 47, 51, 80
Cicero, Town of 9, 18, 35-37, 48,
　　　　　　　　　　　　　　　50-53, 58, 101, 103
Cincinnati, Lawrenceburg & Aurora
Electric Street Railroad 218
Circuit Court
　of Cook County 40, 42, 54, 107, 108
Coben, Augustus 52
Collett, Bert 76, 92, 95, 106, 108, 114-116
Comerford, George 51-53
Concordia Cemetery 10, 30
Cook County Fairgrounds 86
Cook, Andrew 43, 45, 61
Cooper, Henry 29, 34
County Traction
　Company 21, 42, 43, 45, 46, 47, 49-59,
　　　　　　　　　　　　61, 62, 64, 119, 121, 188-191,
　　　　　　　　　　　　193, 194, 207, 208, 214, 226
Crossette, Charles H. 29
Cummings Car & Coach Company 82, 102, 200,
　　　　　　　　　　　　　　　　　　204-207, 211
Cummings, E. A. 9, 11
Cummings, John J. 61
Cummings, Walter J. 61
Cutting, Judge 42

246　　　　　　　　　　　　　　　　　　　　　　　*The Chicago & West Towns Railways*

D

Darlow, James 11
Davis, W. G. Coal Company 119
Des Plaines River 10, 11, 13, 18, 25, 30,
35, 55, 66, 81, 107, 129,
130, 152, 162, 177, 190, 204
Drymalski, Raymond P. 115

E

Escanaba Traction Company 198
Evanston Railway Company 212

F

Flanagan, John P. 83, 86
Foell, Charles M. 64
Forest Home Cemetery 10, 30
Forest Park, Village of 46, 48-50, 52, 54, 55,
61, 62, 65, 76, 109
Forest Preserve District
of Cook County 91, 92

G

Gage Farm 35
Galena & Chicago Union Railroad 9
Galpin, Homer K. 29
Galvin, J. D. 83, 86
Goldblatt Brothers 95, 96
Grant Locomotive Works 26, 28
Grosscup, Judge Peter 43, 45, 48-52
Gurley, W. W. 38, 39, 49

H

Haase, Wilbur N. 63
Hall, Ross C. 48
Harlem Race Track 11, 14, 37, 38
Harris Trust & Savings Bank 43, 58, 91, 115
Harris, A. W. 58
Hawthorne Race Track 18, 38, 73, 81, 109, 141
Hines Hospital 72, 79, 83, 86, 101
Hurst, George 29, 31, 33

I

Illinois Central Railroad 18, 30, 55, 57, 65,
76, 77, 83, 119,
125, 127, 174, 209
Illinois Commerce
Commission 68-72, 74, 75, 79-81,
83, 84, 86, 89, 90,
92-97, 100, 102-111,
115-117, 233
Illinois Railroad and Warehouse
Commission 57
Illinois, State of 29, 40, 81, 97, 117
Indiana Harbor Belt 30, 58, 79, 81, 103, 104,
121, 182, 183, 196, 214
Insull, Samuel 89

J

Jensen, Jens 57

K

Kennedy, D. J 9
Kountze Brothers 34

L

La Grange, Village of 42, 81
LaBuy, Walter J. 115
Lake Street Elevated Railroad 11, 37- 39,
41, 46, 47
Leeds, Charles S. 29-31, 34
Lewis, John L. 109
Leyden Motor Coach Company 232, 233
Loss, C. E. & Company 31
Lyman, David B. 29, 31
Lyons, Village Board of 53, 54, 81

M

Mack Trucks, Inc. 102, 106, 115, 117, 231
Madison Street Loop House 14
Madison Street Transfer 11, 13
Maywood Loop 77, 155
Maywood, Village of 11, 13, 25, 49, 50, 53,
55, 64, 69, 78-80, 111
McCormick, Mrs. Edith Rockefeller 91, 92
McEldowney, C. R. 86
McEwen, William 59, 61, 64, 68
McGuire-Cummings Manufacturing
Company 55, 61-62, 73, 181,
188-189, 194-196, 198, 200,
205- 207, 209, 211-212
McIllvaine, Alan C. 43, 46
Melrose Park, Village of 11, 52, 55,
69, 79, 111
Mesaba Electric Railway 198
Metropolitan Motor Coach Company 87-90
Metropolitan Transit Authority 111
Metropolitan West Side "L" 30, 33-35, 38,
39, 41, 85, 89, 90
Meyers, L. E. 47, 52
Midlothian & Blue Island 195
Minnesota Enterprises, Inc. 233
Mount Carmel Cemetery 84

N

National Industrial Recovery Act 81
National Labor Board 67
Naugle, Holcomb & Company 31, 34
North Chicago Street Railroad 187
Northern Pacific Railroad 23, 26
Northwestern Transit Company 87-90

Index

O

Oak Park Motor Transit 87, 88
Oak Park, Village of 41, 46, 48-50, 53, 57,
58, 63, 65, 87, 89, 92,
94, 96, 101, 225, 229
Oak Ridge Cemetery 84
Oechslin Florist Company 119, 174, 207
Office of Defense Transportation 103, 106
Ogden Street Railway 15, 16-18, 20,
22, 35, 121, 188
Ohmer Fare Registers 62, 63, 198
Owsley, Louis S. 40, 42

P

Pace 144, 146, 159, 173, 236, 239
Parkway 30, 57, 76, 119, 174
Patton Motor Car Company 34
People's Horse Car Company 9
Pohlad, Carl 233
Public Service Company
  of Northern Illinois 109, 227
Public Utilities Commission 63, 66-68

Q

Quebec Railway, Light & Power Company 209

R

Regional Transportation Authority 83, 102, 147,
229, 231-237
Rein, T. E. 43
Richeimer, Frank S. 54
River Forest, Village of 11, 49-51, 53,
58, 63, 64
Riverside, Village of 33, 35, 81
Rosenthal, Emil J. 52

S

Salt Creek 30
Sand Springs Railway Company 117, 218, 219
Schmidt, Emil G. 42, 53-59, 62
Schneider, J. 29
Sears, Roebuck & Company 68
Seattle, Renton & Southern 194
Soo Line 150, 162, 238
Speedway Auto Bus Company 83-86
Sportsman's Park 81, 109, 141
Stump, Irwin C. 29, 31
Suburban Electric Railway 29, 191
Suburban Construction Company 30, 31, 34, 191
Suburban Railroad18, ... 26, 31-35, 38, 40-42,
51, 55-57, 59, 61, 62,
75, 78, 115, 117, 131,
187, 191, 193, 195, 196, 198,
205, 207, 208, 210, 224, 226
Supreme Court of the
  State of Illinois 20, 63, 64, 69,
107, 108, 233

T

Timms, J. C. 52
Townsend, George P. 29, 34
Tri-City Railway & Light Company 212, 213

U

Union Electric Railway 219

V

Vandercook, Charles R. 23

W

Waldheim Cemetery 10, 23, 25, 30
War Production Board 103
Washington & Virginia Railway 196, 198
West Chicago Street Railroad
  Company 9, 13-16, 23, 26, 121,
187, 194, 208, 227
West Suburban
  `Transportation Company 69
Western Electric Company 40-42, 50, 66,
91, 97, 110, 116,
122, 124, 167, 169
White Motor Company 84
Wild, John D. 43
Wisconsin Central Railroad 26, 192
Workingmen's Special Tickets 53

Y

Yerkes, Charles T. 14, 20, 26, 34, 35,
38, 39, 42, 55, 68

A single-truck open streetcar made its way westward on the Madison Street crossing of the Des Plaines River. Circa 1900.

LeRoy F. Blommaert Collection

A group of nine Suburban Railroad trainmen, conductors, and motormen were assembled to pose, in full uniform, for a photo in front of car 520. The uniforms, including the three-piece suit, white shirt with tie, and hat, lasted as the company standard, with minor modifications, well into the 1940s. Circa 1920.

Evelyn Wilson Collection

Near the end of streetcar service, on March 21, 1948, West Towns car 139 stopped on Cermak Road at Cicero Avenue to pick up passengers. The photo was taken from the roof of a Walgreens' drug store located on the southwest corner of the intersection. Tracks in the foreground were used by the Cicero Avenue route of the Chicago Transit Authority.

Robert W. Gibson photo/George E. Kanary collection

FLOOR PLAN

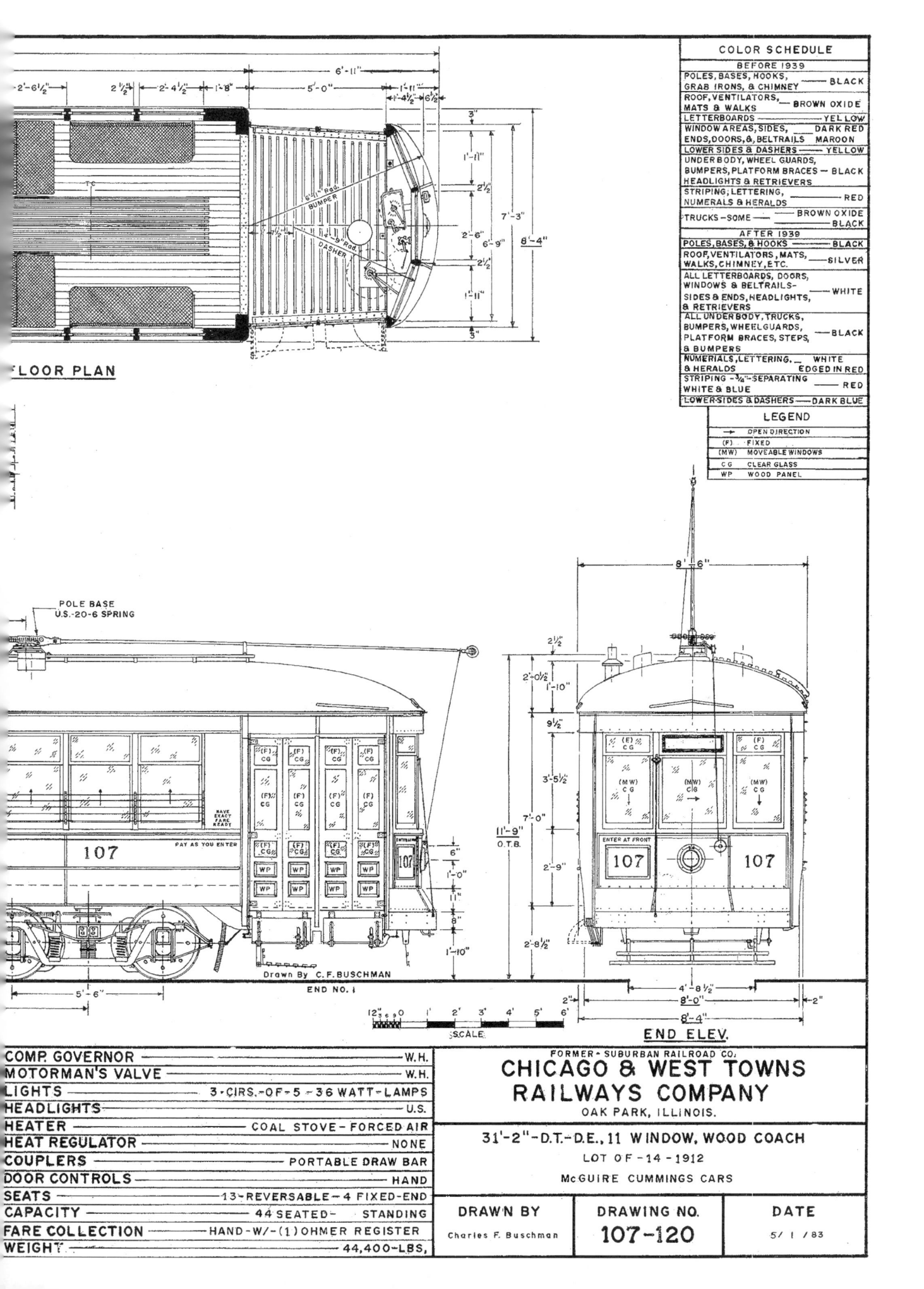

COLOR SCHEDULE

BEFORE 1939

POLES, BASES, HOOKS, GRAB IRONS, & CHIMNEY	BLACK
ROOF, VENTILATORS, MATS & WALKS	BROWN OXIDE
LETTERBOARDS	YELLOW
WINDOW AREAS, SIDES, ENDS, DOORS, & BELTRAILS	DARK RED MAROON
LOWER SIDES & DASHERS	YELLOW
UNDER BODY, WHEEL GUARDS, BUMPERS, PLATFORM BRACES	BLACK
HEADLIGHTS & RETRIEVERS	
STRIPING, LETTERING, NUMERALS & HERALDS	RED
TRUCKS – SOME	BROWN OXIDE / BLACK

AFTER 1939

POLES, BASES, & HOOKS	BLACK
ROOF, VENTILATORS, MATS, WALKS, CHIMNEY, ETC.	SILVER
ALL LETTERBOARDS, DOORS, WINDOWS & BELTRAILS – SIDES & ENDS, HEADLIGHTS, & RETRIEVERS	WHITE
ALL UNDERBODY, TRUCKS, BUMPERS, WHEELGUARDS, PLATFORM BRACES, STEPS, & BUMPERS	BLACK
NUMERALS, LETTERING, & HERALDS	WHITE EDGED IN RED
STRIPING – ¾" – SEPARATING WHITE & BLUE	RED
LOWER SIDES & DASHERS	DARK BLUE

LEGEND

→	OPEN DIRECTION
(F)	FIXED
(MW)	MOVEABLE WINDOWS
CG	CLEAR GLASS
WP	WOOD PANEL

END ELEV.

END NO. 1

Drawn By C.F. Buschman

COMP. GOVERNOR	W.H.
MOTORMAN'S VALVE	W.H.
LIGHTS	3-CIRS.-OF-5-36 WATT-LAMPS
HEADLIGHTS	U.S.
HEATER	COAL STOVE – FORCED AIR
HEAT REGULATOR	NONE
COUPLERS	PORTABLE DRAW BAR
DOOR CONTROLS	HAND
SEATS	13-REVERSABLE – 4 FIXED-END
CAPACITY	44 SEATED – STANDING
FARE COLLECTION	HAND-W/-(1) OHMER REGISTER
WEIGHT	44,400-LBS.

FORMER – SUBURBAN RAILROAD CO.

CHICAGO & WEST TOWNS RAILWAYS COMPANY

OAK PARK, ILLINOIS.

31'-2"-D.T.-D.E., 11 WINDOW, WOOD COACH

LOT OF -14-1912

McGUIRE CUMMINGS CARS

DRAWN BY	DRAWING NO.	DATE
Charles F. Buschman	107-120	5/1/83

HALF ROOF PLAN

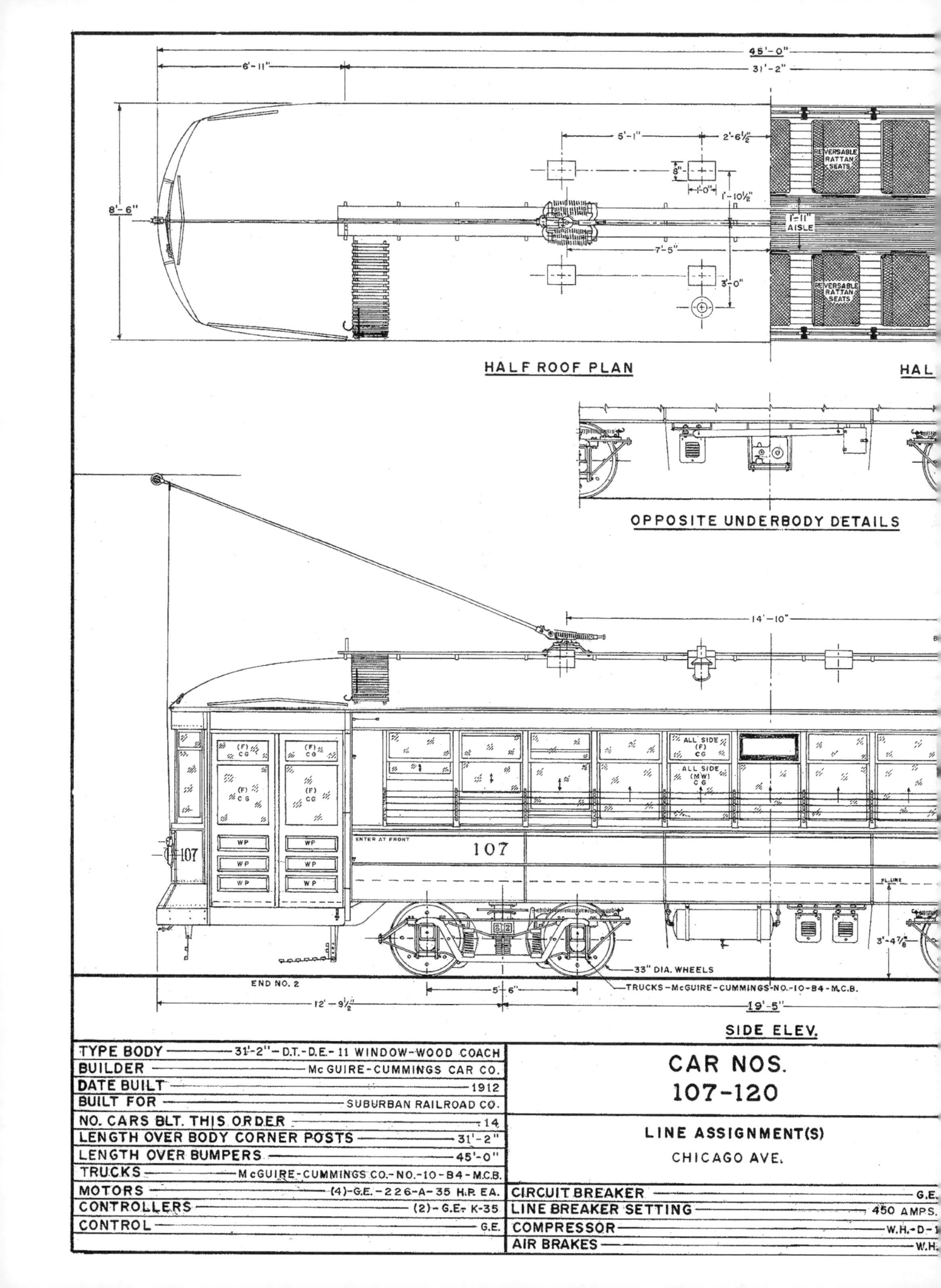

OPPOSITE UNDERBODY DETAILS

SIDE ELEV.

TYPE BODY	31'-2" - D.T.- D.E.- 11 WINDOW-WOOD COACH
BUILDER	McGUIRE-CUMMINGS CAR CO.
DATE BUILT	1912
BUILT FOR	SUBURBAN RAILROAD CO.
NO. CARS BLT. THIS ORDER	14
LENGTH OVER BODY CORNER POSTS	31'-2"
LENGTH OVER BUMPERS	45'-0"
TRUCKS	McGUIRE-CUMMINGS CO.- NO.-10-B4-M.C.B.
MOTORS	(4)-G.E.-226-A-35 H.P. EA.
CONTROLLERS	(2)-G.E.- K-35
CONTROL	G.E.
CIRCUIT BREAKER	G.E.
LINE BREAKER SETTING	450 AMPS.
COMPRESSOR	W.H.-D-1
AIR BRAKES	W.H.

CAR NOS. 107-120

LINE ASSIGNMENT(S)

CHICAGO AVE.

FLOOR PLAN

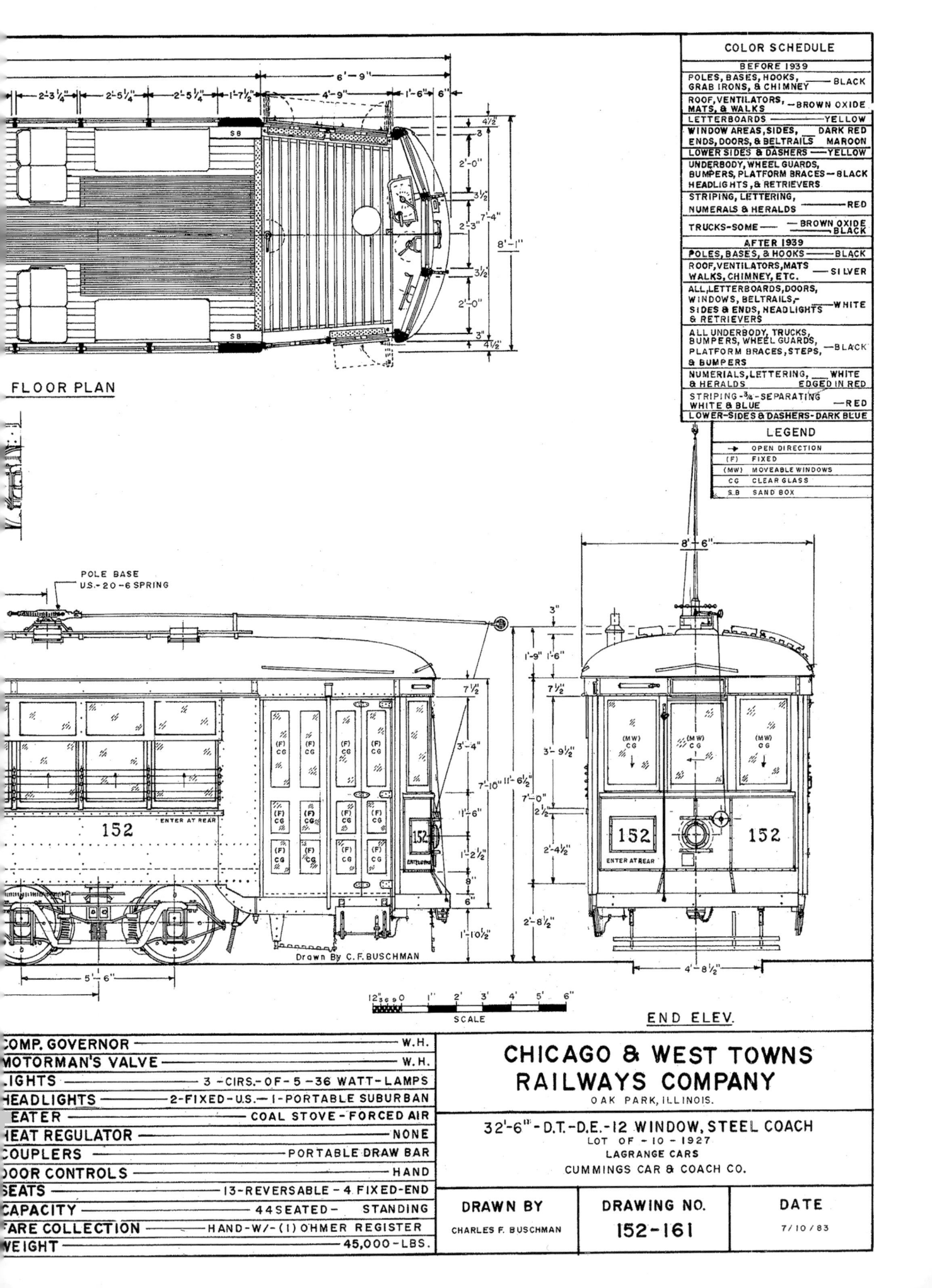

COLOR SCHEDULE

BEFORE 1939

POLES, BASES, HOOKS, GRAB IRONS, & CHIMNEY	BLACK
ROOF, VENTILATORS, MATS, & WALKS	BROWN OXIDE
LETTERBOARDS	YELLOW
WINDOW AREAS, SIDES, ENDS, DOORS, & BELTRAILS	DARK RED MAROON
LOWER SIDES & DASHERS	YELLOW
UNDERBODY, WHEEL GUARDS, BUMPERS, PLATFORM BRACES, HEADLIGHTS, & RETRIEVERS	BLACK
STRIPING, LETTERING, NUMERALS & HERALDS	RED
TRUCKS-SOME	BROWN OXIDE / BLACK

AFTER 1939

POLES, BASES, & HOOKS	BLACK
ROOF, VENTILATORS, MATS, WALKS, CHIMNEY, ETC.	SILVER
ALL LETTERBOARDS, DOORS, WINDOWS, BELTRAILS, SIDES & ENDS, HEADLIGHTS & RETRIEVERS	WHITE
ALL UNDERBODY, TRUCKS, BUMPERS, WHEEL GUARDS, PLATFORM BRACES, STEPS, & BUMPERS	BLACK
NUMERALS, LETTERING, & HERALDS	WHITE EDGED IN RED
STRIPING - 3/4 - SEPARATING WHITE & BLUE	RED
LOWER-SIDES & DASHERS	DARK BLUE

LEGEND

→	OPEN DIRECTION
(F)	FIXED
(MW)	MOVEABLE WINDOWS
CG	CLEAR GLASS
S.B	SAND BOX

END ELEV.

COMP. GOVERNOR	W.H.
MOTORMAN'S VALVE	W.H.
LIGHTS	3-CIRS.-OF-5-36 WATT-LAMPS
HEADLIGHTS	2-FIXED-U.S.-1-PORTABLE SUBURBAN
HEATER	COAL STOVE - FORCED AIR
HEAT REGULATOR	NONE
COUPLERS	PORTABLE DRAW BAR
DOOR CONTROLS	HAND
SEATS	13-REVERSABLE - 4 FIXED-END
CAPACITY	44 SEATED - STANDING
FARE COLLECTION	HAND-W/-(1) OHMER REGISTER
WEIGHT	45,000-LBS.

CHICAGO & WEST TOWNS RAILWAYS COMPANY

OAK PARK, ILLINOIS.

32'-6" - D.T. - D.E. - 12 WINDOW, STEEL COACH
LOT OF - 10 - 1927
LAGRANGE CARS
CUMMINGS CAR & COACH CO.

DRAWN BY	DRAWING NO.	DATE
CHARLES F. BUSCHMAN	152-161	7/10/83

HALF ROOF PLAN

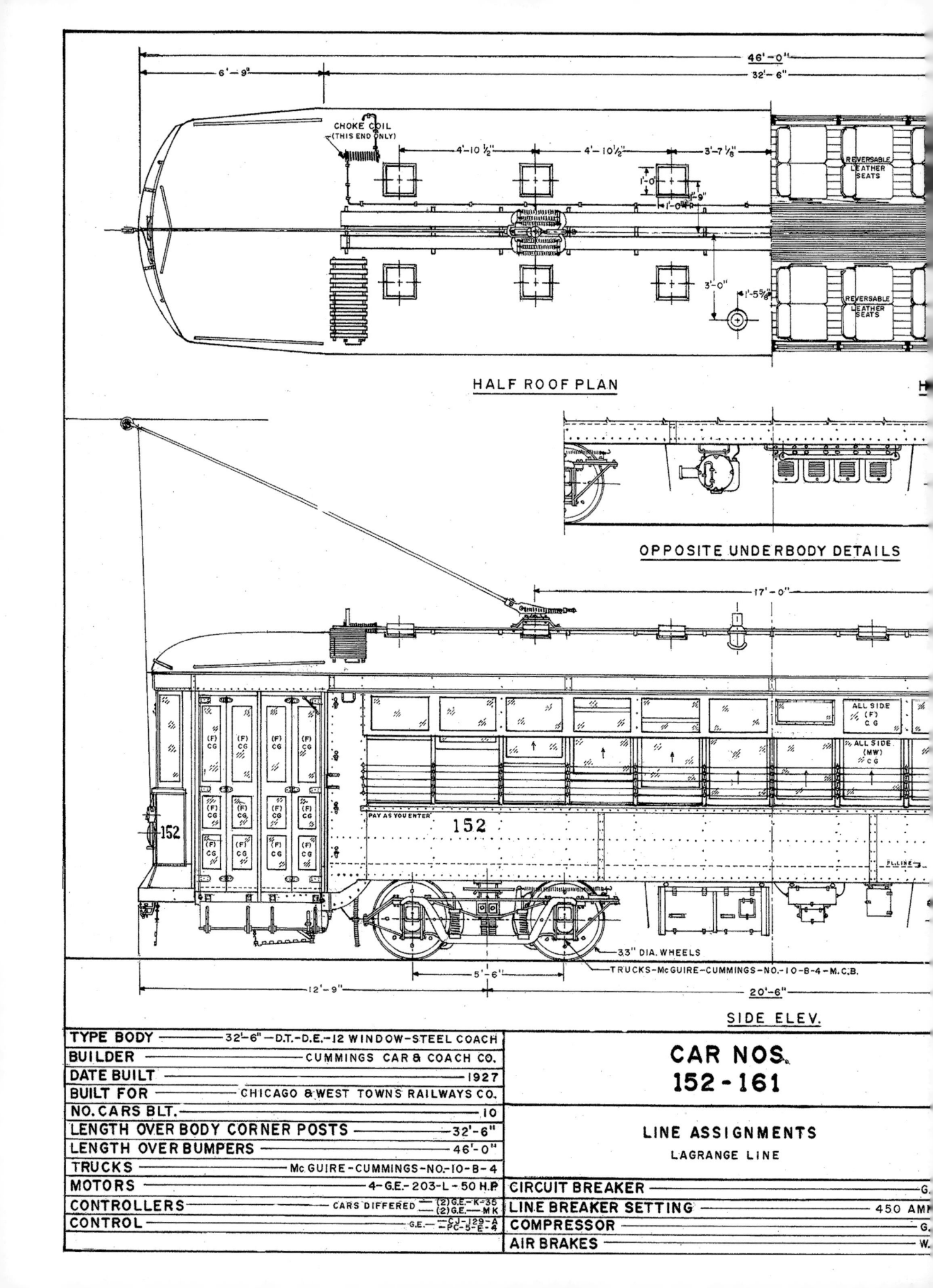

OPPOSITE UNDERBODY DETAILS

SIDE ELEV.

TYPE BODY	32'-6" – D.T.–D.E.–12 WINDOW–STEEL COACH
BUILDER	CUMMINGS CAR & COACH CO.
DATE BUILT	1927
BUILT FOR	CHICAGO & WEST TOWNS RAILWAYS CO.
NO. CARS BLT.	10
LENGTH OVER BODY CORNER POSTS	32'-6"
LENGTH OVER BUMPERS	46'-0"
TRUCKS	McGUIRE–CUMMINGS–NO.–10-B-4
MOTORS	4–G.E.–203-L–50 H.P.
CONTROLLERS	CARS DIFFERED (2) G.E.–K-35 / (2) G.E.–MK
CONTROL	G.E.–CJ-129-A / PC-5-E-4

CAR NOS. 152-161

LINE ASSIGNMENTS
LAGRANGE LINE

CIRCUIT BREAKER	G
LINE BREAKER SETTING	450 AM
COMPRESSOR	G
AIR BRAKES	W

FLOOR PLAN

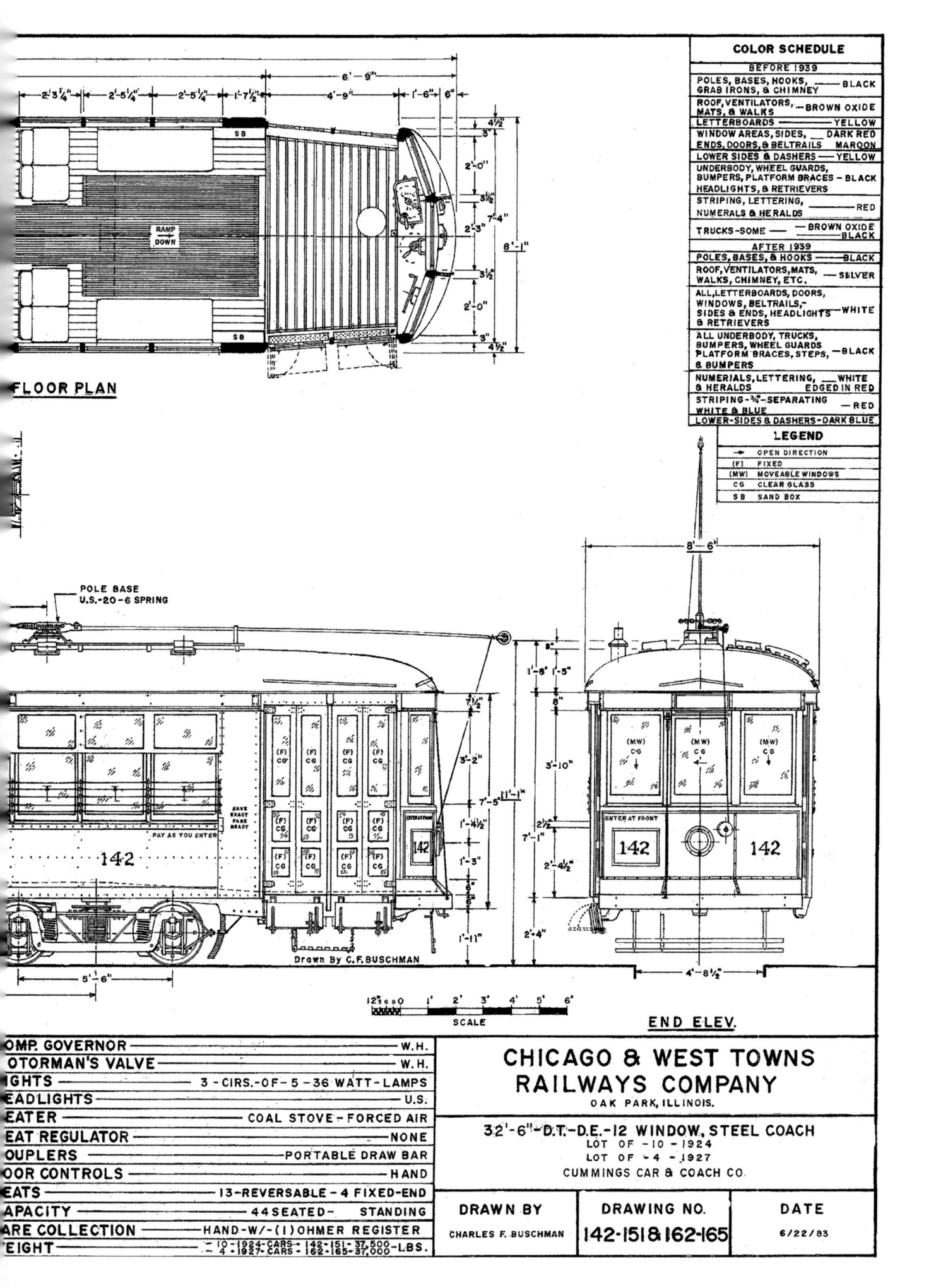

COLOR SCHEDULE

BEFORE 1939

POLES, BASES, HOOKS, GRAB IRONS, & CHIMNEY	BLACK
ROOF, VENTILATORS, MATS, & WALKS	BROWN OXIDE
LETTERBOARDS	YELLOW
WINDOW AREAS, SIDES, ENDS, DOORS, & BELTRAILS	DARK RED MAROON
LOWER SIDES & DASHERS	YELLOW
UNDERBODY, WHEEL GUARDS, BUMPERS, PLATFORM BRACES, HEADLIGHTS, & RETRIEVERS	BLACK
STRIPING, LETTERING, NUMERALS & HERALDS	RED
TRUCKS–SOME	BROWN OXIDE / BLACK

AFTER 1939

POLES, BASES, & HOOKS	BLACK
ROOF, VENTILATORS, MATS, WALKS, CHIMNEY, ETC.	SILVER
ALL, LETTERBOARDS, DOORS, WINDOWS, BELTRAILS, SIDES & ENDS, HEADLIGHTS & RETRIEVERS	WHITE
ALL UNDERBODY, TRUCKS, BUMPERS, WHEEL GUARDS, PLATFORM BRACES, STEPS, & BUMPERS	BLACK
NUMERALS, LETTERING, & HERALDS	WHITE EDGED IN RED
STRIPING–¾"–SEPARATING WHITE & BLUE	RED
LOWER–SIDES & DASHERS–DARK BLUE	

LEGEND

→	OPEN DIRECTION
(F)	FIXED
(MW)	MOVEABLE WINDOWS
CG	CLEAR GLASS
SB	SAND BOX

POLE BASE U.S.-20-6 SPRING

HAVE EXACT FARE READY

PAY AS YOU ENTER

142

Drawn By C.F. BUSCHMAN

ENTER AT FRONT

142   142

END ELEV.

COMP. GOVERNOR	W.H.
MOTORMAN'S VALVE	W.H.
LIGHTS	3-CIRS.-OF-5-36 WATT-LAMPS
HEADLIGHTS	U.S.
HEATER	COAL STOVE - FORCED AIR
HEAT REGULATOR	NONE
COUPLERS	PORTABLE DRAW BAR
DOOR CONTROLS	HAND
SEATS	13-REVERSABLE - 4 FIXED-END
CAPACITY	44 SEATED - STANDING
FARE COLLECTION	HAND-W/-(1) OHMER REGISTER
WEIGHT	10-1924-CARS-142-151-37,500-LBS. / 4-1927-CARS-162-165-37,000-LBS.

CHICAGO & WEST TOWNS RAILWAYS COMPANY
OAK PARK, ILLINOIS.

32'-6"-D.T.-D.E.-12 WINDOW, STEEL COACH
LOT OF -10 - 1924
LOT OF - 4 - 1927
CUMMINGS CAR & COACH CO.

DRAWN BY	DRAWING NO.	DATE
CHARLES F. BUSCHMAN	142-151 & 162-165	6/22/83

HALF ROOF PLAN

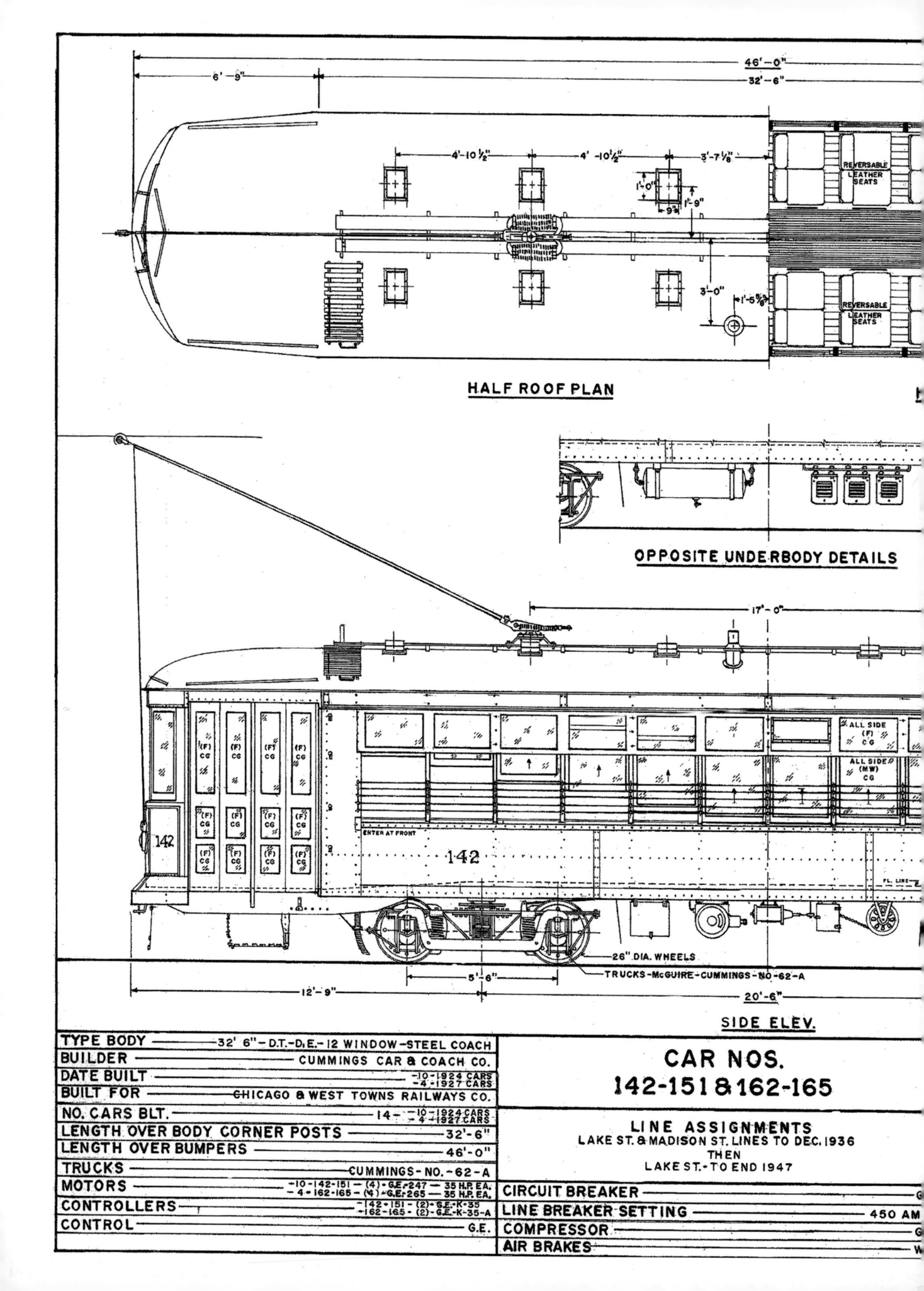

OPPOSITE UNDERBODY DETAILS

SIDE ELEV.

TYPE BODY	32'6"-D.T.-D.E.-12 WINDOW-STEEL COACH
BUILDER	CUMMINGS CAR & COACH CO.
DATE BUILT	-10-1924 CARS / -4-1927 CARS
BUILT FOR	CHICAGO & WEST TOWNS RAILWAYS CO.
NO. CARS BLT.	14 - -10-1924 CARS / -4-1927 CARS
LENGTH OVER BODY CORNER POSTS	32'-6"
LENGTH OVER BUMPERS	46'-0"
TRUCKS	CUMMINGS-NO.-62-A
MOTORS	-10-142-151 — (4) G.E.-247 — 35 H.P. EA. / -4-162-165 — (4) G.E.-265 — 35 H.P. EA.
CONTROLLERS	-142-151-(2)-G.E.-K-35 / -162-165-(2)-G.E.-K-35-A
CONTROL	G.E.
CIRCUIT BREAKER	
LINE BREAKER SETTING	450 AM
COMPRESSOR	
AIR BRAKES	

CAR NOS. 142-151 & 162-165

LINE ASSIGNMENTS
LAKE ST. & MADISON ST. LINES TO DEC. 1936
THEN
LAKE ST. - TO END 1947